SPECIAL NEEDS
ADVOCACY
RESOURCE BOOK

SPECIAL NEEDS
ADVOCACY
RESOURCE BOOK

**WHAT YOU CAN DO NOW TO ADVOCATE
FOR YOUR EXCEPTIONAL CHILD'S EDUCATION**

BY RICH WEINFELD
& MICHELLE DAVIS

PRUFROCK PRESS INC.
WACO, TEXAS

Library of Congress Cataloging-in-Publication Data

Weinfeld, Rich, 1953–
  Special needs advocacy resource book : what you can do now to advocate for your exceptional child's education / by Rich Weinfeld & Michelle Davis.
    p. cm.
  Includes bibliographical references.
  ISBN-13: 978-1-59363-309-7 (pbk.)
  ISBN-10: 1-59363-309-2 (pbk.)
  1. Special education—Parent participation—United States—Handbooks, manuals, etc. I. Davis, Michelle. II. Title.
  LC3981.W37 2008
  371.90973—dc22
                          2007051726

Copyright © 2008 Prufrock Press Inc.
Edited by Lacy Elwood
Cover and Layout Design by Marjorie Parker

ISBN-13: 978-1-59363-309-7
ISBN-10: 1-59363-309-2

At the time of this book's publication, all facts and figures cited are the most current available. All telephone numbers, addresses, and Web site URLs are accurate and active. All publications, organizations, Web sites, and other resources exist as described in the book, and all have been verified. The authors and Prufrock Press Inc. make no warranty or guarantee concerning the information and materials given out by organizations or content found at Web sites, and we are not responsible for any changes that occur after this book's publication. If you find an error, please contact Prufrock Press Inc.

Law is always changing. The information contained in this book is general information and may or may not reflect current legal developments. This book is designed to provide general information in regard to the subject matter covered and sold with the understanding that the publisher and authors are not engaged in rendering legal or other professional services. For legal advice or specific current legal information, consult an attorney.

Prufrock Press Inc.
P.O. Box 8813
Waco, TX 76714-8813
Phone: (800) 998-2208
Fax: (800) 240-0333
http://www.prufrock.com

*To the parents, school system staff, and professional advocates
who dedicate themselves to creating educational opportunity
and possibility for each child.*

Contents

Acknowledgments

Michelle would like to acknowledge her husband for his devotion to children through education and music. She would like to thank her parents and brother for everlasting love, her mentors for leadership, and her friends for inspiration.

Rich also would like to thank his family: Nic, Jake, and especially Sara, for the love, patience, and support that makes everything possible.

We would like to thank Sue Jeweler, whose outstanding vision, tireless efforts, and exceptional skills helped make this book possible.

Jeanne Paynter is largely responsible for the content of Chapter 12. We appreciate her bringing the same expertise that she has brought to the leadership of gifted education in the state of Maryland to this project.

We also would like to thank the following professionals who have reviewed parts of this manuscript and provided us with valuable suggestions and feedback: Linda Barnes-Robinson, Michael Eig, Jennifer Fisher, Brian Gruber, Kristi Messer, Holly Parker, Janet Price, Diana Savit, Steve Silverman, and Karin Tulchinsky-Cohen.

We have been fortunate to work with extraordinary, expert special education attorneys, school system professionals, related service providers, evaluators, special education consultants, and physicians from whom we have learned so much and for whom we are so grateful.

Finally, Rich would like to specially acknowledge Lacy Elwood, who he has been fortunate to have as a Prufrock editor on all four of his books. Lacy has been a wonderful editor with whom to work. She combines the knowledge of how to do it right, the high standards of accepting nothing less than the best, a true interest in the content, and the human relations skills that have brought out the best in my coauthors and myself. We wish her the best in all of her future endeavors!

Introduction

Children are our greatest natural resource. With nurturing, teaching, guidance, and support, they will grow into productive members of society. Our challenge as parents and educators is to uncover and cultivate each student's gifts, while removing the obstacles that may prevent the child from achieving academic success. In the best of all worlds, the home-school partnership accomplishes this far-reaching goal. The reality is, however, that there are times when children do not receive the appropriate programs and services required for their intellectual, social, and emotional well-being.

The information and strategies in this book will empower parents and teachers to navigate and work with school systems to be equal partners in the educational decision making for their children. *Special Needs Advocacy Resource Book: What You Can Do Now to Advocate for Your Exceptional Child's Education* uniquely identifies, from an educational perspective, how effective advocacy can impact relationships and programming and prevent disputes between parents and school systems. As parents and school system personnel, we have an opportunity to advocate for the children we serve and to tap into one another's expertise as we work together. This book will help parents and professionals actively advocate for and support the education of the special needs child, which we define as children with learning difficulties, children with disabilities, and gifted children.

A parent may read this book to learn how best to advocate for her own child. In reading this book, a parent also will gain knowledge that will empower him or her to understand when to utilize an advocate and what to expect from that advocate. Teachers and other school system employees may read this book in an effort to see how to avoid conflicts and work cooperatively with parents in the best interest of students. Still others may read this book as their first step toward becoming professional advocates. Readers will gain valuable information about not only the law and policy, but also about the way an advocate thinks as he strives to get appropriate services and educational placements for children.

The book is divided into 12 chapters that answer the following questions:

1. Why is it important that we advocate for students?
2. What do effective advocates do?
3. What does an advocate need to know about outstanding classrooms or educational programs?
4. What does an advocate need to know about the law?
5. What does an advocate need to know about the IEP process?
6. What does an advocate need to know about evaluating a child's strengths and needs?
7. What does an advocate need to know to work effectively with the parents and family?
8. What does an advocate need to know about the school system, school, and classroom?
9. What does an advocate need to know about educational options beyond the standard public school offerings?
10. What does an advocate need to know about the dynamics of school meetings?
11. What does an advocate do to ensure effective implementation and evaluate the efficacy of individual student plans?
12. How can parents organize into groups and effectively advocate for their children?

Knowledge is power. When partners in education are armed with accurate information, positive outcomes will happen for children. Chapters generally will follow this format to present the most accurate information for parents, teachers, and professionals:

- Chapter title posing an important question related to advocacy
- Introductory narrative related to chapter question
- The answer to the question: Why is this information important for an advocate to know?
- Narrative explanation that addresses, in depth, the answer to the chapter question
- Common problems that relate to the chapter question
- Common situations/examples related to the problem
- What the law says about the issues at hand
- Tips for parents
- Implications for the school system and tips to avoid the problem

At the end of each chapter in this book is a collection of reproducible tools for parents and teachers. These tools are reproducible pages that include checklists, forms, and other materials related to the chapter information.

The following are suggestions for using the book and its reproducible pages:

- Read the book to gain a deeper understanding of advocacy and the actions to take to ensure success for students.
- Use the book as one would a resource book, determining what information is applicable to an individual student.
- Copy the applicable information and specific reproducible pages to assist in ensuring that the needs of the student are being addressed.
- Distribute the information and appropriate reference pages to the parents, staff, and others who work with the student.

- Use and create plans of action to implement successful instructional opportunities, programs, and services for the student.
- Use the reproducible pages to assist you with preparation for and participation in both instructional opportunities and meetings and conferences.
- Use the information as a jumping off point for further exploration on a subtopic of special interest.

Whether you are reading this book to help your own children, the students that you work with each day in school, or the children of parents that have asked for you to become involved in their child's life specifically to help them deal with school problems, we hope this book will provide you with the information, techniques, and tools that you need. It is our hope that the new information you will gain by reading this book will make a difference in the lives of children, transforming their school experience for the better.

chapter 1

Why Is It Important That We Advocate for Students?

E a c h and every child is born with potential. We, the adults in that child's world, must work to make certain that there are educational opportunities in place that ensure each and every child will reach that potential. Realizing potential is crucial both for the individual child and for our society as a whole. When children's individual strengths are recognized and developed, they experience a sense of well-being and fulfillment. They are prepared to go on to further academic study and eventually to participate in personally satisfying careers. As we help each child to reach his or her potential, we also are furthering the progress of humanity. We are helping to cultivate and prepare the next generation of leaders, inventors, healers, and artists who will make the difference for our entire civilization.

There are times when parents and school staff are not able, for a variety of reasons, to effectively plan to meet the needs of an individual child. Involving an advocate often can make the difference in ensuring that the child gets the appropriate instruction and services she needs and deserves.

The education of a child is a very complex process. A parent is a child's first teacher, but once the child enters school, educators become an integral part of the team of personnel responsible for helping a child learn academic concepts and content, organizational skills, social skills, and the life skills essential for functioning in the real world.

As children progress in school, they give clues that indicate how they are doing. They may let us know that the work is too hard or that paying attention is difficult or that they can't remember their math facts or that they have no friends. They also may let us know that school is boring, and that they are not being appropriately challenged. When parents or teachers become aware of a child's obstacles to learning, then together they can plan the appropriate interventions, modifications, adaptations, and accommodations necessary so that the child will access the appropriately challenging instruction. If, however, there is a breakdown in the process, what must be done to ensure that the child receives the services he or she needs and deserves?

Usually, there are a suggested series of steps to be followed when the system breaks down. We are advised, for example, that when we perceive there is a problem, the first step is for the parent and child's teacher to conference. If that does not work, the next step may be to see the principal. While the process continues, the child may be falling farther and farther behind or may be experiencing frustration and exhibiting behaviors that are troubling.

There are many possible roadblocks that can hinder progress within the process of seeking support for a child. For example, laws change. The stakeholders, therefore, need to understand the application of federal and state law to their children's education, among other things.

Staff members and parents at some schools may have the additional roadblock of seeing home and school as adversaries, not equal partners in decision making. This culture of authority may be a major stumbling block. Although school personnel may talk about the importance of parents as members of the team, it may be very intimidating for parents to question the decisions of the "experts," especially when they feel outnumbered by a large group of school staff at the table who seem to all agree on what is best. Having an advocate sitting next to the parent to interpret what is being said and voice what the parent may not feel he is able to say can make the meeting experience very different. Unfortunately, special education law and school policies regarding both special education and gifted education contain many concepts and terminology that can be very difficult to understand. One of the roles of the advocate is to empower parents to take an active role in the meeting by interpreting school jargon and legalese and by providing as much information as possible.

One of the stated goals of the Individuals with Disabilities Education Improvement Act of 2004 (IDEA; 2004) is to create a process where parents truly feel that they are an integral part of the decision making for their children. It is hard to be a true partner in this decision making if one does not fully understand the language and process. The confidence of having an advocate by your side to make sure that you understand all that happens ensures that the process is truly parent friendly.

An advocate who knows and understands children's rights and school system responsibilities under the laws governing the education of children; who can participate with teams to determine whether a disability exists, if so, which disabilities exist, and how to create a school plan to address these disabilities; who can recommend and monitor the implementation of educational strategies based on the student's strength and need areas; who can navigate the school system procedures to secure school services and placement for children with special needs and/or great potential; who can link parents and teachers with a variety of community resources and supports; and who can monitor legal issues and provide intervention when rights are violated ensures that the child will receive the finest educational experience possible.

Advocates bring a high degree of skill and knowledge, based upon their training and experience, to the entire process of helping students reach their potential, particularly students who face the increased obstacles presented by their learning challenges or disabilities. An advocate can help a school team to plan proactively to ensure an individual student's success before serious problems arise. An advocate also can be a crucial part of helping the school team to identify and choose appropriate alternatives when a school problem does exist.

Advocacy, when done appropriately, can be beneficial for any student. It may be especially crucial in cases where the parents don't feel that they are an equal part of the process because of their own cultural, language, or socioeconomic differences. In these cases the advocate can help the parents to effectively understand the process and express their opinions, as well as ensure that the parents' input is treated with the same importance afforded to any other parent.

Advocacy is especially important in situations when the child in question may be the victim, knowingly or unknowingly, of biases on the part of the decision makers in the school. Advocates help to protect the rights of parents whose first language may not be English or who, because of their socioeconomic status or their cultural beliefs, may not feel it is appropriate to challenge the school's viewpoints. Advocates also can listen for other potential biases. Are we excluding the young girl in question from opportunities just because of assumptions we have made about her as a girl? Are we teaching the young man in ways that research have shown will best meet boys' educational needs?

Another of the stated purposes of the revisions of IDEA 2004 is to ensure that special education decisions are not promoting biases that will lead toward a disproportionate representation of certain groups of students in special education. Issues of race may be at play in the decision making in school meetings. It is an unfortunate fact, for example, that Black students are overrepresented in special education, particularly in programs for emotionally disturbed students. It also is an unfortunate fact, that even in integrated schools, many classes or programs are predominantly made up of one racial group or another. An advocate will help protect the rights of the individual student and make sure that decisions are made with that student's best interest in mind, regardless of his or her race.

Many school personnel welcome the presence of an advocate at a school meeting. An advocate can talk about the problems and suggest the solutions that school staff may feel unable to bring up because of the budgetary constraints that they may be aware of and the directions they may have been given by their supervisors. Once the advocate's ideas are out on the table, school staff may feel free to support what they believe is in the student's best interest. The advocate also may have a mediating effect on the parents. By helping to interpret what the school staff is saying and by having a deep understanding of the constraints of the school, the advocate may be able to help the parent understand what is possible and attainable for his child. Although an advocate attends the meeting at the parents' request, the advocate should be there with the purpose of focusing on the needs of the student. He can get the meeting past difficult sticking points by being unbiased and objective and helping the team move toward decisions that are not necessarily the parents' or the school system's position, but are in the individual student's best interests.

The advocate also serves as a truth detector. Sometimes statements are made, particularly about what can and can't be done, that are not based on the law or research. Instead they may be based on an individual's belief about what is right or what he or she has heard from others. The advocate can challenge these statements with the facts of what the law or research does say. In this way, the school team may see that there are other choices for how to respond to the individual child.

In conclusion, it is crucial that we advocate for what each and every child needs in order to help him reach his own unique potential. An effective advocate helps parents and school staff to accurately see the problem and to see all of the possible solutions that may solve the problem that the individual child is experiencing. In the next chapters we will talk more specifically about what an advocate needs to do and know in order to effectively stand up for children.

chapter 2

What Do Effective Advocates Do?

A d v o c a t e s must know how to work with school-aged children and their families as they interact with the school system to pursue necessary educational outcomes for the child. The advocate must understand school law and policies and interpersonal dynamics, and must also understand one's own self. An individual who chooses to be a professional advocate also must know about the best practices involved in the business of advocacy. In this chapter we will introduce the many responsibilities of advocates. In later chapters, we will discuss many of these responsibilities in greater detail.

Here, we will focus on the responsibilities of the professional advocate. We hope that learning about the role of the professional advocate will guide parents in choosing an effective advocate. A parent also may choose to take on these responsibilities for him- or herself. We believe that to be effective the parent must have the same level of expertise and knowledge as a professional. It is our hope that as you read this chapter, either from the perspective of a parent, a professional advocate, or school system personnel, you will see the complexity of effective advocacy, guiding you to increase your skills in order to work more effectively with the children you are seeking to help.

Definition of an Advocate

Although we have chosen to call them *advocates*, people who work with children and their families to help them get appropriate educational services may be referred to as *advocates*, *experts*, or *consultants*, defined here as (Farlex, 2007):

- **Advocate:** To speak, plead, or argue in favor of. One that argues for a cause; a supporter or defender: *an advocate of civil rights*. One that pleads in another's behalf; an intercessor: *advocates for abused children and spouses*. A lawyer.
- **Expert:** A person with a high degree of skill in or knowledge of a certain subject. Having, involving, or demonstrating great skill, dexterity, or knowledge as the result of experience or training.
- **Consultant:** A person who gives expert or professional advice.

In this book, we will consider an advocate to be someone who has a high degree of skill and knowledge about education and gives expert advice about this field for the purpose of supporting children. The components of the definition are defined as follows:

- **High degree of skill and knowledge:** An advocate often is someone who has studied education, special education, and/or gifted education at the undergraduate and/or graduate level. If he does not have a degree in education, he has taken courses and reviewed the current professional literature to further his knowledge of this field. She also may have developed her skills as a working professional in the field of education, often as a classroom teacher, gifted educator, or special educator. Others have developed their skills as advocates by working under the supervision of other professional advocates.

- **Gives expert advice:** An advocate analyzes the situation that the individual child is experiencing by reviewing the child's records; observing the child in her school environment; and interviewing parents, teachers, other professionals, and the student. The advocate synthesizes this information and based on his own skills and knowledge, gives recommendations to the parents and school team about the child's best interests. The advocate must give this expert advice in a way that will be heard and utilized by the parents and school team.

- **Support children:** An advocate's single aim is to support the individual child for whom she is working. Supporting the individual child means staying true to the expert opinion that the advocate has developed and believes will be in the best interest of the child. Hopefully, this expert opinion will be the same as what the parent and the school team believe is in the best interest of the child. Even when the opinion is at odds with one or more of the adults in the child's life, the advocate must keep in mind the primary goal of acting in a way that he believes truly supports the child.

Tasks an Advocate Performs in Order to Be Effective

In order to be effective in his role, an advocate must perform a wide variety of tasks. These tasks may be categorized broadly as gathering information about the child; determining what action steps are necessary for achieving outcomes that are in the child's best interests; knowing the possible outcomes as they relate to the law, policies, community, and school resources; and participating in a wide variety of meetings in varied settings to ensure that these action steps are accepted and implemented. In accomplishing all of these tasks, the advocate must not only have knowledge and expertise about what needs to be done but also about how it needs to be done.

Gathering Information About the Child

Gathering information about the child often begins with an understanding of the parents' desired outcomes that have led to her engaging the advocate. Although the advocate will make it clear to the parents that when they commit to working with the advocate they are hiring an "expert" and not a "hired gun," the advocate will still strive to thoroughly understand the parents' current opinions and feelings related to the child's current school situation.

The advocate will then take time to thoroughly review the child's educational records. This typically includes a review of report cards, other home-school communication, notes of previous meetings, and any assessments or evaluations that may have already been completed. The advocate will look at evidence of strengths and needs, as well as what interventions have been attempted in the past and with what level of effectiveness they have been completed. The advocate will look to see whether the current educational environment is in fact the Least Restrictive Environment (LRE) for the child in question and whether or not it may be able to be modified so that it is an appropriate environment. The advocate will look at whether or not the child may have a disability and whether or not there is an educational impact from that disability. The advocate also will look at whether the current environment is providing the right level of challenge. Although we believe that providing appropriately rigorous instruction is important for all students, it is especially critical for our gifted students.

Assessments, a crucial step in gathering information about the child, are performed to analyze a student's strengths and needs, to determine whether or not a disability may exist, and to ascertain to what extent the disability may be impacting the child's educational progress. Assessments should be performed in all areas where a suspected disability exists. Depending on the suspected disability, assessments can include psychological or neuropsychological, educational, speech and language, and occupational therapy or physical therapy assessments. The advocate will first thoroughly review completed assessments and then may recommend that additional or new assessments be performed. These recommendations may be made because of the belief that the child has changed since the last evaluation, the belief the previous assessment was not complete, or the belief that an area of possible disability or strength was not previously assessed at all.

Some advocates are certified to perform one or more of these assessments themselves. More often, they will refer parents to other professionals who have expertise in the needed areas. Part of the process of gathering information will be for the advocate to speak with as many of the professionals who are involved with the child as possible. These professionals would include both those who have done assessments, as well as those who provide therapy or other supports to the child.

Observation is another critical piece of gathering information. The advocate will want to observe the child in one or more class settings. It is best if the child is not aware of the observation so that he or she is not affected by the advocate's presence. Advocates often will want to see the child both in a setting in which she is being successful, as well as a setting in which she is having difficulties. The contrast of these two settings may provide valuable information about the child's strengths, needs, and needed interventions. As the advocate observes the student in his school environment, it is crucial that she has a picture in her mind about what the ideal classroom would look like (see Chapter 3). How to go about performing an effective classroom observation will be discussed in more detail in Chapters 6 and 11. Observation is one aspect of the advocate's role that is particularly difficult for a parent to perform, because it is desirable to have an observation during which the child does not realize he alone is being observed. However, a parent who frequently volunteers in his child's classroom is better able to observe without affecting the performance of his child.

During the visit to the child's school for the observation, the advocate often will have the chance to interview staff that works with the child. Conducting both informal and formal interviews with the staff who work with the child on a daily basis is crucial. A more complete discussion about how to gather information from staff will be presented in Chapter 6.

As the advocate gathers information, it is imperative that she develops a personal record that accurately and completely summarizes what she has learned. One of the important roles of the advocate is to be the source of all necessary information about the student, so that the parent does not have to worry about this arduous task. This record of information may take the form of a notebook of documents with personal notes attached. It also may take the form of an ongoing electronic log of documents and summary notes that the advocate enters into a file on his computer. Either way, this information should be readily accessible to the advocate, and it must be accurate and complete. It is our recommendation that an advocate only write down notes that he would feel comfortable with if they were made public. Although there are different opinions about whether or not the notes of an advocate can be required to be made public, writing in a factual and objective way is the safest way to avoid future embarrassment to the advocate or unintended harm to the child or his family. All records should, of course, be kept safely and confidentially and be destroyed after an appropriate period of time.

Necessary Action Steps

After the advocate has thoroughly gathered information about the functioning of the child, he will work with the parents, and in some cases the child, to determine what outcomes are desired and, finally, the appropriate action steps that are needed to achieve those outcomes. Depending on the child's current school functioning and strengths and needs, outcomes may involve obtaining or modifying a special education plan for the child. These plans may take the form of a Section 504 plan, an Individualized Education Program (IEP), or some type of less-formal school plan (see the TOOLS section for a Road Map of potential action steps that may be taken when forming these plans).

Section 504 Plans are educational plans that document necessary accommodations or services for people with disabilities. These plans are in action in schools, workplaces, and communities. Individualized Education Programs (which we will refer to as IEPs throughout this book) are legal documents that outline the necessary educational accommodations or services for a child with disabilities or learning difficulties. IEPs are only used in school settings and require participation on the part of the parent, school staff, and other adults with an interest in the child's education. More on 504 Plans can be found in Chapter 4. In addition, while we include IEPs in much of our discussion throughout the book, a detailed discussion of these plans and the stages involved in developing these plans is included in Chapter 5.

The advocate will work with the parents to determine which type of plan may be appropriate and then will guide the parents about how to formally request the type of meeting that will ensure that the right type of plan is developed. The advocate will work with parents to anticipate what roadblocks might appear on the way toward getting the desired outcomes and will make a plan that has contingencies built into it to deal with these possible roadblocks. For example, the advocate will explain to parents their legal rights should the school refuse to develop or modify a 504 or IEP in a way that the parents feel is necessary. The advocate will assist the parents with completing and maintaining a file of the paperwork that may be necessary for reaching the desired results.

Participating in Meetings to Ensure Implementation of Action Steps

Advocates will accompany parents to a wide variety of meetings in a variety of settings where decisions are made about developing new educational plans or modifying existing plans in order to ensure that the appropriate steps for the child's education are accepted and implemented. To prepare for these meetings, advocates often will draft suggested goals, objectives, adaptations, and accommodations. As they develop their draft plans, advocates will utilize all of the information that they have gathered, including reviews of assessments; notes of their own observation and interviews with parents, staff, and other professionals; and reviews of school records. The advocate will prepare parents for the likely process of the meeting, anticipating problems and planning for how to proactively deal with these problems. How to effectively participate in school meetings will be dealt with in detail in Chapters 4, 5, and 10.

Knowing the Law, Policies, and Community and School Resources

An advocate must stay current about federal and state laws, policies of the local school systems, current research regarding special education practices, and both community and school resources. In order to keep up with changes in the laws and policies, the advocate will attend ongoing training through universities and special workshops. Other advocates and/or special education attorneys often present such workshops.

A review of special education and gifted education periodicals and books will help the advocate keep up-to-date regarding new research and best practices. The advocate also may participate in Web groups where parents and professionals share current information. Networking with other professionals in order to keep an updated list of community resources and supports including attorneys, tutors, therapists, assessors, organizational coaches, technology experts, and talent development opportunities, such as gifted education experiences and arts activities, also is essential. The advocate will keep abreast of the ever-changing resources that are offered by the local private and public schools and will visit public and private schools periodically to see for herself the current state of their educational opportunities.

Providing Consultation and Training Opportunities

Due to their special expertise related to a wide variety of gifted education and/or special education issues, the advocate may become a valued expert who provides information to school staff members and parents through group presentations and by working with schools to help them to change or develop a specific program. The advocate may speak at local, state, or national conferences attended by other advocates, attorneys, related service providers, or educators of the gifted or of students who receive special education.

Knowing Yourself

The advocate must be aware of his own strengths and limitations and how they affect the performance of his job. He must be able to call on others to support children in the areas that are not his own strengths. She must understand how her own personality may help or hinder herself in interacting with others, particularly when involved in potentially adversarial interactions.

An effective advocate, whether she is advocating for her own child or professionally for the children of others, must possess and continue to refine a wide variety of skills that allows her to effectively stand up for children. Parents who choose to hire professional advocates will want to ensure that the advocate possesses these skills. At the end of this chapter you will find a tool that will aide you in the selection of an advocate. Parents who will act as an advocate for their own child must strive to find ways to develop their own skills or bring in other experts who can help them in specific areas where they may need help.

Although this chapter summarizes what advocates do, there is much more that advocates need to know in order to do their job effectively. For some advocates, advocacy is or will become a full-time job. We've included some tips for setting up an advocacy business in the TOOLS section of this chapter. However, regardless of whether you are advocating for a career or just to support one child, the information in the following chapters will be vital to your success.

Problem

A well-meaning individual may offer to advocate for appropriate services or programs for the children of others. The person may not have the educational or business expertise to effectively work on behalf of the student.

Common Situation/Examples

A parent may utilize an advocate who does not have adequate knowledge of the educational and/or business requirements of being an effective advocate. He may not be effective in completing all of the tasks required to complete the process and obtain appropriate outcomes for the child.

An individual may decide that he or she wants to help others by offering advocacy services. He may become overwhelmed by the knowledge and expertise that is required of this role and therefore not be able to effectively represent his client.

What the Law Says

Although there are professional organizations and training opportunities that set standards and provide training for advocates, there currently are no laws that set standards for the profession. There are, however, laws related to many aspects of the advocate's work. The advocate must understand the relevant laws related to contracts, incorporation, confidentiality of records and release of information, and the laws (discussed in later chapters) related to a myriad of special education issues.

Tips for Parents

As with any other professional, parents should carefully check on the credentials and reputation of the advocate they may be considering. It is appropriate to ask the perspective advocate about his educational background, certifications, training, and experience. Asking other parents and professionals, including private and public school personnel, for their recommendations also is appropriate. A check on the Better Business Bureau's Web site may be helpful in determining if the advocate in question has encountered previous complaints.

Implications for the School System/ Tips to Avoid the Problem

The school system can foster a working relationship with parents by helping parents to distinguish between advocates who have worked with other parents productively and in the best interest of children. Rather than see advocates as an impediment to working effectively with parents, it is helpful when school system personnel see that the right advocate can help the parents to feel like confident members of the decision-making team and to work more effectively and collaboratively in the best interests of their child.

TOOLS

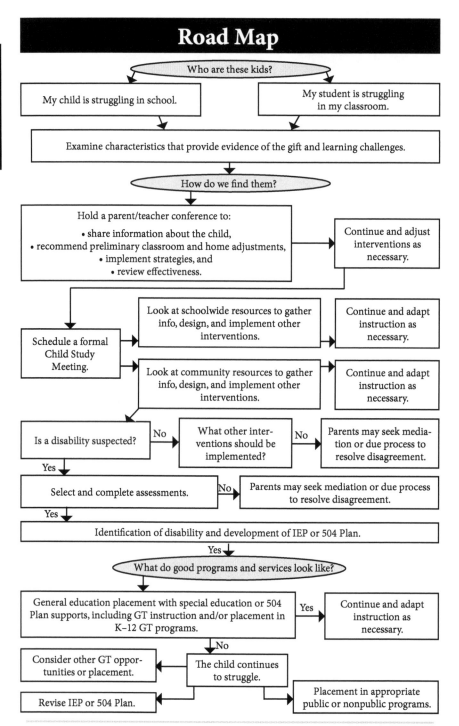

Road Map

Who are these kids?

| My child is struggling in school. | My student is struggling in my classroom. |

Examine characteristics that provide evidence of the gift and learning challenges.

How do we find them?

Hold a parent/teacher conference to:
- share information about the child,
- recommend preliminary classroom and home adjustments,
- implement strategies, and
- review effectiveness.

Continue and adjust interventions as necessary.

Schedule a formal Child Study Meeting.

Look at schoolwide resources to gather info, design, and implement other interventions.

Continue and adapt instruction as necessary.

Look at community resources to gather info, design, and implement other interventions.

Continue and adapt instruction as necessary.

Is a disability suspected? — No → What other interventions should be implemented? — No → Parents may seek mediation or due process to resolve disagreement.

Yes ↓

Select and complete assessments. — No → Parents may seek mediation or due process to resolve disagreement.

Yes ↓

Identification of disability and development of IEP or 504 Plan.

Yes ↓

What do good programs and services look like?

General education placement with special education or 504 Plan supports, including GT instruction and/or placement in K–12 GT programs. — Yes → Continue and adapt instruction as necessary.

No ↓

The child continues to struggle.

Consider other GT opportunities or placement.

Placement in appropriate public or nonpublic programs.

Revise IEP or 504 Plan.

Note. From *Smart Kids With Learning Difficulties: Overcoming Obstacles and Realizing Potential* (p. 8), by R. Weinfeld, L. Barnes-Robinson, S. Jeweler, and B. Roffman Shevitz, 2006, Waco, TX: Prufrock Press. Copyright © 2006 by Prufrock Press. Reprinted with permission.

Special Needs Advocacy Resource Book, Copyright © Prufrock Press Inc. This page may be photocopied or reproduced with permission for individual use.

TOOLS

How to Select a Special Education Advocate/Attorney

Five Things to Look For:

1. *Experience.* Is the advocate/attorney an expert in education policy, issues, and law? How many 504 and IEP process meetings has the advocate/attorney attended? How many due process hearings? Over what issues? Did she achieve the desired outcome for the student? How is her relationship with the school system, including special education personnel, the compliance office, and attorneys?

2. *Personality.* Is the advocate/attorney's personality and personal style a match with both you and your spouse?

3. *Cost and Charges.* Can you afford it? (Think of the investment and whether to spend money on tuition and supports in addition or instead of advocacy/legal services.) Does the advocate/attorney work on any type of reduced fee arrangement when there is a financial need?

4. *Style for Dispute.* Does the advocate/attorney always approach the school system staff as adversarial or as potentially cooperative? What is her thinking behind the pros and cons for dispute options? Does the advocate/attorney shy away from disputes or persist even in the face of challenging situations?

5. *Resources.* Does the advocate/attorney have a wide range of options of experts in different fields? Does she have resources related to the various disabling conditions and areas of both strengths and needs that students may possess?

Sample Release of Information

Letterhead of Advocate

Release of Information

To: _____

Print public school system name and/or private school name

From: _____

Print parent/guardian's name

Re: _____

Child's name

DOB: _____

    I hereby release all confidential and other psychological, educational, medical, or school-related information from:

_____

Print public school system name and/or private school name

To: _____

Name and Address of Consultant

    The signature below authorizes the release of information and includes open and free communication through telephone or e-mail between parties. The signature below also authorizes assigned consultant to conduct program and classroom observations.

_____

Parent/guardian's signature   *Date*

Setting Up a Business Tool

Advocates wishing to start their own advocacy or consulting business will need to keep in mind extra responsibilities beyond those mentioned in this chapter, including:

- *Contracts*: An advocate will utilize a variety of contracts in his work with the families that he serves. The contract should deal with the nature of the work that the advocate will perform, how and how long the services will be performed, structure of fees and payments, and the handling of issues of confidentiality and release of information. We recommend that the advocate consult an attorney for help in drawing up this contract. A written contract or formal agreement with all of those with whom you work can proactively help to avoid or solve any disagreements that may arise at a later point.

- *Insurance*: An advocate should consider purchasing professional insurance from a reputable company. The need to make a claim involving insurance is extremely rare; however, an insurance policy provides some financial protection in the case of an unjust accusation of wrongdoing that may be directed toward the advocate.

- *Incorporation*: An advocate should consider the pros and cons of various forms of incorporation. There are many financial and legal advantages and disadvantages to the wide variety of ways to organize one's business. Again, experts such as an attorney and/or a financial advisor will be able to help look at the advocate's individual situation and advise her accordingly.

- *Record Keeping*: An advocate must keep extensive and accurate records, involving both the financial aspects of his business, as well as all of the information that relates to each and every individual client. An advocate must have a system of recording each time he is involved in working on an individual case. Typically, this will take the form of an entry of the client's name, the date of the work, a brief statement of the nature of the work, and how much time was spent on the work. These entries then will become the basis for a periodic invoice that will be sent to the client. Additionally, the advocate will need to keep accurate records of all business income and expenses for tax purposes.

- *Releases*: An advocate will want to provide his clients with a release that they will sign giving permission for him to communicate with specific people who have information about the client, including professionals who may work or have worked with the child, as well as educators who currently work with the student. A signed release is necessary to share confidential information.

- *Advertising and Marketing*: The best advertising is positive word of mouth from satisfied clients, as well as from others who have been involved with an individual case. Obviously, this includes the child's parents and related service providers that may be working on behalf of the child at the parent's request. Surprisingly, the advocate also may find that her work has been so impressive that she receives new referrals from professionals on the "other side of the table." It also is important to realize that whenever an advocate does an educational presentation for a staff or parent group or writes an article for publication, she also is creating new business opportunities as new individuals become aware of her skills and expertise. Over time, the advocate will develop relationships that will provide ongoing referrals, including attorneys, psychologists, pediatricians, private school personnel, and previous clients. Advocates also may choose to do a variety of traditional advertising and join organizations that provide an opportunity for networking with other professionals.

- *Professional Organizations*: Joining a professional organization provides an opportunity for advocates to learn more about advocacy in general, or about specific topics in special education, business, or the law. Professional organizations include organizations that bring advocates and attorneys together and organizations that bring special educators together, as well as resources found through your local Better Business Bureau or Chamber of Commerce.

- *Creating Your Own Business Team*: There are a variety of professionals who may come together to create an effective support team for the advocate. A strong support team may include a business attorney, a financial advisor, a bookkeeper, an accountant, an informational technology person, and a secretary. Although it is certainly possible for the advocate to do all or some of this related work himself, he may find that the quality of the work done by his team, who are experts in their field, actually saves time and money, making the advocate more efficient and free to concentrate his efforts on the children he is serving.

chapter 3

What Does an Advocate Need to Know About Outstanding Classrooms or Educational Programs?

An advocate often is asked to help parents who feel that the current classroom is not meeting the needs of their child. This feeling on the part of parents may be the result of their belief that their child is not thriving or actually is suffering in the current classroom. As a parent or an advocate analyzes what may need to change in order for the student to be successful, he must have a picture in his mind of what an outstanding classroom or educational program looks like. In this chapter we will describe the attributes of outstanding classrooms and educational programs.

Why Is This Important for an Advocate to Know?

An advocate needs to look at the current classroom where the child is receiving instruction and/or the classroom(s) that may be a future option for the child's placement. An advocate will look at these classrooms to determine if they are a good match for the strengths and the needs of the child in question. The advocate will analyze the current situation to see if it is a good match and if not, if it could be a good match if some achievable changes were made. The advocate will consider whether the classroom that he observes is the Least Restrictive Environment (LRE) for the individual child in question, always keeping in mind that the LRE for one child may not be an appropriate placement for another child (see Least Restrictive Environment section in Chapter 5). Although the advocate will be looking at any environment through the lens of the child for which he is working, the advocate will need to understand what best practices should be observable in all classrooms.

Best Practices in the Classroom

An outstanding classroom teacher must work to provide a balance. On the one hand, he must prepare students for the statewide assessments and high-stakes high school assessments that provide the accountability that ensure that each student is learning the standards that are required by the state board of education and the national government. On the other hand, he must give each student the individual challenge and support that she needs. On the one hand, the advocate must work to provide students with the wide variety of skills that they need to be highly literate citizens of a global society. On the other hand, he must understand each student's unique learning style, interests, strengths, gifts, challenges, differences, and/or disabilities and plan instruction for them accordingly.

What are the characteristics of an outstanding teacher, one who can do all of what is described above? We believe that a good teacher must be both structured and nurturing. A structured teacher communicates what the goals of the lesson are and what she expects from her students. She is clear about the rules of the classroom. Students in her classroom know what to expect in terms of the schedule, the requirements of the assignments, and all other facets of life in the classroom.

But, it is not enough to be highly structured. Students also must feel a connection with their teacher. A nurturing teacher communicates an understanding of the unique strengths and needs of each student in his classroom. Students in his classroom know that the teacher is interested in and cares about them as an individual. Students should feel encouraged to take on new challenges and supported when they are working on improving their weaknesses. The students of teachers who are structured but not supportive will understand what is expected of them, but may not feel motivated to do the work to the best of their ability. The students of teachers who are supportive but not structured will feel a connection with their teacher, but may not be clear about what it is that the teacher expects them to do. Teachers who are both structured and supportive communicate the following to students: "This is important. You can do it. I won't give up on you" (Saphier & Gower, 1997, p. 296).

What happens in the classroom of a structured teacher? The structured teacher begins with a clear understanding of the goals of the lesson. He then communicates to the students about what the goals, the essential question, and the skills are that they will be studying in each unit or lesson. During each period of instruction there is a clear statement of the objective of the lesson. There is time to review the skill or concept that preceded the current concept in order to give the student the scaffolding needed to learn the new concept or skills. There is time to introduce the new concept, and there then is time for the students to practice using the new skill or concept with the aid of a rubric that they can refer to in order to see if they are meeting the requirements. This is followed by an assessment that informs the teacher as to whether or not the student is mastering the new concept. Then there is time for reteaching of the concept to those students who have not mastered it, and finally another assessment to again check for mastery (Hunter, 1982).

What happens in the classroom of the structured teacher who also is nurturing? The structured, yet nurturing teacher teaches the same goals, essential questions, and skills as other structured teachers, but she may give more thought to matching the instructional activities and assessments to the strengths and needs of each individual student. These teachers will utilize a multiple intelligence approach (Gardner, 1983) that engages students in the lesson by hooking them through their areas of interest and talent and allows them to learn and demonstrate their understanding in ways that utilize those strengths.

An observer in a good teacher's classroom will see evidence of the use of a variety of instructional materials and methodology. Materials for students who have verbal-linguistic and mathematical-logical strengths, as well as hands-on tools needed by visual-spatial learners and bodily-kinesthetic learners, will be in evidence. Student projects will be displayed and will show a variety of ways of demonstrating the same understandings. The arts and technological tools will be evident. The observer also will see a variety of ways of learning. There will be time for students to interact in dyads or in small groups, balanced with time to work alone and in large groups.

What is done is probably not as important as how it is done. The structured, yet supportive teacher will provide praise, encouragement, and constructive criticism in a way that students can feel good about what they have accomplished, as well as having an understanding of how to improve. An observer will see teachers providing this nurturing feedback as they shower their students with praise, encouragement, and constructive criticism as the students participate in the large group, in small groups, or individually, and as the teachers provide the students with specific written feedback on their work. The observer also will see evidence in the physical setup of the classroom. He will see student work displayed. He will see a variety of materials and work environments, indicating that learning activities take place in a variety of settings and use a variety of tools and methodologies.

Tomlinson and McTighe (2006) provide a specific framework for the type of teaching described above, which they call WHERETO (see pp. 120–127 of their book, *Teaching for Understanding,* for more on this framework). They encourage teachers to first help learners know what they will be learning, why this is worth learning, and what evidence will show their learning; second, teachers hook and engage learners and help them connect the desired learning to their experiences and interests; and third, they provide learning experiences that develop and deepen understanding of important ideas, while encouraging students to rethink their previous learning, by using self-evaluation and reflection. Next, in a step that is crucial for students who may have learning challenges, they tailor the learning activities and teaching to address the different readiness levels, learning profiles, and interests of the students through the use of differentiated instruction.

When the advocate observes students who are being given appropriate instruction, who are taking ownership for their learning, and who are fully engaged in the learning process, she likely is seeing students who may be experiencing "flow," a mental state in which the person is fully immersed in what he is doing, and feels a sense of energized focus, full involvement, and success in the process of the activity (Csikszentmihalyi, 1998). In order to experience flow in the classroom, the learner needs to have just the right balance between the his or her ability level and appropriate challenge. If the challenge is too great, the learner may experience anxiety and feel unable to perform, and if the challenge is not great enough, the learner may feel bored. In order to create that balance between ability and challenge, a teacher must understand each student's strengths and needs and provide appropriately challenging but achievable goals, learning activities, and assessments.

Differentiated Instruction

How does an outstanding teacher attend to all of the student differences that she may find in a typical classroom? How can she create instruction that truly meets the individual needs of her students? An effective teacher must employ not only whole-group instruction, but also flexible grouping and individual instruction that respond to the needs of each student. Unlike the system of tracking, where ability groups are formed permanently and sometimes across content areas, differentiation calls for the teacher to continually assess students and form groups accordingly. For example, at any given time a student might be in an advanced reading group and a remedial math group. That same child may move to an advanced math group once the math curriculum addresses his strength area of geometry rather than algebra.

When we talk about differentiation we are talking about differentiating content, process, and product (Tomlinson, 1999). It is important to first state what should not be differentiated. The content standards, key understandings, and essential questions of a unit should be the same for the majority of, if not all of, the students. What may be differentiated is the way the knowledge and skills that lead to these overarching goals are taught. Different students will have different levels of expertise with this knowledge and skills and will need different instruction as a result. The learning tasks also will need to be differentiated. Students with different strengths, interests, learning styles, and learning challenges and/or disabilities will need different types of learning activities in order to accomplish the goal of the lesson.

Finally, students will need to be assessed in different ways so that we can ensure that we are assessing what they know about the learning goal in question, and not measuring the effect that their learning challenge or disability may have on their performance. For example, if our goal was to measure a student's knowledge of gravity and the student had a disability that affected her written language, we would want to measure her knowledge orally or by giving her the opportunity to create a model or diagram instead of requesting a written report (Tomlinson & McTighe, 2006). An advocate will be able to see evidence of different content, processes, and products being utilized for different students as they all work toward achieving the same meaningful goals.

Strength-Based Instruction

One of the especially important principles in the best practices of a good classroom is the importance of focusing on students' strengths. First of all, teachers must take the time to get to know the interests and talents of each of their students. They must then incorporate these strengths into their lessons. Teachers should rely on student strengths to hook student interest, to provide the activities that allow students to learn in-depth about a topic, and to provide the opportunities for students to demonstrate understanding of concepts. When we think about offering appropriately challenging or gifted instruction to students, it is crucial that we think about identifying and nurturing the gifts of many students, not of trying to select out only the most "truly gifted" for this instruction. An advocate will look for evidence of rigorous instruction that is focused on the gifts of the individual students in each classroom.

Adaptations and Accommodations

When teachers have identified a student's strengths, they can use these strengths to help students to circumvent their weaknesses by providing appropriate adaptations and accommodations. Adaptations refer to the different ways that information can be presented and the different ways that student understanding can be assessed. It is important to remember that reading is not the only way to learn information and that writing is not the only way to demonstrate understanding. Teachers may adapt how they present information so that they are using guest speakers, field trips, and hands-on experiential learning in addition to or in place of reading about a subject. Teachers may adapt how they assess understanding so that they are having students create PowerPoint presentations, speeches, or projects in addition to or in place of writing about what they have learned. Accommodations allow all students to perform the required task. For example, the opportunity to dictate a response or use a computer to respond will allow a student to demonstrate his understanding on a written assessment if he has problems with writing down his thoughts with pen and paper (Weinfeld, Barnes-Robinson, Jeweler, & Roffman-Shevitz, 2006).

There often is debate about whether providing an accommodation is enabling or empowering. We believe that there are principles that help educators and parents together to determine which adaptations and accommodations are appropriate (Weinfeld, Barnes-Robinson, Jeweler, & Roffman-Shevitz, 2005). Some key points of this decision are that the choice of a specific accommodation should be based on the individual student's strengths and needs; it should be evaluated and faded when no longer needed; the rationale for choosing it should be shared with all staff who work with the student; and we should focus on gradually moving a student from dependence to independence over time. An advocate should be able to see a variety of accommodations that are individualized according to students' strengths and needs being used in the classroom.

Parent-School Partnership

For any classroom to be an outstanding environment for an individual student there must be a partnership between home and school. In order to have an effective partnership there must be regular communication between school staff that includes active listening by both sides. The student's strengths should be identified and celebrated, while challenges are identified and named. Measurable plans must be made and there must be an agreement for follow-up. When parent-teacher conferences include communication that provides for openness and accountability, the student benefits (Lawrence-Lightfoot, 2003).

What Might a Classroom Look Like if It's Not a Good Environment for Children?

Unfortunately, there are times that the classroom may not be meeting the needs of children. What might an advocate see in these classrooms? Some warning signs of a classroom that may not be a good environment for children are:

- The objectives of the lessons are unclear.
- Only whole-group instruction is being used.
- Teachers strive to cover the material, rather than to ensure that students learn the key concepts and skills.
- If there are groupings in the class, they always remain the same.
- The teacher does most or all of the talking.
- There is little or no interaction between students.
- Lessons are always taught in the same way—not accounting for students' learning differences.
- Lessons are not taught in a way that hooks students' interests.
- There is no evidence of adaptations or accommodations, such as the use of a multiple intelligence approach.
- Students are not given choices of how to demonstrate mastery of material.
- Students are not given choices of how to learn content.
- There is no evidence of technology being used to support instruction.
- Student behavior is controlled through fear, criticism, and/or shame.
- Students who need more teacher support are not seated near the teacher.
- Students are not provided with rubrics that make it clear what they are expected to do.
- Assessment is done at the end of instruction in order to see what students have achieved, rather than during

instruction in order to see what students need to be taught or retaught.

- Students are not provided with clear feedback regarding their performance on assessments.
- There is no evidence of a connection between teachers and students.
- There is no evidence of student-directed learning.
- There is no evidence of hands-on, active, project-based, or experiential learning.
- There are a large number of students without additional adults to provide support.
- There is little or no opportunity for clarification of directions or understanding.
- The teacher does not allow for wait time before calling on students.
- The teacher does not use higher order questioning techniques.
- Students are not provided an opportunity to revise or improve their answers.
- Teachers do not provide informative or constructive feedback to students.
- There is a lack of evidence that students have participated in establishing classroom rules and standards of conduct.

As we strive to provide for an outstanding educational environment for our children, we must have a vision of what does or does not constitute a good classroom environment. Having this vision is crucial when a parent is his child's only advocate and having a shared vision is crucial if parents, advocates, and school staff are to work together in the best interests of children.

Problem

You think the classroom is not meeting the needs of your child.

Common Situations/Examples

The student is unhappy; his self-esteem is suffering. Work is too hard and/or too easy. The teacher does not seem to know the unique strengths and needs of the child. The child can't seem to please the teacher.

What the Law Says

The No Child Left Behind Act (NCLB) says that a "highly qualified teacher" must teach the classroom. The school should have evidence that students are making Adequate Yearly Progress (AYP), and this evidence should be disaggregated for a variety of specified gender, minority, economic, and special education groups (NCLB, 2001).

Tips for Parents

Meet with teachers to discuss your child's strengths and weaknesses and to come up with a specific, measurable plan to try to improve identified problem areas. Get more information about your child's strengths and needs through an appropriate assessment, either one by the school or one done privately. Move into a more formal meeting process, either a 504 Plan or IEP consideration, if informal interventions are not being successful.

Implications for the School System/ Tips to Avoid the Problem

Assure that parents understand the instructional goals of the classroom. Assure that parents know how the teacher has identified the strengths and needs of the individual student and what he or she is doing to both meet the needs and build on the strengths of that student. Assure that parents know that the teacher is differentiating for students based on their strengths and needs related to specific skills.

TOOLS

Best Practices Checklist

Parents and advocates observing classrooms should look for the following best practices to be implemented. Good classrooms should provide (adapted from Weinfeld et al., 2006):

- ❏ Appropriately challenging instruction in students' areas of strength.
- ❏ Opportunities for the instruction of skills and strategies in academic areas that are affected by students' learning difficulties.
- ❏ Appropriately differentiated programs, including individualized instructional adaptations and accommodations systematically provided to students.
- ❏ Comprehensive case management to coordinate all aspects of students' Individualized Educational Programs with consistent and periodic review of student's academic progress.
- ❏ Activities that focus on individual students' gifts and interests.
- ❏ Open-ended outlets for the demonstration of knowledge.
- ❏ Instruction that differentiates for learning levels, styles, and abilities.
- ❏ Guided discovery, especially when introducing new topics.
- ❏ Student choice.
- ❏ Collaboratively designed rubrics that show students exactly how and for what they will be assessed.
- ❏ Hands-on experiences.
- ❏ Real-life tasks that use authentic assessment to gauge learning.
- ❏ Integration of visual and performing arts.
- ❏ Multiple texts and varied resources.
- ❏ Interest and learning centers.
- ❏ Interactive journals.
- ❏ Various modes of expression, materials, and technology.
- ❏ Advanced assignments that require higher order thinking skills.
- ❏ Self and peer evaluations.

Adaptations and Accommodations Checklist

Research has revealed that the principles put forth here are the best practices for providing appropriate adaptations and accommodations for kids with learning difficulties in order to ensure access to appropriate educational opportunities.

❐ Accommodations used in assessments should parallel accommodations that are integrated into classroom instruction.

❐ The adaptations/accommodations are aligned with the educational impact of the individual student's disability and the adaptations/accommodations are aligned with the needs described in the student's IEP or 504 Plan.

❐ The adaptations/accommodations are based upon the strengths of the student.

❐ Accommodations are based on what students need in order to be provided with an equal opportunity to show what they know without impediment of their disability.

❐ Assessments allow students, while using appropriate accommodations, to demonstrate their skills without interference from their disabilities.

❐ After selecting and providing appropriate adaptations/accommodations, their impact on the performance of the individual student is evaluated and only those that are effective are continued.

❐ The adaptations/accommodations are reviewed, revised, and when appropriate, faded over time, allowing the student to move from dependence to independence.

❐ A multidisciplinary team, which considers the input of the parent and student, decides upon the adaptations/accommodations.

❐ The appropriate adaptations/accommodations and the rationale for each of them are shared with all staff members who work with the student.

(Adapted from Weinfeld et al., 2006)

chapter 4

What Does an Advocate Need to Know About the Law?

The first thing to know about the law is that it is voluminous and complex. Much of what will be presented in this chapter is very technical. It is meant to help familiarize parents and educators with the law. However, parents or others who wish to serve as advocates for children are encouraged to go beyond reading the chapter and seek out actual training and supervision in advocacy before acting on behalf of other parents' children.

It is important to recognize that, although this chapter is designed to help the reader understand the law, it is not meant to be a comprehensive recitation of it. Reading this chapter does not substitute for legal advice, and individual situations will require interpretation by trained professionals. For legal advice, be sure to consult an expert or special education attorney. To see the actual law and related documents, we recommend taking time to view the Web sites listed in the Resources tool at the end of this chapter.

Interpretations of laws change, laws change, and new case law is being made by administrative proceedings and courts as this book is being read. Keeping up-to-date is the only way to effectively stay abreast of current trends and legal issues. At the end of this chapter, we provide resources, texts, and Web sites that will assist you in keeping up-to-date with special education and gifted education issues.

In addition, there are many issues and individual cases that may not be covered in this chapter. This is another reason that it is critical to continue researching and exploring issues, and at times, consulting with experts in the field. Keep in mind that even experienced advocates, parents, attorneys, and other people in the field consult with one another to expand understanding and application of the law.

Why Is This Important for an Advocate to Know?

Advocates must know the law in order to effectively represent the children they serve. Skilled advocates who understand the law will be able to navigate through the regulations in a knowledgeable and productive way so that the children they serve will receive the appropriate programs and services. There are several different laws that are crucial for the advocate to understand. Depending on the issues that face the individual child, the advocate will be referring to and utilizing general education laws and also specific special education federal laws.

Federal and state laws are designed to protect children from discrimination based on disabling conditions, including the provision of equal educational opportunities for all children. In the area of special education, many regulations exist that clarify the procedures and programming to be provided to children with disabilities. Some of the states even go beyond federal requirements. In the area of gifted and talented education there are no federal laws. Therefore, state laws, as well as local school district policies, must be consulted.

Parents and educators who are able to understand the law and regulations related to the education of children will be better able to make requests and complaints, or express concerns in a way that is directly related to the law.

These issues can contribute to a deterioration of trust, and parents can become even more disgruntled because they do not view the process as child-centered. The scales usually are tipped in favor of school systems when it comes to training and understanding the law and its application. Because school personnel speak this "foreign language" of the law and its implications every day, and parents either do not know the law or have only a partial understanding, this chapter attempts to give parents and advocates a level playing field in terms of knowledge and application of the law. It provides practical applications of the law, and summarizes important facets of the law to forward parent and educator understanding in an effort to collaborate and communicate in a child-centered way.

The overriding concept protecting children with disabilities is the requirement that the public school system provides all children with disabilities with a free appropriate public education (FAPE) at no cost to parents. FAPE will be discussed in more detail later in this chapter.

Brief History: The Law

An advocate needs to be familiar with these statutes:
- Elementary and Secondary Education Act of 1965
- Education for All Handicapped Children Act of 1975
- Section 504 of the Rehabilitation Act of 1973
- Americans with Disabilities Act of 1990
- No Child Left Behind Act of 2001
- Individuals with Disabilities Education Improvement Act of 2004, particularly Sections 614 and 615

- State regulations
- Updates to the application of IDEA 2004 through federal register and state bulletins

The history of special education law has its roots in Civil Rights litigation. The laws related to the education of individuals with disabilities have originated with and occurred at the same time periods as laws related to equal rights and nondiscrimination for all citizens. Before the laws protecting children with disabilities from discrimination, there were separate, special classes in public schools for children with disabilities, but children often were required to do menial, meaningless tasks, and many children and adults with disabilities were placed in institutions that removed them from the community.

In 1954, in a famous case called *Brown v. Board of Education of Topeka*, the courts ruled that it is illegal to discriminate against any group of people; therefore, the "separate but equal" education previously practiced was no longer acceptable. Although this ruling was directed toward Black students, there were implications for the nondiscrimination of students with disabilities because they also were being segregated and denied access to education. This important legislation overturned the case of *Plessy v. Ferguson*, which had previously upheld "separate but equal" train cars and was the basis for segregated schools (Library of Congress, 2007).

The Laws

In the 1960s, parents of children with disabilities became better advocates for their children, and by the 1970s, laws were being passed to assure that all children were being educated equally and included in education opportunities just like children without disabilities. In 1965, the Elementary and Secondary Education Act (ESEA) was instituted by the United States Department of Education. It is extensive and funds elementary and secondary education costs. It provides money for teacher training or professional development, materials, resources, and parental involvement. Title I of the Act provides funding for schools and districts with a high percentage of students in low-income families (ESEA, 1965). The majority of Title I funds are used for elementary schools.

Another landmark case, *Pennsylvania Association of Retarded Citizens v. Commonwealth of Pennsylvania*, occurred in 1971. This case upheld that students with mental retardation could not be excluded from regular classrooms, but further created the requirement that all children receive a free appropriate public education (FAPE). In the same year, from the District of Columbia, a case called *Mills v. Board of Education* (1972) recertified the rights of children with disabilities to a free appropriate public education, solidified due process rights, and secured student rights to FAPE regardless of the ability of the school district to pay for services.

The Rehabilitation Act of 1973 was instituted, but it was not funded; it continues to be an unfunded act today. It has several sections that address various groups and issues. Section 504 states that no people with disabilities can be excluded from any federally funded programs. A qualified person with a disability, including students, has a condition that "substantially limits" a major life function (Rehabilitation Act, 1973, Section 504). Learning is listed as one of several major life functions. The act requires places of employment and schools to provide necessary accommodation to people with disabilities. The act also requires that FAPE be provided. From the Rehabilitation Act comes the terminology for one type of programming plan for students with disabilities, a 504 Plan. A 504 Plan in a school setting provides accommodations, services, or aides for students of all ages. Often offered by school systems when children do not qualify for an Individualized Education Program (the focus of the next chapter), 504 Plans are discussed in detail later in this chapter.

The first federal law protecting and funding programs for children with disabilities was Public Law 94-142, the Education for All Handicapped Children Act (EHA) of 1975. This law has been updated several times, and is now the Individuals with Disabilities Education Improvement Act, or IDEA 2004. Over the decades, the changes in the laws have afforded individuals with disabilities greater protection and respect, as seen even in the titles of the federal law. What once was a handicapped child is now a child with a disability, with the emphasis on the individual person before the disability (ParentsUnitedTogether.com, n.d.).

The Americans with Disabilities Act (ADA; 1990) protects individuals with disabilities from discrimination and allows for any "reasonable accommodation" in the workplace, in government, or in public places. ADA prohibits discrimination against people with disabilities, including people who have had, been known to have, or who are considered to have a mental or physical impairment that limits a major life activity. ADA requires that hiring, recruiting, pay, and other employer practices are nondiscriminatory. It also requires that government buildings and public transportation options are accessible, and that people with hearing, vision, or speech disabilities are able to communicate effectively (U.S. Department of Justice, 2005).

No Child Left Behind

The Elementary and Secondary Education Act (ESEA) of 1965 was upheld and amended in 2001 with President Bush's signing of the No Child Left Behind Act, also called ESEA or, more commonly, NCLB. NCLB emphasizes four concepts: (1) accountability for academic proficiency for the disadvantaged, (2) flexibility in how districts use funds, (3) research-based education to provide interventions that have been researched to be effective, and (4) parent options to expand school choice for students in Title I schools (U.S. Department of Education, 2004a).

Title I, Improving the Academic Achievement of the Disadvantaged, strives to assure a "fair, equal and significant opportunity" for high-quality education and proficiency on state and district achievement tests. It provides funding ($25 billion for fiscal year 2007) to states and districts for a variety of school improvement activities such as reading interventions and services for students who are at risk of dropping out, migratory, or delinquent (U.S. Department of Education, 2004b, p. 1). NCLB has resulted in a pendulum swing in education where all students are to have exposure to the general education curriculum, regardless of the severity of their disabilities. This has put pressure on special educators to prove that their students are performing well on state and district assessments, and fulfilling state graduation requirements, such as high-stakes testing to earn credit for high school courses.

In our experience, this has, so far, led IEP teams (the group of people who evaluate a child's needs and prepare his or her education plan) to consider extensive testing accommodations such as reading aloud the entire test for children with reading deficits. While this does allow a student to score her best without the impact of her disability, parents may feel that with the emphasis on accommodation, there is less focus on skills instruction. Also, special education programs appear to be becoming more inclusive, with the philosophy that special educators cannot deliver the curriculum the way that general educators can. Administrators with special education programs in their schools have voiced concern that the program lowers test scores, resulting in the school being placed on an official monitoring statute or penalizing the school for inadequate performance. We believe that the effect of NCLB has been to increase standardized testing based on curriculum standards, IEP goals based on the curriculum instead of individual needs, and increased accommodation for students on tests. For more information about NCLB, visit this Web site: http://www.ed.gov/nclb/landing.jhtml.

Individuals With Disabilities Education Act

The Individuals with Disabilities Education Improvement Act (IDEA) of 2004 is the most recent statute that provides funding for special education programs, and dictates procedures for the identification, evaluation, and education of children with disabilities. This federal law was first created in 1975 as the Education for All Handicapped Children Act mentioned previously. It has been reauthorized and changed about every 5 years since 1974, with the name changing to the Individuals with Disabilities Education

Act in 1990 and to the Individuals with Disabilities Education Improvement Act in 2004.

IDEA 2004 is separated into four sections, lettered A through D. Part A of IDEA is an overview, stating the purposes and general provisions of the law. This part also includes definitions. Part B of IDEA focuses on school-aged children, ages 3–22. This part is the main focus of this chapter. Part B regulates how school districts evaluate, identify, and serve children with disabilities. It guides school districts with every facet of providing FAPE for school-aged children who are disabled and entitled to services under IDEA. Part C focuses on early intervention programs and issues related to the evaluation, identification, and services for infants and toddlers, ages birth through 3. It dictates the provision of FAPE for children who are too young for schooling. Part D helps the state departments of education and other agencies monitor and improve how children with disabilities are served.

Supreme Court Decisions Relating to Education Law

Several important Supreme Court decisions make it critical that parents continue to be powerful advocates for their children. Because fewer than a dozen special education cases have been heard by the Supreme Court in the last three decades (Philpot, 2002), it is vital that parents understand that in the future more light likely will be shed on issues related to the education of students with disabilities, and it is critical that parents are involved and knowledgeable advocates for their children. Part of this advocacy relates to parents' hiring of experts to either help them through the school system processes, or even more important, to hire experts when parents believe that their children's rights have been denied.

Setting the stage for tuition reimbursement cases in 1985, the Burlington case (*Burlington School Committee vs. Massachusetts Department of Education*) is the precedent case that allows parents to be reimbursed for private school tuition after the IEP is found to be inappropriate, even if the parents place the child in the private school during the due process hearing proceedings (due process hearings will be discussed later in this chapter).

While the Burlington case allows for tuition reimbursement for children who are unilaterally placed in a private school after parent rejection of the IEP, in 1993, the Carter case (*Florence County School District Four v. Carter*) set the precedent that the private schools the parents choose do not have to meet the standards of the state to provide FAPE. In other words, as long as the child is progressing and doing well in the private school, the parents do not need to show that the private school conforms to state standards in order to have tuition reimbursement ordered by the court. For example, parents are allowed tuition reimbursement for schools that may not be certified by the state as special education facilities (Cornell University Law School, n.d.).

In a recent 2007 case, the Winkelmans, parents of a child with a disability, argued that they should be able to represent themselves in federal court in a case related to their child's disability, and the arguments by the Supreme Court further focused on whether IDEA protects children and parents equally. The Court decided that parents are able to represent themselves in federal court, and that parents and children are equally protected under IDEA; parents are entitled to the "full bundle" of rights under IDEA, just as children are so entitled (Supreme Court of the United States, 2007).

In a recent Supreme Court case involving Gilbert F. from New York (*Board of Education of the City of New York v. Tom F. ex rel. Gilbert F.*, 2007), the child had never attended a public school. The parents rejected the IEP and placement proposed by the school system, placed Gilbert in a private school, and sought tuition reimbursement. The reimbursement was denied in the lower courts based on the fact that Gilbert had never attended the public school, or tried the special education program proposed by his IEP (Grenig, 2007). This controversial decision split the Supreme Court 4-4, and agreed that parents may be entitled to tuition reimbursement, even if the child has never attended a public program. Cases will be forthcoming as this is challenged, and will set precedents for the future. Because the Supreme Court decision was tied at 4-4, this case upheld the lower court's decision that the child must not be made to attend an inappropriate public program in order for the parents to seek and get tuition reimbursement for a unilateral placement. Another case on the same issue, *Frank G. vs. Board of Education of Hyde Park* (2006), has been appealed to the Supreme Court, which has not accepted the case as of the writing of this book.

The Murphy case is about the reimbursement of "expert" fees (*Arlington Central School Dist. Bd. of Ed. v. Murphy*, 2006). The Murphys hired an expert who testified for their child, Joe, in a due process hearing. The lower court decided that the Murphys were entitled to reimbursement of the costs of hiring an expert, under the provision of the law that allows for attorney's fees and reasonable costs for parents who win in a due process hearing. However, the court reduced the amount owed to the parent by about $21,000. The Supreme Court decision upheld the school system's position, that IDEA does not authorize the repayment of expert fees to parents (Supreme Court of the United States, 2006). As advocates, we know that is it critical that parents hire experts such as educational consultants or advocates, but we also know that it is costly and expensive for parents. If courts continue to decide that parents are not entitled to reimbursement for expert fees, then parents will not be able to assure equal participation in assuring that the rights of their children are protected.

In the recent Schaffer case (*Schaffer v. Weast*, 2005), the Supreme Court ruled that the party filing the complaint has the burden of proof to show that their children are not provided with an appropriate education. This means that parents must prove that the school system denied their child's right to an appropriate education, rather than having the school system prove that the child's rights were not violated. Although the parents have routinely had the burden of proof in some districts, the Schaffer decision puts the burden of proof on parents nationwide, unless attorneys can compel the state to shift the burden to school systems on an individual basis (*Schaffer v. Weast*, 2005). This puts even more emphasis on the need for parents to be powerful and knowledgeable advocates for their children and reinforces the idea that parents should be entitled to reimbursement for expert testimony in the due process hearing. Parents must have all of the knowledge that the school system has, and this is not possible without parents hiring experts such as educational consultants or advocates.

In our view, having the burden of proof is a daunting task for parents because school systems already have trained and specialized staff with knowledge that parents do not have. School systems hire a variety of special and general educators, specialists, and psychologists and have a wide variety of options for training and development of procedures. Further, school systems have administrators and supervisors who are specially trained to address parents and provide assistance for school teams. Parents come to the process usually only with an understanding of their own child. Although understanding their child is important, it is not enough to prove that school systems were deficient in providing an appropriate education. Most of the parents we meet who have been through a court process have been convinced that they were right about their child's education, but still did not prevail because they simply could not match the expertise of the school system. Parents, now more than ever, require help and expertise from advocates and attorneys who specialize in the special education process.

In our multicultural world, economic, racial, cultural, and other diversity factors can become important for parents as they navigate the processes described in this book. The Office of Special Education Programs and the U.S. Department of Education has acknowledged that, despite efforts of Civil Rights advocates over the decades, children of different racial backgrounds still are being recommended for special education programs or suspended from school more than their peers. IDEA 2004 requires all states to gather and keep data about how often this occurs. Parents of children who are Black or Hispanic, for example, should be aware of the discussions about disproportionality and overrepresentation of these minority groups in special education, as well as those who are subjected to disciplinary action through the school system (U.S. Department of Education, 2007).

If the federal laws cause confusion for parents, then adding to the confusion is that the local school systems have internal policies and procedures as a result of litigation that interprets federal laws. These policies usually are developed based upon direction from the special education administration. States cannot diminish student rights as found in federal laws, but states can establish more protections than the federal law. There are places in the federal law that allows states to create their own policy; for example, timelines for evaluations may be different from state to state.

Important Concepts in the IEP Process

In developing the Individualized Education Program, or IEP, schools must undergo a specific process as defined by federal law in order to ensure that the program meets the individual child's unique needs. This section will discuss some of the important concepts schools, parents, and advocates must consider in the IEP process. A detailed discussion of the stages of the IEP process is included in Chapter 5.

Parental Participation

The most important part of the IEP process is parent involvement. Every time a parent contacts us saying that the school system has held meetings without them, or refuses to allow the parent to observe their child's classroom, we are still surprised. Parents sometimes even allow the school system to conduct meetings on their child's education without parent participation. In our view, this is not at all the intention of the laws, which are in place to *ensure* parental participation in this very important IEP process. According to IDEA:

Almost 30 years of research and experience has demonstrated that the education of children with disabilities can be made more effective by . . . strengthening the role and responsibility of parents and ensuring that families of such children have meaningful opportunities to participate in the education of their children at school and at home . . . (IDEA, 2004, p. 3)

Note the language of IDEA below that requires steps that *must* be taken to ensure parental participation as equal partners in the IEP process:

Each public agency must take steps to ensure that one or both of the parents of a child with a disability are present at each IEP Team meeting or are afforded the opportunity to participate. This language emphasizes the need for school systems to allow parents to participate via phone or by other alternative means: If neither parent can attend an IEP Team meeting, the public agency must use other methods to ensure parent participation, including individual or conference telephone calls. (IDEA, 2004, p. 251)

Here is what IDEA says about school systems holding meetings without parents:

A meeting may be conducted without a parent in attendance if the public agency is unable to convince the parents that they should attend. In this case, the public agency must keep a record of its attempts to arrange a mutually agreed on time and place, such as—
  (1) Detailed records of telephone calls made or attempted and the results of those calls;
  (2) Copies of correspondence sent to the parents and any responses received; and
  (3) Detailed records of visits made to the parent's home or place of employment and the results of

those visits. (U.S. Department of Education, 2006, p. 46789)

Parent participation is vital in the IEP process; parents must insist that meetings are held on a date and at a time that is convenient for them, and parents should not give permission for the IEP meeting to be held without their participation. If the school insists on holding the meeting without the parent, the parent should ask for the records of calls, copies of correspondence sent, detailed records of visits to the home or place of employment, or any other actions taken to assure parental participation. As with any other action, parents should write a letter to the school system if they are unable to attend on a suggested meeting date. To be clear, the parent should state that the date should be "mutually convenient" and the letter should specify that the parent does not give permission for the school team to meet without parents present.

FAPE: Free Appropriate Public Education

An advocate needs to know what defines and constitutes FAPE for children with disabilities. FAPE means that all students, even the students with the most severe disabilities, must have access to an appropriate program, including individually designed instruction to meet their unique needs. FAPE means that regular and/ or special education and related aides and services are provided to meet a child's unique needs. FAPE relates to any aspect of a child's education that is related to the special education process. If a child is receiving FAPE, he is accessing the curriculum and making meaningful progress. Meaningful progress is discussed in more detail in Chapter 11. Parents and children have certain protections, called *procedural safeguards*, and an advocate must know and understand these protections in order to effectively guide others through the IEP process. Procedural safeguards will be discussed in more detail later in this chapter. Gifted and talented students who do not have a disability do not have a legal right to receive FAPE. Advocates and parents of gifted students may argue that for them, however, access to curriculum should be access to appropriately challenging instruction.

Free appropriate public education means special education and related services that:

- are provided at public expense, under public supervision and direction;
- meet the standards of the Department of Education, including the requirements of IDEA;
- include preschool, elementary, or secondary education; and
- are provided in conformity with an IEP that meets the requirements of IDEA. (108th Congress, 2004, pp. 7–8)

A central concept of IDEA 2004 and the other laws and regulations is to provide children with disabilities with a free appropriate public education. FAPE relates to every aspect of the stages of the IEP process in the next chapter, and every aspect of the development of the child's IEP. In addition, FAPE relates to the implementation of the child's IEP and entire educational program. As stated in the in Congressional findings of IDEA in 2004,

Almost 30 years of research and experience has demonstrated that the education of children with disabilities can be made more effective by—

(A) having high expectations for such children and ensuring their access to the general education curriculum in the regular classroom, to the maximum extent possible, in order to—

(i) meet developmental goals and, to the maximum extent possible, the challenging expectations that have been established for all children; and

(ii) be prepared to lead productive and independent adult lives, to the maximum extent possible. (108th U.S. Congress, 2004, p. 3)

Children who are receiving FAPE are making educational progress, accessing the curriculum, and are otherwise being afforded an overall appropriate education at public expense. FAPE is guaranteed and protects children who are eligible under IDEA through the IEP, and under the Rehabilitation Act of 1973 through the 504 Plan. Each of these plans will be discussed in detail later in this and the next chapter.

Prior Written Notice and Meeting Invitations

Perhaps some of the most important words to remember through the IEP process are *Prior Written Notice*. The term is a bit confusing, because the Prior Written Notice is provided after the IEP meeting, but before a change is made or an action step is done for the child. The notice is meant to, among other things, inform parents in writing of anything that the parent requested with which the IEP team did not agree. The Prior Written Notice is a *required* record of the concerns expressed and the commitments made by the IEP team members. The notice must be in the parents' native language and document actions discussed, refused, considered, or agreed to by the IEP team.

Each Prior Written Notice should:

- describe what the district proposes or refuses to do, or what action the district will take, and why it made the decision;
- include what evaluations, procedures, assessments, records, or reports the district used to make the decision;
- be provided in a reasonable time period before the action will occur;
- include a statement of parents' rights, procedural safeguards, and how parents can get them, including how to contact someone for help understanding them; and
- be understandable for the general public (108th Congress, 2004).

A parent also is entitled to a written invitation to meetings about the child. The invitation should be received well enough in advance that the parent will have an opportunity to attend. Many districts have specific guidelines, such as assuring that the meeting invitation is received at least 10 days before the meeting is scheduled. The notice of the meeting must indicate the purpose, time, and location of the meeting. When the purpose of the meeting is to discuss preschool, infants and toddlers, or transition services, parents must be specifically informed of those purposes as part of the meeting invitation. Parents must be informed about who will be attending. The notice is required to state what areas will be addressed, so parents have time to think about whether an advocate or attorney need to attend the meeting with them and how to prepare for the meeting.

The Multidisciplinary Team (MDT)

The multidisciplinary team or MDT is so-called because it is a team of different and multiple disciplines, or areas of expertise. Depending on the state or district in which you live, the MDT meetings are also called ARD meetings: admission (A), review (R), and dismissal (D). The team can admit students to special education, review progress and IEPs, and dismiss students from special education, hence the ARD team name. The meeting also may simply be called IEP team meetings.

The advocate, who serves as part of the MDT, has a responsibility to speak up and voice concerns about the IEP. Advocates must understand that it is important to give the MDT feedback, with an opportunity to correct concerns and revise the IEP to address parents' concerns. The advocate should advise parents to keep an open mind about the IEP developed by the school system, including possible placement options. Having positions or opinions before the MDT meeting is natural for parents and professionals; being stuck on positions without considering other possibilities can stymie the development of an appropriate educational program for children. An advocate's silence at the IEP

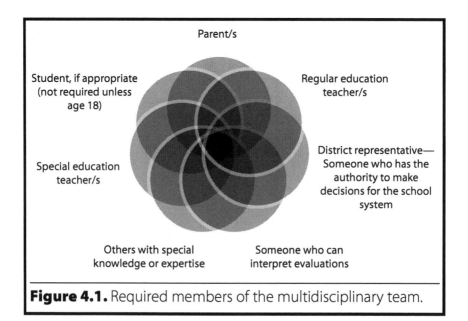

Figure 4.1. Required members of the multidisciplinary team.

meeting is not appropriate. Parents and experts have been found to have contributed to the development of an inappropriate IEP, because they did not voice the concerns they had about the IEP until after the MDT meeting.

Required Members

It is critical that required members of the IEP team are present during the IEP process. Otherwise, the IEP that results from an inadequate team meeting may be disregarded as invalid. Required team members are to attend the entire IEP meeting. If a member arrives late or he or she leaves early, for example, before a placement is discussed, they may be subject to the new procedures under IDEA for excusing team members, which are discussed later in this section. The required members, as shown in Figure 4.1, include the parent. Required members of the team are defined by IDEA 2004.

Here, the parents are defined as guardians, care providers, or those appointed by the court as parents. The regular and special education teachers should be those who teach the child, unless special circumstances apply. The school district's representative should be knowledgeable about the curriculum and the school system's resources. This representative should have the authority to make decisions for the school system and should be able to provide or supervise the provision of special education services. The individual qualified to interpret evaluations for parents and other team members can be a related service provider or other individuals who can help the parent and team interpret the results of evaluations.

A general education teacher is not required if the child is attending a program that is completely removed from the general education setting. If that student, however, is being considered for inclusion or "mainstreaming" (participation in the general education setting), the general education teacher is a required member. Other members with special expertise or knowledge about the child may be part of the IEP team at the discretion of the parents or school system.

Dual roles, where the special educator also is designated as the district representative, are acceptable, as long as the person performing the roles can fill each position as its purpose is intended (Norlin, 2007). The important thing to consider when determining if the MDT is in compliance with this section of the law is whether the team is able to fully discuss appropriately programming for the child. Unfortunately, we have been involved in meetings where the person playing the role of the district representative is not knowledgeable about all of the school system options and also may not be able to commit the school district's resources as is required in the law. This particularly happens in school districts that require a two-tier IEP system, in which the district only allows the second tier meeting to make decisions to place students in certain types of placements. There are questions about whether the two-tier system complies with IDEA. Eventually the courts will interpret the law and decide this issue.

Attorney Participation in the IEP Meeting

The Office of Special Education Programs notes that the presence of attorneys at IEP meetings is "strongly discouraged" because it "could potentially create an adversarial atmosphere at the meeting, which could interfere with the development of the child's IEP

. . ." (U.S. Department of Education, 1998). Attorney involvement can make the IEP process less child-centered. Attorneys are not required members of the IEP team. Parents sometimes invite a special education attorney to attend the IEP meeting, and the school system may choose to send their attorney to the meeting in these situations, as well. If a parent attends the IEP meeting without an attorney, and the school system sends their attorney to the meeting, we believe that the meeting should not be held until both parties are equally represented.

Excusals From Meetings

A required member may be excused from the MDT meeting if the school system and the parent agree to the excusal in writing. This applies to the excusal of the member for the whole meeting or even part of a meeting. This also applies to related service and other providers of the IEP, only if their area or curriculum will be modified or discussed. For example, if occupational therapy goals and services are not an issue, and will not be modified or discussed at the IEP meeting, the occupational therapist may not be a required member of the IEP team. There is a relationship between the meeting purpose, attendees on the meeting invitation, and the parent decision about whether to allow a member to be excused from the meeting.

Parents must agree in writing to the member's excusal. Also, before the meeting, the member who wants to be excused must submit a written report to the IEP team and parents that provides input into the development of the IEP.

If the excusal of IEP team members becomes a routine and regular practice for school systems, the state should investigate this as an inappropriate practice. Overall, parents should consider heavily whether a written report will suffice for the IEP member's participation, or whether the IEP meeting should be rescheduled for a date and time that the member can participate in person or even by phone.

Scientifically Based Methods and Peer-Reviewed Research

IDEA was reauthorized in 2004 with the understanding that there have been obstacles to student progress since the first education act in 1975. It calls for the use of "scientifically based instructional practices, to the maximum extent possible" (U.S. Department of Education, 2006, p. 89). The scientifically based practices are not just best practices in the field. They are specifically defined as research-proven practices that are "approved by a panel of independent experts" through "scientific review" (U.S. Department of Education, 2006, p. 89).

Emphasizing the need for the use of scientifically based methods for student instruction and for teacher training, the findings of the 108th Congress state,

> Since the enactment and implementation of the Education for All Handicapped Children Act of 1975, this title has been successful in ensuring children with disabilities and the families of such children access to a free appropriate public education and in improving educational results for children with disabilities. However, the implementation of this title has been impeded by low expectations, and an insufficient focus on applying replicable research on proven methods of teaching and learning for children with disabilities. Almost 30 years of research and experience has demonstrated that the education of children with disabilities can be made more effective by—supporting high-quality, intensive pre-service preparation and professional development for all personnel who work with children with disabilities in order to ensure that such personnel have the skills and knowledge necessary to improve the academic achievement and functional performance of children with disabilities, including the use of scientifically based instructional practices, to the maximum extent possible. (108th Congress, 2004, pp. 3–4)

Parent Demand for Specific Programs, Devices, or Methods

There is nothing preventing the MDT from specifying a research-based, scientifically sound educational method on the IEP. However, parents cannot make the school system put a specific reading method, assistive technology device, or any other specific educational methodology in the IEP. So far, the way to get a resolution to a dispute in this area is through a formal dispute process, as defined at the end of this chapter. School districts may resist putting a specific methodology on the IEP due to several reasons: School systems may resist training in a specific methodology due to cost or philosophy; school systems may not want to be responsible for implementing a specific program or method correctly with all required components; or school systems believe they should have the authority to make decisions about instructional methodology. Parents also may have a concern about who is delivering the methodology. Parents have a right to know the qualifications of the person delivering services, as we will discuss in the section on highly qualified teachers in Chapter 11.

Response to Intervention

Response to Intervention (RTI; see Figure 4.2) is a concept of increasing or changing supports, instruction, and interventions as student needs increase. A professional thinking in an RTI model may say, "If a small amount of service does not work, add more and/or different services, and see how the student responds." It relates to every stage of the IEP process described in Chapter 5. RTI means that, if a child has difficulty with reading, a research-based, peer-reviewed reading program should be put into place to address those needs.

If data show that intervention is successful, and the student is responding to that intervention, no additional interventions are needed. If however, the data show that the intervention has not been successful, either the intervention would be changed,

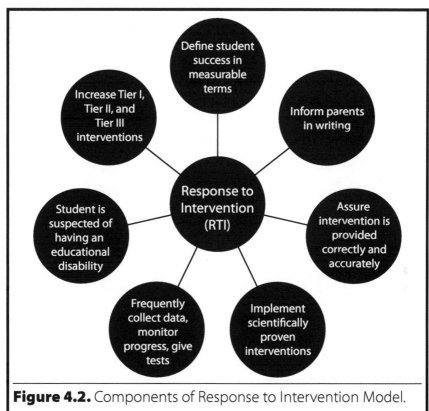

Figure 4.2. Components of Response to Intervention Model.

added to, or revised, or the length and intensity of the intervention would increase.

Similarly, perhaps a child is having behavioral problems at school. The multidisciplinary team may conduct a functional behavior assessment (discussed in Chapter 6) and develop a behavior intervention plan. Special education services often are considered to be an intervention, along with related services.

During an evaluation phase of the IEP stages, the MDT may decide to put into place interventions while evaluations are being conducted; a component of RTI is data collection to monitor the child's progress in the curriculum. RTI is specifically mentioned in IDEA 2004 as a way of determining learning disabilities. However, parents and advocates may find that schools are also using this approach with other suspected disabilities.

As shown in Figure 4.2, data collection is a necessary component of the RTI model. Data collection is more efficient when the student's needs have been stated directly in measurable terms. Accurate collection of data allows for data-driven decision making to occur after interventions are put into place. As a result of data collection, parents and school teams work together to determine whether interventions are successful or whether a higher level of intervention is required.

Problem

Parents want to specify educational methodology in the IEP, with specifics about how often the service will be provided and by whom it will be provided.

Common Situations or Examples

A parent of a child with autism spectrum disorder believes that applied behavior analysis (ABA) should be the specified methodology on his son's IEP. A parent of a child with a specific learning disability caused by dyslexia believes that the Wilson Reading System should be specified on her child's IEP.

Tip for Parents

If the school team refuses to put a specific methodology in your child's IEP, use the structure of the IEP goals to "drive" the services you believe are appropriate. For the child with autism, whose parents believe ABA is the appropriate and only methodology to show progress, the IEP goals may read:

> Given a structured work time of 10 minutes with tokens earned every minute, a 30-second break at regular intervals, and data collection in an individual session, Jeremy will imitate 5 consecutive gross motor movements after no more than two verbal prompts in 9 out of 10 trials.

The way goals are written will allow you to make requests about how and with what methodology services are provided. Hiring a professional advocate who is an expert in the area of IEP goal development will improve the information parents provide as input to the IEP process. Understanding the IEP process (as discussed in Chapter 5), including evaluation of student needs and developing clear, measurable goals, allows the advocate to more effectively document the need for specific services, methodology, or devices.

Parental Consent

There are two times that parental consent is necessary and important: (1) when parent permission is required for evaluation—either initial evaluation or reevaluation, as described in the evaluation stage of the IEP process in Chapter 5, and (2) parents must give consent in writing when they approve and agree to the *initial* IEP and placement. No initial special education services may be provided per the IEP without parent signature.

Timelines for evaluations begin when parents sign permission for the evaluation. If parents refuse to give permission for the initial evaluation, the school system can take parents to court or a due process hearing to try to convince the judge to force the parents to give consent. However, if an independent hearing officer does order the parent to allow the evaluation of the child, and the MDT eventually determines that the child has a disability, the parent cannot be forced by an independent hearing officer to allow the school system to provide any special education or related services. This is new as of IDEA 2004. Previously, a parent could be forced by a due process hearing to consent to services.

Parents must provide consent, but the district must assure that parents are informed before providing this consent. This concept is known as *informed consent*. In order to make the parents fully informed, the district must do several things. The district must use the parent's native language or mode of communication to provide information. When a parent signs to consent for any evaluation or to agree to the initial provision of special education services, the school district must clearly explain for what it is seeking consent. Also, the school district should make it clear to the parent that her consent can be revoked, but not after the action is already completed (National Center for Learning Disabilities, 2006).

The only time that parents must sign the IEP in order for it to be implemented, or in order for any special education or related services to be provided, is during the planning for the very first IEP, or the "initial IEP." A parent signature is not required on subsequent IEPs in order for the school system to implement special education programs. The recourse for disagreeing with an initial IEP is not to sign the IEP at all. Therefore, if parents have any question at all whether the initial IEP and special education placement are appropriate, if there is any doubt, then we generally would advise parents not to sign the IEP. Certainly, parents should not feel pressure to sign the IEP at an IEP meeting, especially without reviewing the final product and thoroughly understanding the placement, services, and all parts of the IEP.

All subsequent IEPs are developed by the school team and parents. With or without a parent's signature on a future IEP, the school system can go ahead and implement that IEP, even if parents do not agree. If the IEP is approved by the school system, the IEP will be implemented. Parents will need to consider options for how to stop the implementation of the IEP if the school system continues to implement an IEP that the parent is challenging. The recourse for disagreeing with the IEP when it is not the first IEP is to exercise due process, mediation, or other dispute processes (see the dispute section of this chapter), or keep providing new information to the MDT to continue to revise the IEP.

The new federal law does not allow school systems to take parents to a due process hearing to force the parent to approve the initial IEP. School districts, therefore, may be motivated at times to develop the initial IEP such that parents agree and services can be initiated.

504 Plans

Students with disabilities may be eligible for services in two ways: (1) under IDEA, or (2) under Section 504 of the Rehabilitation Act of 1973. The previous sections of this chapter have focused on requirements of IDEA. The 504 law mandates that all people with disabilities must have access to any programs and services that receive federal funding. It applies not only to services during the school day, but also to services outside of a school day, such as a publicly funded homework club, sport activity, or afterschool activity. For adults, the Rehabilitation Act of 1973 may require a 504 Plan in the workplace. Section 504 of the Rehabilitation Act prohibits discrimination, but it is not funded; there is no money allocated for programs under this law like there is under IDEA 2004.

In order to qualify for or be eligible for a 504 Plan, a disabling condition must significantly impair one or more major life functions. Learning is a major life function. Specifically in Section 504, the law defines a person as disabled if the person has a physical or mental impairment that substantially limits one or more major life activities, such as blindness, deafness, or mental illness (U.S. Department of Health and Human Services, 2006). In addition, the law defines as disabled those who previously had an impairment or are regarded as having an impairment. 504 Plans may apply to disabling conditions that are considered to be either short- or long-term conditions.

Eligibility under IDEA 2004 differs in several ways. First, a disabling condition is different from one of the federally defined educational disabilities; a disabling condition does not need to be defined as one of the federally defined disabilities discussed in detail in Chapters 5 and 6. Second, the educational impact question in the 504 process relates to impairment of major life functions (including learning), not to whether the disability adversely affects the child and requires special education services, as in the IEP process. Also, 504 Plans are available for people of any age, not just school-aged children. Lastly, 504 Plans address activities and environments that are beyond the typical school day. If the student is eligible under IDEA 2004, the student also would qualify for a 504 Plan. However, the opposite is not always the case; students who are eligible for 504 Plans likely have not qualified for services under IDEA 2004. Students eligible under IDEA may need a 504 Plan to address afterschool activities, if these services are not addressed in the student's IEP.

A myth about 504 Plans often is perpetuated by school systems when they tell parents that children with 504 Plans are not entitled to special education or related services. According to the U.S. Department of Education Office of Civil Rights (OCR; 2005, Question 4), "An appropriate education for a student with a disability under the Section 504 regulations could consist of education in regular classrooms, education in regular classes with supplementary services, and/or special education and related services." Special education is a publicly funded program, so students with disabilities under Section 504 of the Rehabilitation Act are not prohibited from receiving services in a special education program. Students with 504 Plans may even be entitled to related services (see related services section in Chapter 5). Although students who are eligible under IDEA must receive special education in order to receive related services, students with a 504 Plan may receive related services without receiving special education services (Norlin, 2007).

Another myth about 504 Plans is that gifted students are not eligible for 504 Plans. Some parents are wrongly informed that, in order to consider eligibility for a 504 Plan, the gifted child is compared with his or her "average" peers. This is an inappropriate and discriminatory practice. Gifted students may be eligible to receive necessary accommodation in gifted or Advanced Placement courses; there is nothing within the Rehabilitation Act of 1973, Section 504 that discusses the peer group against which students should be compared to qualify for services under a 504 Plan.

Students eligible under Section 504 are entitled to FAPE, as are students under IDEA 2004. The 504 Plan should not be seen as a consolation prize when students are not eligible for the IEP. Although the IEP has annual goals against which progress is measured and although the IEP has other required sections as described above, a 504 Plan does not, unless the team determines that goal development is a necessary accommodation. The 504 Plans provide for the possibility of a vast array of services and accommodation, for evaluation, and for the provision of FAPE. The 504 Plan allows for periodic reevaluation for the provision of FAPE, as does IDEA 2004. The 504 Plan also does not specifically exclude any of the parts of the IEP. The dispute options described in the following section also apply to the student who has the 504 Plan. The tenets of the Least Restrictive Environment described in the next chapter related to the placement of children with disabilities also relate to placement of children who receive services under the 504 Plan.

If a child attends a private school, and that private school receives any federal assistance or funding, the private school must provide students with disabilities a FAPE, including the development of a 504 Plan. This applies to colleges and universities, as well.

The most common complaints we receive about the 504 plan are that the accommodations listed in it are not being followed, the accommodation is too vague, and that all staff are not aware of the 504 Plan. Every child is different, but we have found that overall, teachers are doing their best to implement accommodations, if they are aware of the 504 plan. If teachers are doing their best to implement the 504 Plan, and the child's disability continues to adversely affect his achievement or educational performance, the MDT should take steps to discover whether the child is eligible for special education and related services under IDEA 2004.

Tips for Parents

Make a 504 binder resource for your child's teachers and staff every year, so all of the staff will be aware of your child's 504 Plan. When parents believe the 504 Plan has not been followed, request evaluation to determine if the child should be receiving additional services, should be receiving services under IDEA with the development of the IEP, whether the child is making progress, or whether the lack of accommodation is harming the child or impacting her in the classroom.

Tips for School Personnel

When school systems consider a 504 Plan, or implement one, they are acknowledging that there is basis for suspecting an educational disability under IDEA 2004. In other words, any time a child has a 504 Plan, he or she has a suspected IDEA disability. Whether eligible for services under IDEA with an IEP or under a 504 Plan, parents have options to disagree with the determinations of the MDT. These dispute options are held in common because students who are eligible under either law are entitled to receive a free appropriate public education (FAPE).

Dispute Options
and Procedural Safeguards

A parent may complain that her child has been denied FAPE, and she may either write a state complaint, request for mediation, or request for a due process hearing. States also have other dispute processes available. Each one of these dispute options are discussed in detail here.

While advocates frequently help parents through the dispute process, this section is not meant to be legal advice, to substitute for law, or to guide parents in which dispute route to take. We advise the reader to consult with a professional advocate and/ or attorney for advice about which dispute option to use in individual circumstances.

IDEA 2004 clarifies that FAPE is not denied just because school systems fail to follow procedures. There must be some detriment or harm to the child as a result of the procedural failures; if the procedural problems stack up enough to impact the child, it could be that the child has been denied FAPE. For example, if the school system repeatedly fails to evaluate a child within timelines, that delay may cause a delay in the services the child receives. The procedural breakdowns must have impacted the child negatively in some way for the school system to take notice and for parents to have a reasonable complaint that may deserve a remedy.

Advocates often are considered to be experts on the child and his needs. Because parents may need experts during the IEP process, parents also likely need experts during dispute processes. We are not attorneys, so we will spend part of this section helping the reader understand when consultation with a special education attorney is vital in our opinion.

Professional advocates will have experience filing state complaints and mediation complaints, but in our opinion, even professional advocates should not generally file a request for a due process hearing without a special education attorney. However, as previously described in this chapter, it is legal for parents to pursue their due process rights without an attorney. At the same time, it is important for parents to know that they are entitled to be informed about free or low-cost legal services.

State Complaint

Literally a letter or form completed by parents or their advocate or attorney, the state complaint is sent to the state that oversees the school system. Many states require the issue of concern described in the state complaint to be connected to the law in order to fully investigate the issue. The state has 60 days to issue a report that either agrees that the issues in the complaint are valid or not. The state may direct the school system to do action steps to correct the problem, or the state may direct the school system to hold a particular type of meeting. It also may state that the child is entitled to a particular type of service, such as compensatory education services. We have found that the state complaint can be an effective way to dispute procedural violations, but is not useful to remedy more substantive complaints such as student placement. As with each dispute option, the state complaint has advantages and disadvantages.

The advantages of the state complaint include:
- State corrective actions (things they require the school system to improve) help children.
- The state becomes aware of issues of concern for parents.
- Having state oversight provides more attention to a child, and therefore, the school system attends to the child's case better.

The disadvantages of the state complaint include:
- Not useful for many issues, such as placement of the child.
- The state has a long time to investigate.
- Parents believe that there may be subtle or overt retribution for issuing a state complaint.

- Once the state's findings are issued against the parent, it is very difficult to complain about the same issue in another forum.
- Corrective action may be more about staff policies and/ or procedures than about the child.

Mediation

Mediation is a voluntary meeting between the school system and the parents that is run by or facilitated by a qualified mediator from the state. The parent and the school system meet together, usually with many or all of the same people who were involved with the issues that caused the dispute. However, having a qualified mediator and an opportunity to solve the problem to prevent a due process hearing is sometimes very helpful. To file for a mediation, it is important to connect the issues of concern to a denial of FAPE. There usually is a form used by the school system located online, in schools, in the Board of Education, and in the Procedural Safeguards Manual (a booklet schools are required to give to parents before any changes to their child's educational program) to use in filing a mediation. A mediation is not appropriate for all issues in our opinion, but it can legally be used to try to work out any issue related to the education of children with disabilities. A mediation is confidential, and there are rules about what information from a mediation may be used at a subsequent due process hearing, if the issues are not solved.

School systems sometimes ask parents to put into writing that they will not file for due process in the future about the issue mediated. School districts also may ask parents to give up certain rights in exchange for certain agreements in mediation. We believe parents should not make these decisions without consulting an expert advocate or attorney, and parents should have a thorough understanding of the implications of such agreements.

A written, legally binding decision can be a product of the mediation if the parties agree. Parents who go through the mediation process without help may not insist on correct language of this agreement, and we encourage parents to at least consult with a professional before mediating.

The school system may encourage the parent to mediate. This does not mean that there will be agreement at the mediation.

The advantages of mediation include:

- confidentiality;
- prevention of due process hearing;
- another chance to talk about child's needs;
- mediator may use caucusing with either side and help reveal another point of view;
- negotiations are possible;
- a written, binding agreement; and
- a special education attorney is not always needed.

The disadvantages of a mediation include:

- confidentiality;
- no reimbursement for attorney's fees, unless agreed to;
- school district may not send a representative who can negotiate; and
- can be expensive for parent, in terms of both time and money.

Due Process Hearings

The most intense and complicated dispute option is the due process hearing. To initiate any dispute process hearing, the parent must write and file a complaint to the district or to the state, requesting a due process hearing. The school district usually has forms to complete that may be available online and usually are available in the Procedural Safeguards Manual.

An expert special education attorney who we very much respect recently reminded us that the due process hearing and record of the hearing is only four steps away from taking a dispute to the Supreme Court. The stakes are high in the due process hearing for this and many other reasons.

First, the due process hearing creates a record of evidence, transcripts, and testimony that may be heard by higher courts of appeal, and there are rules that govern whether this record can be added to on appeal to higher courts. Next, if a parent loses the due process hearing, there is no way to do it over, or get another chance to complain about the same issues. Once the decision is issued, if the parent does not agree with the decision, the parent has no choice but to appeal to the higher court. The parent cannot lose a due process hearing, and then go to mediation, for example, complaining about the same issues from the due process hearing. It is critical that, while there is nothing prohibiting a parent from filing a request for a due process hearing without an attorney, parents understand that it is perilous to do so. Parents generally do not know how to write a sufficient due process hearing complaint, gather disclosure documents and submit them timely to the district, put on evidence, question witnesses, make and write motions, make objections, and use precedent law to make points. Therefore, a parent at a due process hearing without a skilled attorney may be unable to successfully present a case for her child.

Further, there is nothing in the Procedural Safeguards Manual to teach parents how to do all of these things. The procedural safeguards are not required to disclose this information to parents. Procedural safeguards and requirements are discussed later in this section.

A due process hearing is like a court proceeding, with an administrative law judge or independent hearing officer who is the decision maker, witnesses, evidence, and testimony. The hearing officer hears both sides, and makes a legally binding decision. IDEA has requirements that dictate how the due process hearing request is written, what information it should contain, and how it should be distributed. Parents now may be responsible for the school system's attorney's fees if the school system proves that, "the parent's complaint or subsequent cause of action was presented for any improper purpose, such as to harass, to cause unnecessary delay, or to needlessly increase the cost of litigation" (108th Congress, 2004, p. 78).

The school system must respond in writing to the due process hearing, and a parent needs an attorney to determine whether the response is sufficient. Then, 15 days after the request for due process is received, the school system must schedule a dispute resolution session that strives to resolve the problem and prevent going forward with the due process hearing. We also believe that an attorney is needed for the due process complaint and hearing from the beginning when the due process complaint is filed because parents cannot raise any issues in the hearing that are not in the request for the hearing. Figure 4.3 shows the process after the request for the due process hearing is filed.

The advocate may provide expert testimony in due process hearings. The advocate understands that despite the best efforts of parents and school systems, disputes arise and the parents' dispute options are a necessary part of the special education process and may, in fact, be an important catalyst for change. Due process hearings can be stressful, time consuming, expensive, and difficult. At times, however, this dispute option is the only choice and parents' use of the dispute processes available to them results in decisions that can set precedents that further protect children with disabilities.

The advantages of a due process hearing include:
- A due process hearing is sometimes the only option after mediation and state complaints.
- A decision maker makes a legally binding decision.
- The due process hearing is a necessary part of parents challenging the school system.
- When parents continue with the IEP process after the due process hearing, the school system attends to the IEP process better, in general.
- Prevailing parents are entitled to legal fees and expenses if represented by counsel.

The disadvantages of a due process hearing include:
- Due process hearings are expensive for families and school systems.

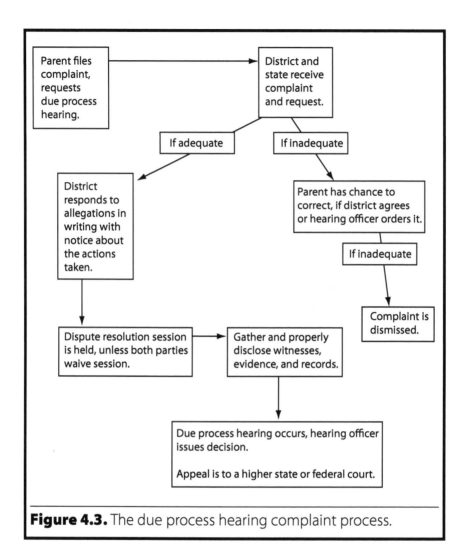

Figure 4.3. The due process hearing complaint process.

- Parents must hire experts, and there is controversy about whether expert fees can be reimbursed after winning a due process hearing.
- Due process hearings are stressful for families and educators.
- Due process complaints, if done incorrectly, can devastate a parent's chance of using this process successfully.

Parents often believe that, because they did not sign the IEP, they are now disputing the school system. This is not true; not signing the IEP does not constitute a formal dispute. Different dispute options are effective for different situations. Parents or school systems may initiate any of these options. Because the school district's MDT is the decision-making body, the majority of the time that a disagreement occurs, it is the parent disagreeing with the MDT's decisions. School districts may, however, bring a parent to a due process hearing in order to try to force the parent to give permission for evaluations, or to defend an evaluation in reaction to a parent complaint. The school system may not bring a parent to a due process hearing to try to make the parent agree to initial special education services or placement.

Disputing Proposed Programs

The MDT may make a placement, and if it is approved by the school district, it will go into effect even without parent approval. This means that a parent who does not agree with moving her child to another placement likely will be put in a position in which she must exercise a dispute option to stop the district from changing the child's program. As discussed earlier in this chapter, this does not apply when the classroom- or school-proposed move is because of the child's first IEP. If the parent does not sign the initial IEP, no services will be provided.

The majority of the time, a change of placement would mean placement in a different classroom, or even a different school. If the proposed placement means a classroom change for the child, it is very important in our view to become familiar with the proposal before officially rejecting it. To become familiar with the proposed program, the advocate will conduct one or more observations, interviews, and data collection about the various aspects of the proposal, including the service delivery model for special education and related services.

The advocate is an expert in the placement of children with special needs. He will form an opinion about the proposed program and articulate his findings to the school district when participating in the dispute processes. At times, the advocate may find that the proposed program is unable to implement the child's IEP. At other times, the IEP is not appropriate and will not allow the child to benefit from his program. It may be advisable that the advocate work with the special education attorney when a dispute arises.

Stay Put

Also called pendency during a due process hearing, stay put is a confusing concept and can be even more confusing in real-life situations. In developing IDEA, Congress discussed what would happen with students' placements during the time that parents and school systems are involved in the due process hearing.

If the school system is intent on placement in a different school or classroom, and proceeds with placement in a different location, the parent only has one option to stop that action: File a due process complaint and request a due process hearing. The filing of the complaint and request for due process makes the stay put provision kick in. Stay put means that the child stays in the last agreed upon placement during the due process hearing proceedings, until the administrative law judge or independent hearing officer determines the child's placement in her decision. The exception to this is when the change of placement is to an Interim Alternative Education Setting (IAES). Placement to an IAES is a result of discipline of the student with a disability. The school district may change the child's placement for up to 45 school days, in which case stay put is not in effect. Parents may disagree and file a request for a due process hearing, but that filing does not mean that the child stays in the current or last agreed upon placement when discipline is for one of three serious behaviors related to drugs, weapons, and serious bodily injury. In these and other cases, school districts or parents may request an expedited due process hearing to determine student placement and other issues of FAPE.

Procedural Safeguards

Parents must receive a copy of the Procedural Safeguards Manual one time per year. But, the parents also should receive a copy of the booklet when the child is first referred for special education services, when the parents file a complaint, and any time the parents request a booklet. The procedural safeguards booklet may be posted online and/or e-mailed to the parents, but the school system cannot require the parent to use the online booklet.

According to the law, the procedural safeguards booklet must contain information about the following:

(A) independent educational evaluation;

(B) prior written notice;

(C) parental consent;

(D) access to educational records;

(E) the opportunity to present and resolve complaints, including—

   (i) the time period in which to make a complaint;

   (ii) the opportunity for the agency to resolve the complaint; and

   (iii) the availability of mediation;

(F) the child's placement during pendency of due process proceedings;

(G) procedures for students who are subject to placement in an interim alternative educational setting;

(H) requirements for unilateral placement by parents of children in private schools at public expense;

(I) due process hearings, including requirements for disclosure of evaluation results and recommendations;

(J) state-level appeals (if applicable in that state);

(K) civil actions, including the time period in which to file such actions; and

(L) attorneys' fees. (108th Congress, 2004, p. 73)

Now that you have an overview of the law, to further equip you to achieve a successful, individualized education plan for your child, you'll need to understand the various stages of the IEP process. Although these stages are dense, gaining a knowledge of what will happen (and what is required to happen by law) when the school system begins planning for your child's special education needs is imperative to ensuring that your child receives the education he or she needs and deserves.

Resources

The following Web sites will help you stay current with law and education issues:

- http://www.nichcy.org/reauth/PL108-446.pdf
- http://www.nichcy.org/reauth/IDEA2004regulations.pdf
- http://www.nichcy.org/idealist.htm
- http://www.educationlawadvocates.com/Supreme_Court_Cases.shtml
- http://www.pattan.net/files/OSEP/CY2004/Parker01.pdf
- http://idea.ed.gov/explore/home
- http://www.hhs.gov/ocr/504.html

For finding general information regarding special education law:

Russo, C. J., Osborne, A., & Borreca, E. A. (2005). *Individuals with Disabilities Education Improvement Act vs. IDEA '97: Charting the changes.* Horsham, PA: LRP Publications.

Tips for Parents

- Read the Procedural Safeguards Manual, understanding that its contents should be supplemented by other information from the law as described in this chapter.

- Only sign forms if you fully understand their contents and implications.

- Don't let your emotions distract you from the goal of getting your child what he needs.

- Review the child's records periodically.

- Put concerns in writing; make a written record of personal or teleconferences.

- Make copies of school system documents

- Consult a professional who is knowledgeable about writing complaints regarding the denial of FAPE. In your complaint, reference important items in your state's regulations, which will be very similar to those described in this chapter. Focus the complaint on issues that relate to the required aspects of the IEP, and connect the issues to the regulations in your state.

- Research the result of complaints and due process hearings in your state and region to understand the history of decisions, both in general and specifically those that are similar to your case.

- Consider professional help when writing any type of complaint, whether a state complaint or a request for mediation or a due process hearing. Put your requests and school response or actions in writing. Remember, if it hasn't happened in writing, it hasn't happened.

- Contact the free and reduced cost service providers in your Procedural Safeguards Booklet. Contact the parent centers in your district that are responsible for helping you understand the rights of you and your child. Contact agencies in your area that provide services for children with disabilities and explore whether they will help pay for expert advocate fees.

Tip for School Systems

Bring to the mediation someone who is able to and has the authority to negotiate with parents. Be flexible; avoid predetermined outcomes, or positions that cannot be changed. Inform parents and their representatives well in advance if the school system declines to mediate.

TOOLS

How to Spot a Scientifically Based Practice

Utilize these criteria, as described on the National Institute for Literacy Web site, to determine if the interventions being suggested or used for the child are truly "scientifically based" as required in IDEA 2004 and NCLB.

To meet the NCLB definition of "scientifically based," research must:

- employ systematic, empirical methods that draw on observation or experiment;
- involve rigorous data analyses that are adequate to test the stated hypotheses and justify the general conclusions;
- rely on measurements or observational methods that provide valid data across evaluators and observers, and across multiple measurements and observations; and
- be accepted by a peer-reviewed journal or approved by a panel of independent experts through a comparatively rigorous, objective, and scientific review. (National Institute for Literacy, 2005)

chapter 5

What Does an Advocate Need to Know About the IEP Process?

The IEP process can feel like a maze to parents and even school staff. To effectively navigate the IEP process, the advocate must understand the stages of the process, how the stages relate to each other, and the aspects of the law guiding each stage. Understanding the IEP process provides an opportunity for parents and school teams to listen to each others' concerns about a child and make decisions in a way that is consumer-friendly to parents; an informed advocate will anticipate the future steps of the process and know how they relate to the past.

Most parents who have navigated this complex process say that it introduces them to a completely different language. Often, school personnel talk about the law in jargon that parents do not understand, so the advocate speaks the language of the MDT and in a sense, interprets for parents. Parents often do not know the stages of the special education process or where they are in the process with their children. Parents may not know how best to respond to the purpose of the meeting or how to respond when there is disagreement. Even clients with familiarity with some of the processes may have the experience of leaving a multidisciplinary team meeting thinking, "What just happened to my child in there?"

Why Is This Important for an Advocate to Know?

The school team has the decision-making authority in the process. The MDT is able to make decisions about a child, even when parents do not agree. It is up to parents to enter into a dispute if there is disagreement, so it is in every stakeholder's best interest to work effectively through the stages of the IEP process to effectively program for children with as much agreement as possible. The school system must follow all of the processes and procedures laid out in the federal and state laws so that FAPE will be provided. Parents only will be aware whether FAPE has been denied if they understand the law as it relates to the IEP process described in this chapter.

Advocates continually update knowledge of the application of the law and so do school system staff. Parents must become better informed to be able to take action when their children are being denied FAPE. Court cases and legal decisions also affect how the school systems perceive that FAPE should be provided. FAPE can relate to the identification, evaluation, or instruction of children with disabilities in any of the stages of the process. Parents and other advocates must be aware of the issues that constitute FAPE so that they can focus on the issues of concern in a way that can be heard by the multidisciplinary team and focus on the child's needs in a productive and powerful way.

Stages in the IEP or Special Education Process

There are stages in the process to identify the need for special education and other services, and each stage relates to the provision of FAPE for students with disabilities. The stages are:

- Stage 1: Prereferral, Prescreening, General Education Intervention
- Stage 2: Referral and Screening Stage/Process
- Stage 3: Evaluation Planning and Evaluation
- Stage 4: Eligibility Determination
- Stage 5: IEP Development
- Stage 6: IEP Is Implemented
- Stage 7: The Child's Progress Is Reported
- Stage 8: IEP Is Reviewed in a Periodic Review or Annual Review Meeting
- Stage 9: Reevaluation

It is imperative to understand how the stages relate to one another, and when to return to a previous stage in order to forward the process. For example, many parents complain that the goals the school system has developed are not specific and not designed to meet their children's needs. An effective advocate explores whether the goals are created from accurate information, including taking a careful look at the prior evaluation planning stage. Perhaps updated information needs to be gathered before appropriate goals can be developed. Understanding the stages and their interrelatedness will help parents experience the process in a powerful way that allows them to be an equal partner with the team. Each stage is described in more detail in the following sections.

Stage 1: Prereferral, Prescreening, General Education Intervention

Some states have regulations requiring school systems to put into place services for struggling students before placing them in special education environments or before providing special education services. The best practice is to use the RTI model during this stage to provide all students with specialized, research-based interventions based on their unique needs. School teams (MDTs) that identify children who are struggling and make a plan to address the areas of need before officially beginning the process for special education services may have a better handle on that child's needs. There are some times when the MDT will proceed more quickly to evaluations based on individual situations. This practice of implementing prereferral interventions prevents teachers who just want to "get rid" of students from simply placing children in a special education classroom and segregating children without due process of law. When students are in regular classrooms and having difficulty or struggling in any area, or there is negative educational impact, they are said to have a "suspected" educational disability until the MDT makes a decision about eligibility for services.

It is important to note that children who are suspected of having an educational disability are protected under federal and state laws and regulations, just like their disabled counterparts. This is especially important for children suspected of having an educational disability who have disciplinary infractions, as will be discussed in the IEP development stage later in this chapter. Interventions to address these learning or behavior problems would be identified by a school-based team before referring the child for evaluations or certainly before providing special education services. The prereferral school-based teams usually are coordinated by the guidance counselor or administrator and are comprised of people from multiple disciplines such as a school psychologist, general class teacher, special education teacher, and guidance counselor. The multidisciplinary team has many important purposes and functions, which are driven by the stages in the special education process. Its compilation of members depends on what stage the child is in the special education process and the purpose of any meetings that are convened with the parent.

The prescreening and prereferral general education intervention team is called by many different names, such as Student Support Team, Student Services Team, Collaborative Action Plan Team, and Educational Management Team. These teams usually are called by acronyms, adding to the "alphabet soup" of special education. The teams generally are chaired by the administrator or guidance counselor at the school. The purpose of the team is to make instructional recommendations for the general classroom setting before evaluating a child or providing him or her with services under a 504 Plan or IEP. The purpose of the team meeting is to define and evaluate interventions to address learning problems or interfering behaviors. The problems with learning or behavior can point parents, educators, and advocates to a suspected disability.

The MDT continues to meet with parents and discuss interventions and their effectiveness. At some point, someone on the team, such as the parent, may request that the team move to the next stage for referral and screening.

Tip for Parents

When you first notice your child struggling in any area, begin to keep a portfolio of work samples and examples of assignments that represent your child's strengths and areas of need. Through the referral, screening, and evaluation process, it is very important to keep a calendar so that you may document discussions with school staff, behaviors that occur at home, correspondences with the school system, or any other important events related to the IEP process. Have more frequent meetings with school staff during the referral and screening stage, and observe your child in the classroom as many times as possible. The more effective and frequent communication you have with the school, the more you will understand the IEP process and the less you will be surprised during it.

Stage 2: Referral and Screening Stage/Process

Regardless of where the child attends school, a general process for referral and screening is followed. Referral means a written request for evaluation and special education and related services as appropriate. Screening is the process of administering global methods to determine whether a child has a suspected disability, and whether the child should have evaluations to determine if he qualifies for special education and related services. In the screening process, student performance is assessed using broad tools and techniques that are used to identify struggling students. Many classroom-based tests are screening tools because they are administered to the whole class or to the whole school. Screening is defined as the process of analyzing information from tests and activities that all students take. Parents do not need to give written permission for any type of test that also is given to children without disabilities in the regular classroom. Screening can lead to or be part of interventions through the Response to Intervention model described in Chapter 4.

Children from birth through the year in which the child turns 21 years old who attend public schools or live in the public school's local system, may be referred for screening or evaluation by anyone: a child's doctor, psychiatrist, parent, teacher, administrator, or tutor. The referral must be in writing, and once a school system receives written referral, federal and state timelines apply. When a parent or advocate makes a referral to the MDT, the most important action step for him to take is to put his concerns and requests in writing. Once again, keep in mind that "if it didn't happen in writing, it didn't happen." A referral letter should state the following: (1) the child is suspected of having an educational disability; (2) the child is in need of evaluation in all areas of the suspected disability; (3) the parent requests that the multidisciplinary team meet to discuss the steps required in order to consider the child eligible for special education and related services;

and (4) the parent requests that the multidisciplinary team meet as soon as possible, acknowledging that the receipt of this letter begins legal timelines (see sample letter in the TOOLS for this chapter).

This process is much easier if there has been clear and open communication between school staff and parents. The referral in most cases will not come as a surprise to the school system. However, in cases where the school system may not be aware of parental concerns, it is a good idea for parents to communicate with the person in charge of coordinating the screening and referral process. Submitting a written referral is the process that parents must use as the initial step to secure special education and related services, specialized services, therapies, accommodations, and modifications for their children. A possible result of the referral and screening, including possible attempted interventions, may be a recommendation for evaluation or testing, which will be discussed later in this chapter.

Example or Common Problem

At the age of 7, Jimmy was diagnosed by a private psychiatrist as having Attention Deficit/Hyperactivity Disorder (ADHD). Written reports by the psychiatrist were provided to the school system. Although Jimmy did well through elementary school, now that he is in middle school, he has become disorganized and is having trouble completing his assignments. The MDT recognizes that his learning is impaired, and develops interventions along with a data-collection plan, without formally referring him for a special education screening. The MDT tells Jimmy's parents that they will review how well this informal plan is working. At the review meeting, the MDT discusses how Jimmy's grades have dropped and teachers report that he participates less in the classroom, even with the attempted interventions. The MDT refers Jimmy for complete psychological and educational evaluations, and tells the parent that Jimmy may now qualify for special education and related services under IDEA 2004 as a child with an Other Health Impairment.

Children Placed by Parents in Private, Independent, Religious, or Parochial Schools

Parents of children who attend private schools also may refer their children for screening by the local school system using this same referral process. Some private schools are specially and specifically certified and approved by the state to serve children with disabilities. Some of these special education private schools receive some funding from the local school system or local education agency. Some of these schools only receive funding from the local school system. Other schools are not equipped nor designed to serve students with special needs. Still others may have minimal special education services or programs. When students are attending any of these types of schools at parent expense, the referral should be made to the child find coordinator of the local school system. This individual is called the child find coordinator because it is his or her responsibility to "find" students with known or suspected disabilities who are placed in private schools by parents so that the school district may consider special education and related services.

Children who are attending private, religious, parochial, or independent schools at parent expense may or may not have attended a public school before they attended the private school. In order to make a referral for special education services, parents in either situation should send a written referral and request for services to the child find coordinator of the local school system, and copy the request to the administrator of the school in the parents' neighborhood (the school the child would attend if he or she were attending a public school). The IEP process should begin, and parents should be invited to a meeting with the local school system. The rest of the IEP process described in this chapter applies.

For example, Felicia is a third-grade student who has been attending a private school for children with learning disabilities since the first grade; her parents have been paying for the placement there. Felicia has never attended a public school or received services from any public school. The private school is under no obligation to develop an Individualized Education Program because there has not been any involvement by any school district. However, because the private school is a special education school, the staff has developed goals for Felicia with a listing of accommodations, modifications, and services she requires based on classroom and formal evaluations. The parents must make a referral to the special education office in the school system in order to have the school system consider funding that placement, or providing some supplementary special education or related services through a services plan. The following stages of the special education process would apply, and Felicia would have to be found to have a disability and be eligible for special education services so that the IEP would be developed.

One interesting change in the federal law under IDEA 2004 relates to which school system is required to provide FAPE to a child when he lives in a different school system than the school system where the private school is located. The location of the private school dictates which local school system the parent must approach in order to request or obtain services. For example, if the child lives in school system A's neighborhood, but attends a private school in school system B's neighborhood, the parent would work with the special education department in school system B to determine if his child will qualify for and receive services.

Private schools and public schools are required to collaborate, share information, and participate in the child find process, including evaluation, eligibility, and IEP development, as appropriate. However, this collaboration is a complex issue that is still being sorted out between parents and school systems.

Services Plans: Special Education Services for Students Eligible for Special Education

Students eligible for special education under IDEA 2004 through the school system also may be eligible for services while attending the private or parochial school under what is called a *services plan*. Federal law also specifically states that services by a public school system *may* be provided on the grounds of private, religious, or parochial schools, as long as they comply with the definition of "school" under other laws. Students may be eligible to receive special education and related services under this type of plan when students are attending private school at parent expense. Like an IEP, the services plan is determined using the same process through the MDT.

Once screening tools have identified students who may have an educational disability and be in need of more intensive or special education services, the parent participates in one or more meetings to explore whether evaluations are necessary. These meetings should include thorough review of the child's records, review of work samples, reports from the child's teachers, observation performed by someone other than the child's teachers, and input from the parents. These meetings may result in a decision to move to the next stage, evaluation planning or evaluation.

Tips for Parents

Have one or two professionals from the private school attend the local school system MDT meetings with you. Provide as much written documentation as possible about the child's areas of difficulty to the school system, including a student work portfolio. Provide written evidence that the child is not performing as expected, and document all interventions that have been attempted to address the problem areas. The school system does not know your child, so it is important to educate the MDT about who your child is and in what areas he is struggling to access the curriculum. Learn the buzz words in this chapter such as *access to curriculum* and *suspected disability* to increase your familiarity and comfort level during the meetings.

When children are attending their local public school, the referral process can be much easier. Members of the MDT will likely know the child, and often, it is a member of the MDT who has made the referral for special education and related services. In the case of children attending the public school, parents do not need to work through the local school system's child find office—the referral is made to the administrator or special educator assigned to the child's grade level.

Stage 3: Evaluation Planning and Evaluation

During the evaluation stage of the IEP process, the MDT, including the parents, will have a discussion about evaluating the child wherein the team discusses what type of evaluation is needed to figure out what the child's disability is and how the child's current level of functioning in all areas is related to the possible disability.

The most important aspect of this stage is the need for *informed parental consent*, as discussed in Chapter 4. The members of the MDT already have expertise handling the types of evaluations the MDT considers and have experience with the implications of such assessments. Parents may not comprehend this process and may need to depend on the explanations of the MDT members to understand the evaluations that are being discussed for the child. Parents must be adequately informed about the evaluations being proposed, and parents must provide written consent. Timelines for evaluations begin when parents put their consent in writing by signing a school system form, or by writing a letter and authorizing evaluations. It is critical that parents understand the types of evaluations being considered, the reasons why the evaluations are being considered, and implications for the evaluations.

If at this stage, parents do not know to ask for a certain type of evaluation, it is possible that evaluations will be conducted without the appropriate type of evaluation that will address parent concerns. There are reasons this may occur. The correct team member may not be at the evaluation planning MDT meeting or the parent may not know which evaluation relates to her area of concern. In any case, this section is designed to help answer these questions, and provide information about the evaluation process.

Evaluations are critical to the IEP process, to a child's educational program, and ultimately, to their lives.

Evaluations: What the Law Says

Evaluations must be conducted in all areas of suspected disability. In the prior stages, the suspected disability or disabilities have been identified based on the problems in the regular classroom and on the red flags that have been observed for any of the problems in the classroom. Psychological and educational evaluations generally are required for every suspected disability. The type of evaluations that may be considered related to the different suspected disabilities will be discussed in greater detail in Chapter 6. When the advocate asks about "suspected disabilities," her question is meant to do several things. First, it compels the team to look at other possible disabilities or areas that should be addressed in the child's IEP. Next, it puts the school system on notice of all possible suspected disabilities, especially in the case of students who have not been formally identified for special education services. Framing the evaluation discussion in terms of suspected disabilities protects students who *may* have disabilities or who are in the *process* of the evaluations. Lastly, it also protects students because the school system must assure that FAPE is provided, even for students who are not yet identified as having a disability. This may be especially important for those students who are facing any type of disciplinary actions.

Evaluations must be conducted in a language and form that will yield the most accurate results; evaluations must be in the child's native language. If a child is not a native English speaker, uses sign language, or is not verbalizing words, this is an important consideration. The evaluation method must be discussed by the MDT and understood by the parents. This is a requirement of IDEA unless it is clearly impossible or not feasible to provide evaluation in the child's native language or form most likely to yield valid results.

Evaluations must be conducted by qualified and trained examiners, who must follow the test guidelines and publisher requirements for the evaluation. The tests used must be both valid and reliable measures for the skills and abilities they are supposed to evaluate. In addition, evaluations must be conducted in a manner that does not discriminate against students based on racial or cultural factors.

The MDT must use different measures and methods for evaluation so that multiple sources of information are used to make decisions. In other words, the team may not rely solely on one tool or score to make educational decisions or to determine an educational program; *multiply-confirming data* (information gathered from more than one source or method) should always be used when evaluating student classroom or functional performance, academic achievement, or developmental performance. This important concept has its history in litigation from the 1970s and 1980s, during a time when discriminatory practices were the standard practices.

One landmark case, *Larry P. v. Riles* (1984), discussed the bias inherent in psychological evaluation. In the *Larry P. v. Riles* case in California, using IQ (cognitive psychological) tests as the assessment measure for placing Black students in special education programs as mentally retarded was found to be discriminatory. Schools in California were mandated to reduce the disproportionate representation of Black students in special education. In *Larry P. v. Riles* (1984), the court determined that IQ tests were discriminatory against Black students in three ways:

1. IQ tests actually measure achievement rather than ability. Because Black citizens throughout their educational history have been denied equal educational opportunities through schools segregated by race, they will inevitably have achievement scores lower than the norms and thus be discriminated against in testing.

2. IQ tests provide artificial ranking of student intelligence; occurrence of intelligence based on the bell curve is an unproven assumption.

3. IQ testing leads to tracking, or placement of students who are Black in stagnant classrooms as compared with White counterparts.

More recently, in *Ford ex rel. Ford v. Long Beach Unified School District* (2002), the school district was not required to use an IQ test to determine the student's specific learning disability. The 9th Circuit noted that "such tests have come under increasing criticism in recent years because of cultural bias and other factions tending to diminish their reliability" (Norlin, 2007, p. 2:13). The MDT, including parents, should be aware of possible bias in psychological and other evaluations when discussing results and student needs.

Whether it is an initial or reevaluation that is occurring, the MDT must review existing data, including previous evaluations and information. It also must review and consider information provided by the parent, including evaluations done at the parent's expense. The MDT further must consider the child's performance on state, district, and classroom tests; classroom performance; and observations by the teachers, educational professionals, or any other MDT member. Through the review of this information and the collection of all data, the MDT must be especially thoughtful about biases inherent in the evaluation process.

For the Initial Evaluation

During the initial evaluation for the child who has never been evaluated by the school system, *evaluation* means that the different members of the MDT conduct assessments or tests, then collect and analyze the data from those assessments. The collection of classroom information and data also is an important part of the evaluation process.

It is very important to include hearing and vision screening in the planning for any evaluation, but especially during planning for the initial evaluation. Problems with vision or hearing must be identified first before other conditions or disabilities can be ruled in or out through the evaluation process. This is especially true for younger children who may not be able to verbalize problems with vision or hearing. Behavior, attention, and learning problems can be affected by problems with vision and hearing. During planning for the initial evaluation, the MDT, including the parents, should discuss the types of formal, standardized tests that will be used to gather information. The MDT also should consider the types of informal evaluations or assessments that may be needed.

The advocate needs to know how to determine the types of evaluations that are needed for each discipline involved in the child's education. The suspected disability, to a large extent, determines the type of evaluations that may be conducted. Knowing the conditions that commonly occur within different disabilities is a useful skill that professional advocates use frequently and one that parents need to better develop. This section focuses on evaluation as it relates to the IEP process. More information about which evaluations should be conducted and the use of evaluations to define educational plans will be discussed in the next chapter.

After the above-mentioned review of all existing information, the MDT must determine what other information is needed to determine whether the child has a disability, to define the disability, or to determine whether the child needs special education or related services.

The initial evaluation generally must be completed within 60 days of the date that parents give permission for the evaluation; however, federal law allows different states to establish their own timelines. Parents should know their state's timeline for evaluation. If states have not established a timeline, evaluations must be completed within 60 days.

The school system must consider any information provided by the parent, including evaluation information. Parents may prefer to have evaluations done by a private, independent examiner. This may be due to lack of trust in the members of the MDT, parent preference to have someone outside the school system conduct evaluations, parent need to supplement public evaluation or to obtain additional information, or the unavailability of tests in the school system.

There are pros and cons to conducting an evaluation privately, at parent expense. These are described in more detail in Table 5.1.

Table 5.1

Pros and Cons of Private and Public Evaluation

	PROS	CONS
Private Evaluation	Parents select the examiner; parents interface with the examiner through the evaluation process and may be able to express concern or family history more freely; parents can review results before giving them to the school system; evaluators may select from a wide variety of sound assessments.	Expense to parents; no guarantee that the school system will accept the findings; school systems may still want to conduct their own evaluations; private evaluators may not be familiar with school system process; proficiency of examiner is important; school system may not approve of an assessment tool that has been used.
Public Evaluation	They are free; school systems are more likely to accept their own findings; various members on the MDT can more easily consult with one another; the examiner may be familiar with the child and vice versa; public evaluations are equally practical.	Parental involvement may take more work and effort on the part of the parent; examiners may not be qualified and it may be difficult for parents to know qualifications; school system examiners may consult with one another and reach a decision before discussion with parent; evaluation tools and tests may not be available because the school system has not purchased a test; examiners may have pressure from the school system due to directives or trends; school system may only choose which assessment to administer from a narrow list of tools that they have approved.

Tips for Parents:

Be sure that the private examiner gets classroom-based information through an observation, checklist, rating scales, interviews, or other method as described in the next chapter. School systems sometimes complain that private evaluations do not include classroom-based information, so it is important to include the school system input, particularly the observation if one has not been done privately, when conducting private evaluations. Parents may want to have private evaluators include an observation of their own or one done by another professional of the parent's choosing. Be aware of the differences between a diagnosis and a disability. More is explained about this in the eligibility stage of the IEP process (which is detailed in the next section). Use a private evaluator who is willing to attend the IEP meeting and/or dispute proceeding, if necessary. The advocate's observation also may be used to supplement others' evaluations.

As long as the private examiner has used the techniques, tools, and methods that the school system would have used, the evaluation must be *considered* (not necessarily accepted) by an MDT or IEP team.

Parental Disagreement With the Results of a Public Evaluation

Whether it is an initial evaluation or reevaluation, parents and their advocates may not agree with the results of the school system's evaluation. Parents may disagree with any part of the evaluation, including diagnoses, conclusions, or recommendations. Parents may believe that the evaluation does not reflect their child or that methods of evaluation were not appropriate. Because evaluation results, along with classroom information, drive the development of the educational program, it is important that evaluations are correct and complete before the development of the educational program.

At this juncture, parents have several options:

- Note the disagreement and proceed to eligibility or IEP development.
- Seek out and schedule a private evaluation (an Independent Educational Evaluation; IEE) at parent expense. Reimbursement for the cost of this evaluation is possible, but usually only if the school team accepts the evaluation and uses it to develop the IEP or educational program and

parents go through another process (see dispute section of Chapter 4) to seek reimbursement. If the public agency brings the parent to a due process hearing and the independent hearing officer agrees that the public evaluation is sufficient, the parent can still obtain an IEE, but it will be at parent expense.

• Request an Independent Educational Evaluation at public expense (see below).

Requesting Independent Educational Evaluations

When parents make a written request for an IEE at public expense, school systems have two choices: either agree to fund the IEE or take parents to a due process hearing to defend their evaluation (see Chapter 4 for information on due process hearings). School districts may ask parents to explain their concerns with the public evaluation, but the parent is not required to tell the district her concerns, and this may not delay the district's response to the parent request for an IEE at public expense. Of course, during the due process hearing (if there is one), the parent will need to provide evidence regarding the allegation that the public evaluation is insufficient. It is important that parents and advocates carefully consider whether they have information to prove that the school system's evaluation was deficient before making this request. Parents should be fully aware of the implications for initiation of a due process hearing by the school system, which in our opinion would require that the parent retain a special education attorney.

Parents only get one opportunity to have an IEE at public expense for each disputed evaluation. For example, a child's parents disagree with the school system's speech and language evaluation and request in writing an IEE at public expense. The school system gives the parents a list of certified, independent speech and language pathologist examiners, and the IEE is completed at public expense. The IEE, however, shows the same results as the school system evaluation. Parents cannot then request another IEE at public expense. There is a limit of one IEE at public expense for each time a disputed evaluation is conducted. In other words, parents are not entitled to two speech and language IEEs at public expense when disputing the school system's speech and language evaluation.

Parents are not required to select from the school district's list of examiners who are qualified to perform the IEE, but the examiner selected by the parent must meet state standards and be qualified in the same manner as the school district examiner. The school district may impose limits on the IEE, such as cost or location of the examiner (Norlin, 2007).

An IEE does not have to be only an academic or achievement evaluation. Although called an Independent *Educational* Evaluation, this evaluation may be a psychological, speech and language, occupational therapy, or other type of evaluation. When parents request in writing an IEE at public expense, parents are disputing the results of the school system's evaluation, and leave themselves open to a due process hearing. Parents must be sure that they can prove that the public evaluation is deficient, and must be ready to provide evidence to an independent hearing officer when they request an IEE at public expense.

Tips for Parents

Be prepared to go to a due process hearing when you request an IEE at public expense. Do not request an IEE at public expense without consulting with an expert in the field to determine whether you are justified in disputing the evaluation. Ideally, parents should consult with a special education attorney before requesting an IEE at public expense.

Common Problem/Example

Javier is a third-grade, 8-year-old student who does not yet write all of his letters, is not reading more than five words, and who has trouble with daily living skills like eating and using the restroom. At the evaluation planning meeting, the school psychologist tells Javier's parents that she would like to test Javier for "cognitive skills and adaptive behavior skills." An advocate understands that the suspected disability is mental retardation based on the advocate's understanding of the definition of mental retardation: significantly below average intellectual, academic, and adaptive behavior skills. However, most parents do not know to interpret this statement as, "We on the MDT believe your child may be mentally retarded." Many times, after the evaluations are completed and the next meeting is held to define the disability, parents are surprised to hear which disability is being considered.

Tips for Parents

Parents must ask the MDT what the suspected disabilities are, and for written definitions of each suspected disability. Then, parents must be informed by asking questions and doing research about which evaluations are proper based on the suspected disabilities.

Stage 4: Eligibility Determination

After evaluations are complete and discussed and considered at the MDT meeting, the MDT determines whether the child is in fact a child with a disability, whether the disability adversely impacts the child's education, and whether the child requires special education. Another way of saying this is that the MDT must determine eligibility for special education and related services after a disability is found and defined.

A child is not automatically eligible for special education and related services once the disability is defined. As shown in Figure 5.1, and described below, the defined disability must affect the child's education, and the child must be in need of services, per the MDT decision.

Once it has been determined that a disability exists, the next step in determining whether or not the student qualifies for an IEP is the consideration of whether or not the student's disability

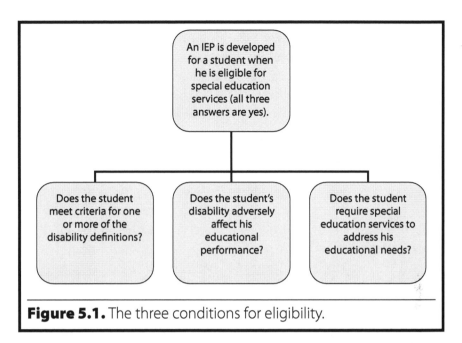

Figure 5.1. The three conditions for eligibility.

adversely impacts his education. Inherent in each of the disability definitions in the TOOLS at the end of this chapter is the concept of *adverse impact*, which is the second part of the determination of disability. A child is eligible for special education and related services under IDEA if he meets criteria for the definitions of the disability, including the adverse impact, and if the child requires special education because of the disability.

The process of determining adverse impact often is a very difficult decision that can be somewhat contentious. The parents may see the adverse impact in the fact that the student is anxious and depressed, is "spending long hours outside of school studying in an effort to keep up, and/or that his or her self-esteem is plummeting" (Silverman & Weinfeld, 2007, p. 138). School staff may not see the educational impact, as the student may not display his emotional issues during the school day and his grades may be adequate or even strong. "How to determine educational impact is not defined in the law and often is the source of disagreement at school meetings" (Silverman & Weinfeld, 2007, p. 138). Some school officials have described adverse impact as including academic impact, as well as other things that may prevent a child from participating in the life of a classroom. As Silverman and Weinfeld note, "this unofficial definition at least opens the door to look beyond grades and test scores to the student's participation in the entire school day" (p. 138). As advocates for students, it is important to look at every aspect of a child's life that may impact the child's involvement in and progress in the general education curriculum. For some students, this will include aspects beyond reading, writing, and mathematics. The advocate considers the child's entire experience of the school environment to determine whether the identified disability adversely affects the child's ability to access her education.

There are several important legal factors to consider when determining eligibility. A child's eligibility must be determined by a team of qualified professionals. Parents must receive a written report of the evaluation results and a written statement of the documented disability. Children who have not received instruction in reading and math, or who have Limited English Proficiency, may not be found eligible for services. Children who have been adopted from another country, children of migrant workers, children who have been neglected or abused, or children who have not been properly homeschooled may fall into this disqualifying category. If children have not received instruction in the curriculum, then they should receive proper instruction, and then the MDT should return to a meeting to discuss eligibility for special education services.

If the team determines that there is not a disability, the child returns to the regular classroom with no services through an IEP or 504 Plan. The MDT may determine that the child has a disability and is entitled to services under Section 504 of the Rehabilitation Act of 1973. The MDT also may determine that the child does not have an educational disability or need special education or any services other than those provided in the regular classroom. In this case, eligibility has been denied. If eligibility for any special education or related service under IDEA 2004 or under Section 504 of the Rehabilitation Act of 1973 is denied, the child is not entitled to any accommodation modification or supplementary aides and services. If the parent disagrees with the eligibility decision of the MDT, she must enter into a dispute process such as a due process hearing, as described in the previous chapter.

Disabilities that are defined by IDEA 2004 are listed in the TOOLS at the end of this chapter. It is vital that parents understand which disability or disabilities are being considered by the MDT or which disabilities are suspected as they go through this process. Parents also should keep in mind that definitions of disabilities are different from diagnoses. A psychologist may make a diagnosis of dyslexia or reading disorder, but that does not mean that the child is educationally disabled until an MDT meets to discuss the evaluation and makes the child *eligible* for services under the category of Specific Learning Disability. In this case, the diagnosis of dyslexia is translated to the closest match from the list of federally defined disabilities.

Diagnoses vs. Disabilities

When conducting intakes of new clients over the years, we have found that when asked, "What is your child's disability on his IEP?" parents infrequently are able to name the disability. Instead, parents usually describe the child's weaknesses or often describe the child's diagnoses. There generally are two sources that psychiatrists, physicians, neuropsychologists, or psychologists use to diagnose disorders in children: the *Diagnostic and Statistical Manual of Mental Disorders*, 4th edition (DSM-IV), and the *International Classification of Diseases* (ICD). Each source classifies human disorders in categories, provides definitions for the disorders, provides classification criteria for the disorders, and is widely used in private practice. School psychologists do not widely use these sources to diagnose and classify disorders because they are more interested in the child's educational disability as defined by IDEA.

Private providers usually make diagnoses, while the multidisciplinary team determines educational disabilities. The MDT should consider any information, including diagnoses, provided by parents. Whether or not children have been evaluated and have been diagnosed with particular disorders or conditions, the MDT still will need to translate the disorders or conditions to a federally defined disability in order to develop the IEP and provide special education and related services. The TOOLS section of this chapter includes a list of some common diagnoses or conditions, the possible corresponding disability, as defined by IDEA, and the types of evaluations that may be necessary to determine if a child has an educational disability that requires special education services.

Special Education Services Defined

Special education is a service, not a location or abstract concept. Special education is, in large part, what results from the implementation of the goals as defined in the Individualized Education Program.

Special Education is:

- free;
- "specially designed" or specialized instruction that adapts content, methodology, and delivery of instruction;
- designed to "meet the unique needs of a child with a disability" and address needs that result from the disability;
- delivered in the classroom, at home, or in other settings;
- instruction to "ensure access to general curriculum;" and
- instruction to allow the child to meet the educational standards of the school system. (U.S. Department of Education, 2006, p. 46762)

A certified special education teacher generally provides special education services, and services that are being delivered by a paraprofessional or aide must be directly supervised by a certified special educator. The trend in some school systems is toward believing that special education can be provided in the general or regular classroom by the general or regular teacher. This needs to be determined by the child's IEP through the MDT, and is a major function of the special education process, as discussed in this chapter.

Special education services, when provided through the child's Individualized Education Program, are provided as spelled out on the IEP. The IEP is developed as a result of the eligibility determination of the MDT.

Again, it is important to consider that there are children who have educational disabilities but do not require special education services. The MDT must determine whether the child with the educational disability requires special education and related services. If the team determines that there is an educational disability including adverse impact and special education services are required, then the Individualized Education Program or IEP is developed.

Eligibility of Infants, Toddlers, or Preschoolers

Children from ages birth to 2 may be eligible for services under an Individualized Family Service Plan (IFSP) under part C of IDEA 2004. Children ages 3 to 5 may be eligible for services under the IEP or IFSP. Many parents of children with disabilities are unsure about how to start the process for special education and related services, especially if the child is at home or in a private preschool or daycare setting. Because children this age are entitled to FAPE, the IEP process applies. Children with disabilities in need of special education and/or related services will have an IEP and services will be determined by the MDT. Children with disabilities may be eligible if the disability impacts the child's ability to do the same things his peers can do at a developmentally appropriate level. If the child is suspected to be or is in need of special education services, the public school system must provide the child with FAPE under part B of IDEA 2004.

Stage 5: IEP Development

Once the MDT, including the parents, determines that a child is eligible for special education and related services, the MDT begins to develop the Individualized Education Program (IEP). This may happen in the same meeting as the eligibility meeting, or the MDT may convene another meeting to develop or craft the IEP.

The meeting to develop the IEP must be held within 30 calendar days of the determination of eligibility. In addition, the IEP must be developed and in effect by the beginning of the child's school year. This is true whether the school uses a semester, trimester, or year-round education program.

The 10 required parts of the IEP are the same for each state because IDEA 2004 spells out what each part should contain. States and counties or local school districts within the state (including Washington, DC, and U.S. Territories) may add to these required parts of the IEP, but the structure of the IEP is generally consistent from state to state based on federal law.

Part I: Identifying Information

The first part of the IEP is usually the child's identifying information, including date of birth, name, grade placement, school, ID number, and the like. Parents should assure that this information is correct.

Part II: Present Levels of Academic Achievement and Functional Performance (PLOP)

When developing the IEP, the MDT must consider the following:
1. the strengths of the child;
2. the concerns of the parents;
3. the results of the most recent evaluations; and

4. the child's functional and classroom performance including academic, developmental, and functional needs of the child.

A critical and often overlooked part of the IEP is the Present Levels of Academic Achievement and Functional Performance (PLOP). This lists student strengths and weaknesses or areas of need. It lists information based on formal and informal evaluations describing the current levels for all areas of need, so that progress can be measured from that starting point. The information in this section establishes a baseline for student performance. Standardized testing information from the various evaluations should be included in this part, and classroom-based information should be included from data collected in the classroom. Needs are identified based on the child's disability and from formal (testing) and informal (classroom) information.

Parents and school teams often do not spend enough time discussing this part of the IEP, which can be viewed as the blueprint for building the next parts of the IEP. Every area of need, as documented in the PLOP section of the IEP, should be addressed by the annual goals, accommodations, supplementary aides and services, or modifications needed to address the child's areas of need. MDTs that are proficient in crafting a thorough PLOP will have a better chance to develop an IEP that will meet student needs. The PLOP also should include an "impact statement"—a statement on the IEP that tells how the student's needs affect his performance in the classroom. The impact statement should be complete and address each area of need that is affected by the student's disability. A house cannot be built without a blueprint, and an IEP cannot be crafted without an adequate PLOP section.

Common Example

Mr. and Mrs. Jones are in an IEP development meeting for their son, Charles. In the Present Levels of Academic Achievement and Functional Performance part of the IEP, the MDT has listed the following needs: reading comprehension, spelling, and math calculation. The MDT begins to develop goals in these areas. At the end of the discussion about goals, Mr. and Mrs. Jones tell the MDT that they want a goal added to the IEP for organization. They state that their child forgets his homework, doesn't turn in completed assignments, and loses many assignments. The MDT refuses to add a goal for organization, stating that in the classroom, Charles seems to be organized, and although he does not turn in each assignment, his organization is not affecting him in the classroom, only at home.

The parents' mistake here is that they did not ask the MDT to consider organization skills in the PLOP as part of the IEP discussion; they waited until goals were being developed to bring up concerns. Instead, parents should have a full discussion in the PLOP part of the IEP, assuring that all areas of concern are addressed and identified as needs before diving in to develop goals to address the need areas. In this case, Mr. and Mrs. Jones can ask for data from the classroom (assessment in the area of organization) to determine whether organization is, in fact, an area of need that should be addressed by a goal. This brings the MDT backward to previous stages of the process, to the evaluation planning and consideration of data stages in order to identify needs on the IEP. In fact, after data was collected, it was determined that Charles only turned in 55% of assignments. This was added to the PLOP section of the IEP, and the MDT developed a goal to meet this educational need, so that he received special education services to address the goal.

Part III: Statements of Assessment, Curriculum, and Outcome

Another part of the IEP speaks to a child's curriculum and the type of testing in which he will participate. In other words, the IEP must dictate whether the child will take the state-mandated tests or whether the child will take an alternate assessment.

Because curriculum and assessment are two sides of one hand and are interrelated, children who are being taught the regular curriculum take the regular state and district tests, whereas children who are being taught an alternate curriculum take the alternate assessment and do not participate in the state or district tests.

No Child Left Behind works in collaboration with IDEA 2004 in this area. NCLB requires every child with a disability to be counted in the state and district testing. NCLB further requires that only the children with the most significant disabilities should be excluded from the state and district tests. The IEP must state whether the child will take the alternate assessment, which alternate assessment will be given, and reasons why the child cannot take the regular state or district tests.

Usually, children who are learning the regular curriculum and taking the regular state or district tests would be scheduled to earn a high school diploma, and students who are taking an alternate curriculum and alternate assessments do not earn a diploma; they earn a Certificate of Attendance. Some states have "tiered" diploma programs, with various levels of diplomas granted.

Part IV: Transition Services

Starting at age 16, and earlier if the MDT determines it necessary, the MDT discusses the student's need for transition services. Transition services can be special education and/or related services, or other services or activities, as determined necessary for the student to progress and improve in functional and academic achievement (see Figure 5.2 for a full list of transition services). These services and a coordinated set of activities including community participation may be listed in the IEP to facilitate the student's move to postsecondary options, after graduation, or after exiting the IEP by aging out. Transition services include vocational assessment, career exploration, and future planning to meet individual goals for the student's life after high school. If the school system fails to provide the transition services in a student's IEP, the MDT must convene an IEP meeting to identify different interventions and strategies to put into place such that the transition objectives in the IEP can be met. Transition services are determined based on the student's strengths, interests, abilities, and preferences. They include instruction, related services, experiences in the community, daily living skills, and functional vocational evaluation.

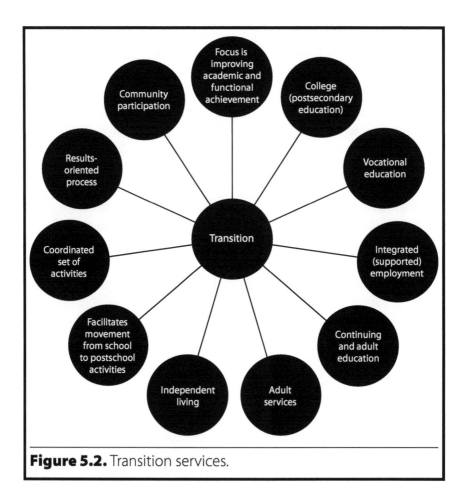

Figure 5.2. Transition services.

Advocates will encourage the use of the vocational assessment, and utilize various agencies in the community in conjunction with the school system to adequately plan for and implement the student's transition plan (U.S. Department of Education, 2006).

Vocational education is a type of transition service defined as a structured program related to employment of the student, whether the student is paid or not. Vocational education also can prepare the student for a career that does not require an undergraduate or advanced degree (108th Congress, 2004). Depending on the student's abilities, interests, and aptitudes, the student may go to college or university. In this case, transition services would strive to prepare him for the college experience. Other times, the student will participate in a post-high-school vocational training program. In still other situations, the student may plan to live in a supervised residence and need support in a job setting. Whatever the student's individual outcome, the transition section of the IEP first plans ahead for the child's future, and then supports the transition to that future by providing assessment, services, and activities through the IEP. Often, multiple agencies support transition services for young adults. It is important to have multiple agency participation in the planning for transition from school to life.

Part V: Annual Goals and Short-Term Objectives

The most well-known part of the IEP contains the annual goals that address all areas of need. Measurable annual goals will address academic and functional needs or any other needs identified in the PLOP part of the IEP. The requirement that only annual goals need be listed on the IEP is new. Before 2004, all students with IEPs had both annual goals and short-term objectives listed in the IEP. Now, only the measurable annual goals are required and progress reports only are required to address the annual goals. Short-term objectives are still optional, and many school districts continue to put short-term objectives that lead up to the annual goal on the IEP, but again, we must stress that short-term objectives are no longer a requirement. The exception is that students who are not taking the standard state and district tests as described in the section above still must have a description in the IEP about short-term objectives or benchmarks.

While the PLOP statements tell the reader of an IEP where the child is currently functioning, annual goals tell the reader of the IEP where we want the child to be functioning within a school year. Annual goals are written so that the child will be involved in and make progress in the general education curriculum. The exception to this occurs when students are not taking the regular curriculum and are participating in alternate assessments based on alternate curriculum standards. For these students, annual goals and short-term objectives still will be included in the IEP.

A best practice to develop annual goals is to think of goals in four parts:

- Condition Statement (what a child needs to perform the behavior);
- Observable Behavior (what a child will *do* that can be observed);
- Mastery Criteria (how well the child will perform the behavior); and
- Timeline (over what time period the achievement will occur).

A parent or professional should be able to look at the PLOP statements to determine a child's current level of performance or functioning, and match them to the annual goals. In the example below, this is the annual goal for the school year. If the goal is for the student to read at the second-grade level, it would make sense that the PLOP statements indicate she is currently at the first-grade level of reading, regardless of her age. The needs identified by the PLOP part of the IEP should be addressed by annual goals, and for each annual goal area, there should be a PLOP statement identifying where the child currently is functioning.

Common Example

Given a second-grade reading passage of fewer than 200 words and 10 inferential question (CONDITION), Sally will orally answer questions correctly using complete sentences (OBSERVABLE BEHAVIOR) as evidenced by 9 out of 10 questions grammatically correct (MASTERY CRITERIA) daily for 4 consecutive weeks by the end of the first semester (TIME PERIOD).

Part VI: Accommodations, Modifications, and Supplementary Aides and Services

The term *supplementary aids and services* refers to aids, services, and other supports provided in regular education classes or other education-related settings to enable children with disabilities to be educated with nondisabled children to the maximum extent appropriate. The IEP also must provide a statement of the necessary supplementary aides and services for the child to participate in nonacademic services and extracurricular activities. This includes school trips, dances, clubs, and a wide range of services or activities. The MDT should consider student involvement in the community when appropriate. Limitations on participation may be viewed as discriminatory.

Accommodations are put into place to change the student's environment, way of responding, equipment, delivery of direction or instruction, or format of the curriculum. Accommodations change the educational program and assessment procedures, but do not change the content of the curriculum or the criteria for assessment. Modifications, in contrast, change the curriculum demand and assessment criteria such that the level, content, or criteria for the curriculum and assessments are altered (Cohen & Spenciner, 2007).

Part VII: Related Services

The first thing that parents need to know about related services is that these are services that the child needs *in order to benefit* from her special education program. Related services are titled such because they are related to special education instruction.

Sometimes, parents contact advocates because they believe the amount or level of related services should be increased. Often, the first response from the school system is that the child is receiving benefit in the special education program (read more about this in the meaningful progress section in Chapter 11), and therefore, there is not a need for an additional related service. Parents who are prepared to discuss this concept are much better equipped to make such a request; therefore parents must learn how to be prepared for this discussion.

The next thing parents need to know about related services is what services may be included in this section of the IEP.

According to IDEA 2004, the following list provides examples of related services. But, IDEA 2004 also more broadly defines related services as "developmental, corrective, or other supportive services" that allow a child with a disability to benefit from special education.

Examples of related services include (this list is not exhaustive):

- transportation;
- speech or language pathology;
- audiology services;
- interpreting services;
- psychological services;
- physical therapy;
- occupational therapy;
- transition services;
- travel training;
- recreation, including therapeutic recreation;
- early identification and assessment of disabilities in children;
- social work services;
- school health services;
- school nurse services;
- counseling services, including rehabilitation counseling;
- parent counseling and training;
- orientation and mobility services;
- medical services; and
- vision therapy.

There are some special considerations about related services that are important to know. The language of IDEA 2004 requires transportation to be a related service. It is one to which each child with a disability is entitled, if the child must take transportation to get to the school program. Medical services are limited to diagnostic and evaluation purposes with a few exceptions, such as the use of a catheter. As described in the section considering exceptions to assistive technology service, IDEA 2004 does not allow surgically implanted devices as a related service.

The last thing parents need to know is that the IEP must specifically define how often (frequency), how long (duration), and where (location) the services will be provided, along with which discipline will provide the service (names of individuals are not included on the IEP, only the title or discipline of the service provider).

Tip for Parents

A private therapist may view the need for therapy differently from the school district. Some of these differences in points of view may follow the law, and others may not. While each situation is different, it is appropriate to some extent that your private provider works on different goals. To effectively supplement the IEP, parents may provide private services at any time. It is important to share information from the private provider with the school district, including recommendation for service. The private provider should fully understand the eligibility criteria for related services in the school district and make recommendations tied to achievement and functioning in the classroom. The school district needs to see how the related service is needed for the child to benefit from the special education program.

Part VIII: Consideration of Special Factors

In this section, we will explore the section of the IEP that requires the MDT to consider the following special factors for children with disabilities: interfering behaviors, language needs of speakers of other languages, communication needs, Braille for students who are blind or visually impaired, and assistive technology.

Interfering Behaviors

It's common knowledge that many students with disabilities display behaviors that interfere with their own or other students' learning. These behaviors are appropriately called *interfering behaviors* under the law, and there are times when it is either a good idea or a requirement that the MDT address these behav-

iors through the IEP process. Students do not need to be identified with an emotional disturbance to have interfering behaviors.
Students with specific learning disabilities, autism, mental retardation, or other health impairments such as those due to ADHD
may demonstrate behaviors that require certain actions through
the IEP process. Any child with a disability may show behaviors
that interfere with learning.

There is sometimes dispute about whether an IEP should
address areas other than academics, such as attendance and
behavior. Sometimes, school teams either do not find that a child
qualifies for an IEP or tell parents that the IEP does not need to
address behaviors such as attendance or social skills, saying that
these behaviors do not negatively impact the child's education.
As common for a child with Asperger's syndrome, for example,
she may not have academic deficiencies, yet she may display poor
social or emotional skills. Parents who have challenged this have
been successful as in the case of *Mr. and Mrs. I v. Maine School
Administrative District 55* (2006), which concerned a child with
Asperger's syndrome and social-emotional problems. The IEP's
contents and goals may span across a child's day and address
attendance, social skills, executive functioning skills (see more
about this in the next chapter), coping skills, or adaptive skills
(daily living skills), among others; the IEP content may not be
limited to academic areas.

Therefore, parents must understand that interfering behavior
must be defined individually for each child, and these behaviors
may need to be addressed in the IEP if the behaviors negatively
interfere with the child's education. Behaviors may not necessarily result in poor achievement or academic skills to be addressed
in the IEP; students with average or higher academic skills may
still require interventions and services to address nonacademic
or behavioral skills.

In our view, it is important to correctly define behavior, not
just describe it. For example, when standing in line to go to lunch,
a student with other health impairment due to ADHD touches
other students' hair and clothing. Some interpretations of this

Table 5.2

Ways to Define Behavior.

Behavior in Observable Terms	Words to Avoid That Interpret Behaviors
Walking away from teacher after given a direction to sit in seat	Disrespect to authority
Turning in 20 blank assignments	Disorganized student
Touching other students during instruction	Aggression to peers
Saying "I don't care" when given in-school suspension	Unmotivated student

behavior may be that it is aggressive, inattentive, or inappropriate. The members of the MDT, including the parent, should refrain from defining behaviors through words that interpret behaviors. Instead, the behavior should be specifically defined, such as a videotape recording the behavior. Table 5.2 includes some examples of things to avoid when attempting to define interfering behaviors.

When children demonstrate interfering behaviors, the IEP team must consider whether the child requires positive behavioral interventions and supports to address interfering behaviors. The IEP may address interfering behaviors in several ways:

1. Behavior needs may be documented through statements in the Present Levels of Educational and Functional Performance (PLOP) section.
2. Annual goals may be written to address interfering behaviors.
3. Related or other services such as psychological services, counseling, or parent education and training may be listed on the IEP, and provided according to the IEP statement.
4. A functional behavior assessment (FBA) and behavior intervention plan (BIP) that becomes part of the IEP may be developed.

In our view, the most effective and yet overlooked way for the MDT to evaluate and address interfering behaviors is through an assessment called a functional behavior assessment (FBA). Details about conducting the FBA can be found in Chapter 6.

According to IDEA, an FBA is required as part of the manifestation determination process (see next section), specifically when the process described below results in a decision that the behavior is a manifestation of the child's disability. This occurs when students with disabilities are suspended or removed from school more than 10 days in a school year or are recommended for expulsion.

Suspensions, Expulsions, and Manifestations Determination. Parents contact advocates frequently when their children are being disciplined by the school district. The school district may use many methods in relation to discipline of behaviors. Children with disabilities may be treated under the law just like their non-disabled peers until the student with a disability is removed from the classroom so often that the removals equate to a change of educational placement. This means that students with disabilities may be removed from the classroom, suspended, and given in-school suspension and other short-term removals like their nondisabled peers up to and including the 10th day of removal or suspension during a school year. In other words, school districts are allowed to treat students with disabilities the same as any other child in many circumstances, including removal of the student for a few days of the year.

Since the 1988 *Honig v. Doe* Supreme Court decision, the law is clear that children with a disability may not be suspended or removed from school more than 10 school days per year without necessary action steps being taken to evaluate whether the behavior is related to the child's disability (manifestation determination review) in a particular way. In other words, after 10 days of removal or suspension of a child with a disability, the MDT must take certain actions to determine whether the child's behavior is a manifestation of the child's disability or conduct a manifestation determination meeting.

The intention behind these protections is that students with disabilities should not be excluded from school for such a long period of time that the removals are similar to changing that child's placement. In other words, if a disabled child is removed too often from the classroom, that pattern can constitute a change of placement. This can apply to in-school suspensions or other time-out or short-term removals from school that add up to deny the child an education in a way that it is equal to the placement being changed. Per the IEP, students with disabilities also must receive education when they are removed, suspended long term, or expelled.

There are three exceptions to this process in which a student with a disability may be treated like his nondisabled peers without regard to the manifestation process. When any of these three exceptions apply to children with disabilities who are being removed from school or recommended for expulsion from school, the child may be placed in an Interim Alternative Educational Setting (IAES) by the IEP team for up to 45 school days (not calendar days). When these three exceptions apply, a child with a disability may be expelled or removed from school, as if the child did not have a disability.

The first exception relates to situations where a student "carries a weapon to or possesses a weapon at school, on school premises, or to or at a school function under the jurisdiction of [a school system]" (U.S. Department of Education, 2006, p. 46798). And, the term *dangerous weapon* means

> a weapon, device, instrument, material, or substance, animate or inanimate, that is used for, or is readily capable of, causing death or serious bodily injury, except that such term does not include a pocket knife with a blade of less than 2.5 inches in length. (U.S. Department of Education, 2006, p. 46723)

The second exception relates to situations where students are in possession of or selling illegal substances or drugs, specifically, when a student "knowingly possesses or uses illegal drugs, or sells or solicits the sale of a controlled substance, while at school, on school premises, or at a school function under the jurisdiction of [the school system]" (U.S. Department of Education, 2006, p. 46798).

The last exception occurs when a student with a disability causes another person serious bodily injury. Serious bodily injury is defined through other laws, and IDEA 2004 has adopted those definitions, as discussed below. Note that serious bodily injury is different from bodily injury. If a student has inflicted serious bodily injury upon another person while at school, on school premises, or at a school function, the student may be removed to an IAES for up to 45 school days under U.S. federal rules of criminal procedure.

Serious bodily injury means bodily injury that involves (a) a substantial risk of death; (b) extreme physical pain; (c) protracted and obvious disfigurement; or (d) protracted loss or impairment of the function of a bodily member, organ, or mental faculty. The term *bodily injury* does *not* qualify for 45-day removal. It means (a) a cut, abrasion, bruise, burn, or disfigurement; (b) physical pain; (c) illness; (d) impairment of the function of a bodily member, organ, or mental faculty; or (e) any other injury to the body, no matter how temporary (Equip for Equality Legal Advocacy Program, 2007).

Interim Alternative Educational Setting (IAES). An IAES is a setting other than the student's current placement that enables the student to continue to participate in the general curriculum and progress toward meeting the goals set in his or her IEP. The IAES must enable the student to participate in the general education curriculum, although in another setting. In addition the IAES requires progress toward meeting the goals set out in the IEP. According to the National Center for Learning Disabilities (2007), students in an IAES should also receive, as appropriate, a functional behavioral assessment, behavioral intervention services, and "modifications that are designed to address the behavior violation so that it does not happen again" (¶ 6).

Special education services must be provided to students with disabilities, even when they are removed from school. Services within the IAES will vary greatly from state to state, and from district to district. Much of the time, IAES placements consist of schools or classrooms that have been set up to teach students with and without disabilities with varying behavior, legal, substance, and social problems. While the IAES is not required to implement the IEP to the letter, it is important that advocates help fully inform parents about the way services are being provided, and whether those services are adequate to allow the child to make progress on the IEP goals and be involved in the curriculum. Special education and related services may be provided in a variety of settings.

Manifestation Determination Review Questions. When the IEP team considers whether the child's behavior is a manifestation of the disability, the IEP team must answer two questions with either a "yes" or "no" response. Only one of the following questions needs to have an answer of *yes,* for the behavior to be determined to be a manifestation of the child's disability.

1. Was the conduct in question caused by, or had a direct and substantial relationship to, the child's disability? or
2. Was the conduct in question the direct result of the local educational agency's failure to implement the IEP? (108th Congress, 2004)

There are some important changes in IDEA 2004 in this regard. Now the child's behavior must have a "direct and substantial relationship" to the disability, or the behavior must be caused by the child's disability. If the relationship between the behavior and the child's disability is direct and substantial, or the behavior was caused by the child's disability, the behavior is said to be a manifestation of the child's disability. This means that there was such a relationship between the disability and the behavior that the child should return to school without serving the remainder of the disciplinary removal. Also, the behavior may be a manifestation of the child's disability if the school system failed to implement the child's IEP, including failure to implement any behavior intervention plans. This means that the behavior resulted from the school system doing something or not doing something required in the child's IEP or behavior intervention plan, which is part of the IEP. This is one of the reasons that it is so critical to list all of a student's services, accommodations, aides, and interventions on the IEP.

This critical manifestation determination process dictates whether a child may be returned to school and the limitations of disciplinary action from the school system. If the student's behavior is found to be a manifestation of his disability, he is returned to school without further disciplinary action, likely on the same day that the multidisciplinary team meets and has this discussion. However, if the child's behavior is not found to be a manifestation of his disability and the child's behavior is not a result of the school system's failure to implement the IEP, further disciplinary action may be taken, including expulsion from the school system.

When behavior is a manifestation of the disability:
- The child returns to school.
- FBA is required to be conducted or reviewed.
- BIP is required to be written or reviewed.
- IEP may be revised to address behavior of concern.

When behavior is not a manifestation of the disability, the school system may proceed with disciplinary action, unless parents appeal the manifestation determination review decision.

Language Needs of Students With Limited English Proficiency

As mentioned in the evaluation stage discussed earlier in this chapter, evaluations must be conducted in the child's native language or in the child's mode of communication, unless it is not possible or it is unreasonable to do so. It is important to make sure that a child is proficient in English before administering tests in English.

The IEP team must determine whether the child requires special education and/or related services, as described in the IEP process, based on his eligibility as a child with a disability under IDEA. This special factor requires IEP teams to consider the language needs of the child with Limited English Proficiency (LEP), as the language needs relate to the child's IEP (U.S. Department of Education, 2006). We have found great variability in the provision of special education services and services to students with Limited English Proficiency depending on the culture and climate from school to school and community to community. If the child is bilingual, the school district is required to have available a bilingual team and make translation services available to the child.

Communication Needs

The IEP team also must consider (not accept or agree to, just consider) whether the child has communication needs including the need for direct instruction in the child's language and communication mode. There is a specific statement that also applies in this section to students who are deaf or hard of hearing. In these cases, the IEP team should consider chances for the child to communicate directly with peers and adults along with his or her academic level and full range of needs.

This section of the IEP brings to mind a case we experienced with a 10-year-old fifth-grade student with dyspraxia (a disorder that affects motor development) and mild mental retardation who is not hard of hearing or deaf. Due to her motor problems, she is unable to speak clearly, but she is able to use a form of sign language along with nonverbal communication such as smiling, pointing, or taking an adult's hand to lead him to a desired activity. The IEP team considered her communication needs in her mode of communication; in this case it was called *approximated signing*. The MDT agreed to provide her with a type of interpreter to address these communication needs in her unique way of communicating, along with assistive technology devices and services.

Use of Braille for Students Who Are Blind or Visually Impaired

The use of Braille, being one mode of communication for students who are blind or visually impaired, must be considered by the MDT. Braille may be considered to be the child's native language or mode of communication. Instructional materials and assessments may be converted to Braille. The school district is responsible for Braille transcription and conversion.

Need for Assistive Technology Devices or Services

An assistive technology (AT) device, according to the definitions in IDEA 2004 is "any item, piece of equipment, or product system" that is purchased "off the shelf, modified, or customized" that increases, maintains, or improves the "functional capabilities of a child with a disability" (Section 602). Functional capabilities can include just about any area of need in a child's IEP. For students with autism, AT devices may need to be considered to improve the child's functional capabilities in the area of communication or social skills. For students with mental retardation, an AT device may be necessary to improve the child's functional capabilities in the area of self-care. For a child with a specific learning disability, an AT device may be necessary to improve the functional capabilities of the child in the area of reading or spelling. There are a wide variety of devices that are available, and through an evaluation, parents are able to better determine which devices may be necessary to include in the IEP.

In 2004, the definition of AT was revised in part *not* to include any surgically implanted devices, such as a Cochlear Implant which is used with students who are deaf or hard of hearing. Parents who understand this language are able to request evaluation of their children's needs by asking the IEP team this question: What assistive technology devices does my child need to improve his functional capabilities? An assistive technology evaluation can be seen as an assistive technology service, based on the definition below.

An assistive technology service helps the child with a disability to select, get, and use an assistive technology device. The

AT service can include evaluation, purchase, selection, designing, fitting, customizing, adapting, maintaining, and repairing of AT devices. AT service also can include training and technical assistance for the child, for the child's providers or caretakers, or for the child's family.

At times, a Catch-22 for parents lies inherent within these new definitions of AT devices and services. On one hand, the child may need a service, but on the other, the school system may not have the devices. In our experience, at times this results in school system or IEP team members telling parents that students do not need a service, including an evaluation. Parents should not accept a blanket statement that "our county does not have that device," or "we don't do that here." These are statements that should raise red flags for parents. If parents feel completely stonewalled, they should explore requesting an IEE in the AT area, or they should privately obtain an evaluation and submit it to the IEP team for consideration (IDEA, 2004).

Part IX: Extended School Year Services

Extended School Year (ESY) services are available only to children with disabilities. These services are provided during times that the school system does not usually have school, such as during winter or spring break, during summer vacation, during weekends, or before or after school hours.

School systems are not supposed to limit ESY services in any way due to a child's age or systematically limit ESY services to students with disabilities by providing, for example, only one ESY option for the summer. School systems may not limit ESY services based on a disability, by the type or amount of service, or by how long the service lasts.

ESY services are determined by the MDT, and a student is eligible for ESY services if she needs these services to be provided a free appropriate public education. ESY services are special education and related services that are provided as spelled out on the child's IEP. In most districts, goals for ESY are identified by the IEP team, along with the level of service and placement for ESY.

The federal law and guidelines talk about three reasons a student would need ESY services, but different states have come up with additional reasons why ESY services are necessary. IDEA discusses the risk of regression, likelihood of retention, and risk of lack of recoupment as eligibility conditions for ESY services. Any time retention is discussed for students with disabilities, it is important to discuss ESY services that may be needed to prevent the retention. It is vital that advocates and parents understand their own state criteria for ESY services.

Court cases deciding important ESY decisions have provided language that guides the way the MDT determines whether a child is eligible and how the child will receive services. In *MM v. School District of Greenville County* (2002), the court found that ESY services should not be given only on the basis of a likelihood of regression, because all children regress to some extent over the summertime. The court offered language that encourages MDTs to consider whether the progress the child experienced through the previous school year would be significantly jeopardized if ESY services were not provided.

The school districts tend to discuss ESY in terms of particular preplanned programs that the district has already decided to make available during summer months, but do not as often discuss or inform parents about different types of ESY services that may be available to students. ESY programs should be individually defined for each child, including a full range of services during times when school is not in session, as well as before and after the school day.

Problem

The school district tells parents that ESY services are for students with very severe disabilities such as mental retardation and for children who need practice over the summer with functional life skills or critical goal areas.

Common Example/Situation

Parents sign an agreement that their child is not eligible for ESY services, based on the MDT making brief statements at the IEP meeting such as "your child is not eligible for ESY services." Parents are not aware that ESY services are for any time of year, before or after school, or any time school is not usually in session. Parents agree to summer school, thinking that summer school is the same as ESY services.

Tips for Parents

Be sure to get your state regulations about ESY, and do not rely on the school system's brochure on ESY to inform you of your rights. Be prepared to discuss progress and need for ESY services based on data, not opinion. Collect data during school breaks to show the need for ESY services.

Tips for School Systems

When discussing ESY with parents, be sure to include the required member on the MDT who is able to consider and authorize parent requests for atypical ESY services.

Part X: Educational Placement and Least Restrictive Environment

Every child's IEP must include a statement justifying the student's placement, including written justification for any removal from the general education setting.

Level of Service and Location

The educational placement on the IEP has two prongs: level of service and location for services. The level of service is the statement for how much and what type of special education and related services will be needed to address the child's needs as laid out in the IEP. The MDT often reviews the goals, accommodations, and other sections of the IEP to consider what part of the child's week will require specialized instruction and related services.

In the level of services statement on the IEP, the type of service, provider, duration, and frequency of the service should be specified. The environment in which the service will be provided also should be specified. The level of special education services usually is documented in terms of hours per week and percentage of time the child will participate with nondisabled peers. A child could, for example, receive 20 hours per week of special education service, where 10 of those hours are provided in the general education classroom setting.

The location for services is the second prong of the child's placement. The location is usually the name of a school where the services will be delivered. The location for ESY services, home-based services, or other special services must be specified. If the IEP states that the location for services is the neighborhood school, we advise parents to request that the name of the school is specified. The reason for this is twofold: Placement location is a requirement, and neighborhood school boundaries can change with the building of new schools or changes in the community. The location for services should not change without parent involvement in the MDT meeting. Districts also may propose a special education program with a specific name or acronym. This usually is specified in the IEP, and the location for services should be stated as specifically as possible.

It is possible for parents to agree with the level of service proposed for the child, but for the parents to disagree with the location for services. For example, Sally is a fifth grader who is reading at least 3 years below grade level, and she recently has been diagnosed with Attention Deficit/Hyperactivity Disorder. Based on her IEP that identifies her as a child with a Specific Learning Disability and Other Health Impairment, Sally's parents and the school district agree that Sally needs a full-time, special education placement in a separate school; all agree that her disability requires removal from the general education setting. However, the school district proposes the placement location to be the public school for students with behavior problems. Sally's parents request that she is placed in a local private special education school that is certified to serve children with specific learning disabilities.

Each state is required to have schools for students who are deaf or hard of hearing and blind or visually impaired. A residential placement may be deemed appropriate by the IEP team because the distant location of the program makes it impossible for the student to attend as a day student.

Related services also should be specified in the same manner. Related services impact the delivery of special education services, and this is a topic discussed by the MDT. Some school districts have a standard practice of indicating whether a service will be a group or individual therapy, while other districts need more convincing to specify these details in the IEP.

Extended school day (ESD) services may be required for some students, especially when the MDT is considering ways to prevent a more restrictive, residential placement. Although other agencies also are able to provide wraparound services where the family and child receive services to provide structure, instruction, or therapy outside the confines of the school day, ESD services are specified in the IEP and are the responsibility of the school district, as determined by the MDT.

Tip for Parents

Do not allow the district to indicate you or your child as a service provider on the IEP. This does not mean parents should not participate in the education of the child; parents should not be service providers or in any way responsible for the delivery of the IEP. Providing service is a responsibility of the school, not the parents.

Continuum of Services (Consultative to Residential)

Each school district must have in place a continuum of services, from the general education classroom to a residential setting. Different districts construct self-contained, special education classrooms differently. Some school districts separate special education classes by disability or by need area, and develop separate classes for students with emotional disturbance and specific learning disabilities. Other districts have set up special education classrooms in which children with different disabilities are placed. These are said to be "noncategorical" classrooms because the child's IEP category or disability does not determine the placement. As discussed in Chapter 9, residential, special education private schools also may have different programs designed and certified to serve students with particular disabilities.

In many districts, the special education programs are located in particular schools that serve children from different regions. This means that a student with special needs may be placed in a program that removes him from his neighborhood school. Because it is rare that the continuum of service is located within one school, unfortunately students with special needs may be subject to school changes more than their nondisabled peers. This practice makes transportation costs very extravagant in some districts, and moreover, necessitates school changes in order for students with disabilities to have an appropriate education.

Different districts and states have different ways of describing the same basic continuum of services. The advocate must learn how the district discusses its continuum and use the correct vocabulary between districts. The continuum of services runs from least restrictive to most restrictive. The word *restrictive* is used because the restrictive placement restricts the child from interacting with her nondisabled peers. The less restrictive placements look more like general education classrooms, while more restrictive placements look less like general education classrooms. Figure 5.3 illustrates a general continuum of services and does not indicate the continuum from any law; there is no legal definition of the components of the continuum of services.

Least Restrictive Environment (LRE)

The idea of Least Restrictive Environment is that children with disabilities are educated with their nondisabled peers to the greatest extent possible. The concept includes the provision of accommodations, modifications, supplementary aides and services, specialized instruction, and related services in the general education setting, unless the child must be removed from the general education setting for all or part of the school day or week. While the LRE for one child is in his neighborhood school, the

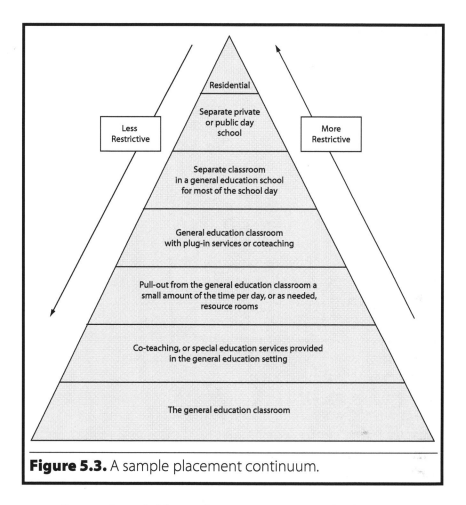

Figure 5.3. A sample placement continuum.

LRE for another child may be a separate special education class or school. It is an individualized decision based on what each child needs. Students should remain with their nondisabled peers unless the nature and severity of their disability warrants such removal, when accommodations and modifications cannot be provided in the general education setting, or when behaviors are so disruptive to the student and his or her peers that access to the curriculum is prevented.

For most students, the concept of LRE ensures access to the curriculum that had not been available earlier in the history of special education. *Inclusion* is a term that often is used to explain a philosophy of educating children with special needs in their home school and in the general education classroom. It is not a location, program, service, person, or classroom. There are advocates and advocacy groups who believe that all children, regardless of the nature and severity of disability, should be included in the general education setting.

There are mixed research studies on the efficacy of inclusive practices. For example, in the area of reading improvement, in various studies, inclusion of students with mild specific learning disabilities has not yielded an improvement in reading skills (Holloway, 2001). However, skill acquisition varies from one student to another, and benefits of participation with nondisabled peers may include other areas; it is important to view how all of the child's learning needs may be impacted by the delivery of special education services in the general education setting in a child's neighborhood school. For some students, there are harmful effects of participation with nondisabled peers. All of these discussions should be held at the IEP meeting table with the parent and multidisciplinary team.

Litigation and court decisions have driven school districts to comply with laws related to the inclusion of students with disabilities in the general education curriculum and setting to the extent possible given the nature and severity of the child's disability. LRE and special education legislation relates to the civil rights of individuals in general, and specifically for people with disabilities. The most important thing to remember about LRE is that it is different for everyone, and should be determined for each individual child through the IEP process.

Legal precedent helps guide the MDT in determining placement, including the decision about when children with disabilities should be removed from the general education setting. *Daniel R. R. v. State Board of Education* (1989) is one of the leading cases opening the door to increased placement of children with disabilities in the general education classroom. The court developed a two-pronged test for consideration of placement in the general education setting. The first question relates to whether the child can be satisfactorily educated in the general classroom with the use of supplementary aides and services. If the child requires a separate setting, the school district must ask the second question: whether the child has been placed in the general education setting to the extent appropriate. Other courts followed this case using and modifying this two-pronged test for removal of children, while continuing to strongly favor placement in the general education classroom. When considering a child's academic and social needs, the MDT does not have to attempt every aide or service possible to include the child, but its effort must be a genuine attempt to educate the child with his nondisabled peers.

In addition to *Daniel R. R.*, other cases have supported inclusion of children with disabilities in the general education setting. In cases such as *Oberti v. Board of Education of Borough of Clementon School District* (1992), the court added to the considerations of placement the possible benefits or disadvantages of inclusion to nondisabled children. Although again strongly favoring placement in the general education classroom, this case highlighted instances that justify removal from the general classroom: when students are receiving little or no benefit from inclusion or when student behavior is disruptive to the educational setting. In *Greer v. Rome City School District* (1991), the district was not able to show it had taken appropriate steps to program for the child in the general education setting, therefore failing one of the *Daniel R. R.* prongs, and the court ruled that the child should be educated with his nondisabled peers regardless of the cost to do so.

In *Sacramento City School District v. Rachel H.* (1994), a four-pronged consideration was developed to determine the extent to which the child was placed in the general education setting. These factors include the cost of the supplementary aides and services needed in the general education classroom, the educational benefit to the child, the nonacademic benefit or social benefit, and the impact of the child with a disability on the teacher and students in the general classroom. These cases highlight the need for consideration by the MDT that social skills development, communication skills, improved self-esteem, and role modeling for language are benefits to children with disabilities that justify placement in the general education setting (Howard, 2004).

However, simply being in the same room with nondisabled peers does not necessarily mean that the disabled child is getting benefit from his placement. If a student with disabilities is not learning from being with nondisabled peers, or is not interacting with nondisabled peers, placement with nondisabled peers should not be the reason for including the child with a disability. For example, in *Hudson v. Bloomfield Hills Public Schools* (1997), the court found that the child "remains naively responsive and vulnerable to a certain segment of unscrupulous classmates who tease, taunt, and ridicule her" (Norlin, 2007, p. 5:21). One witness accurately described the child as "an island in the mainstream," and accordingly, the court found that removal from the general education setting was appropriate (Norlin, 2007, p. 5:21).

In determining whether it is appropriate to place a student with disabilities in the regular education setting, the student need not be expected to learn at the same rate as the other students in the class. In other words, part of the required supplementary aids and services must be the modification of the regular education curriculum for the student when needed. The court in *Daniel R. R. v. State Board of Education* (1989) noted, however, that the school need not modify the program "beyond recognition." Also, in looking at whether it is appropriate for the child to be in regular education—in other words, whether the student can benefit educationally from regular class placement—the school must consider the broader educational benefit of contact with nondisabled students, such as opportunities for modeling appropriate behavior and socialization (Hager, 1999).

IEP Versus IFSP

By the age of 3, the IEP for preschoolers must be developed and in effect (U.S. Department of Education, 2006), if the child is eligible and requires special education and related services. For children in this age group, an Individualized Family Service Plan (IFSP) may be developed. The IFSP focuses on preliteracy and early intervention. The family must be fully informed about the differences between the IEP and IFSP. When the child turns 5, the IEP team must consider the necessary services to transition the child to a school-aged IEP. Parents should contact the service coordinator in the school district or hire an advocate with special expertise in programming for preschool-aged children with disabilities for more information. Providing a continuum of services for preschoolers with IEPs or IFSPs has proven difficult for some school districts because of the limited general and special education options in the public school system.

Stage 6: IEP Is Implemented

All staff working with the child, and especially those staff with responsibilities for implementing the IEP must be informed about their responsibility and role for implementing the IEP, including specific accommodations, modifications, and supports for the child (U.S. Department of Education, 2006). Staff members to inform include regular teachers, aides and paraprofessionals, special education teachers, related service providers, or any other person who is responsible for providing services through the child's IEP.

The IEP needs to be in effect by the beginning of each school year. In *Justin G. v. Board of Education of Montgomery County* (2001), the court held that the failure to have an IEP in place at the beginning of the school year through no fault of the parents resulted in the denial of FAPE. In *Kitchelt v. Montgomery County Public Schools* (2004), the court again held that the failure to have an IEP in place at the beginning of the school year resulted in the denial of FAPE. "At the beginning of each school year, each public agency shall have in effect, for each student with a disability within its jurisdiction, an IEP" (U.S. Department of Education, 2006, p. 46789).

Stage 7: The Child's Progress Is Reported

An advocate needs to know how to strive to ensure that all aspects of the educational program are in place and adjusted as needed, as described in Chapter 11. In this stage, parents, consultants, and school system professionals should make every effort to collect data and implement the services on the IEP in the way it was intended. Progress on the IEP is measured against the annual goals that spell out what the child reasonably should achieve within a year's time. The way progress is to be measured should be spelled out specifically within the IEP.

Each of these methods of measuring progress comes with a product or something that the IEP team or teaching staff can provide to parents in addition to oral reporting or report card comments, which are usually based on impressions and not data. This discussion again highlights the need for parents to be knowledgeable and powerful advocates for their children, and to hire experts as necessary to get help interpreting progress and developing tools to measure progress. Progress reporting can determine the direction of the child's program for the upcoming school year because the goals will change or remain the same based on information collected, including progress reports.

Minimum progress or lack of benefit requires that the IEP team meets to consider ways the IEP should be changed or revised. Parents should request that the IEP team meet to discuss progress, especially when there are concerns. Progress should be reported based on the IEP measurable goals at least as often as nondisabled students receive report cards. Because the IEP calls for specification of the type and frequency of the progress reports, the MDT discusses and determines how progress should be reported. The IEP should specify what information should be provided with the progress reporting.

School districts and states have developed codes, such as numbers or letters, to indicate progress on the IEP. These codes may or may not be in line with the intention of the law. If advocates are concerned about the standard way in which progress is reported, they may request that alternative ways of reporting progress are specified in the IEP. Some examples of alternative ways to report progress include a lettering system as follows:

- P = Progressing
- LP = Limited progress
- NA = Not addressed
- M = Mastered

Another method uses numbers instead of letters:

- 1 = Not addressed
- 2 = Minimal progress, goal likely will not be met
- 3 = Adequate progress, goal may be met
- 4 = Excellent progress, goal close to being met
- 5 = Mastered

The MDT may determine different ways to report progress.

Tips for Parents

Parents should be sure that data collection methods are required in the reporting of progress. In our view, it is not appropriate for the IEP to call for teacher observation as the only way to measure progress, unless the observations are written and accompany other types of data. The most formal and reliable way to measure progress is through formal testing or evaluation (see evaluation section). Of course, classroom data and information are very important. Data could be collected through the use of portfolio assessment, work samples, checklists, or curriculum-based assessment.

Request progress reports and data used to report progress. If the IEP calls for 9 out of 10 correct words spelled on work samples, request a portfolio of work samples and count the number of words. Be sure goals are written in a way that provides data and written documentation of progress. If not, go back to the IEP development stage (Stage 5), rework the IEP goals, and continue to request progress in line with IEP goals. Request more frequent teacher conferences, and find an opportunity to review your child's record in conjunction with the reporting of progress. If a parent is dissatisfied with the reporting of progress, she should review the PLOP statements and goals in the IEP to determine how progress should be reported. The IEP should be revised if needed.

Stage 8: The IEP Is Reviewed in a Periodic Review or Annual Review Meeting

At this stage, educators have had the chance to follow the IEP, collect data to measure progress, and provide the services listed in the IEP. Parents hopefully have been very involved in their child's education, and have collected work samples, researched curriculum demands, observed in the classroom, met with or spoken with service providers, and done any number of things to develop expertise on the implementation of the IEP. Parents may request a periodic review at any time. A periodic review is an MDT meeting to discuss any part of the child's IEP.

Changes to the IEP do not have to be made during or as a result of the periodic review meeting. IDEA 2004 allows for changes to be made outside the context of a meeting, as long as the change is agreed to in writing by the school district and the parent. Some districts have developed an amendment form to make these changes. Parents who have any question about whether the proposed change is appropriate should not use this method of making changes to the IEP and instead should request a periodic review to discuss changes with the MDT.

Stage 9: Reevaluation

There are processes for the review of any educational plan and the reevaluation of children who already are receiving special education services. Students who already have an IEP may be reevaluated at any time. There are many reasons to reevaluate a child who already has been identified with a disability. Perhaps there is an additional disability that had not been found previously, or the parent or MDT is wondering whether the child is making adequate progress. IDEA 2004 encourages the consolidation of reevaluation meetings with other types of meetings.

After the review of all existing information, the MDT must determine if the child's disability is correct or whether there is an additional disability. The MDT may determine that a child does not have a disability any more and does not, therefore, require special education services. Evaluation is *required* before the MDT determines that a child is no longer a child with a disability or before the child is dismissed or considered ineligible for special education and related services. A full battery of evaluations must be conducted before a child is dismissed from special education or related services.

School teams must consider all existing information, including information provided by the parents, and determine if any more information is needed to define the disability (either keep the current disability, change it, or add to it) or for educational planning or programming. If the MDT determines that no additional information is needed, the MDT must put in writing to the parent reasons that reevaluation planning did not result in evaluations. The MDT is not required to conduct the reevaluation, unless the parents request such assessment. No assessments would be completed, unless parents request them to determine their child's educational needs, or to make decisions about the educational disability. As with any issue regarding the education of children with disabilities, if a parent disagrees with any of the MDT's reevaluation decisions, the parent should utilize one or more of the dispute options available to her, as detailed in Chapter 4.

Reevaluation must be considered every 3 years. The key word here is *considered*, because consideration does not mean that the reevaluation *must* be conducted every 3 years. Reevaluations may be conducted more frequently, up to once per year. Reevaluation more than once per year requires agreement between the MDT and the parent.

After the reevaluation planning, the necessary evaluations are conducted. The evaluations contain recommendations that should be considered for inclusion in the IEP.

Parents should request reevaluation, and in the process, go back to stage 3 of the IEP process. Going back to stage 3 where evaluation information is considered by the IEP team, then moving to stage 4, Eligibility, then into IEP development, is a cycle that is necessary for continual planning from year to year.

The advocate's intimate understanding of the stages in the IEP process is critical in developing an appropriate program for a child with a disability. Parents can be equal partners with the school district when implications of each stage of the IEP process are fully understood. The advocate's ability to navigate each stage and assist in the development of an IEP with its required components builds trust between parents and MDT members and ultimately best serves the child.

Tip for Parents

Any time reevaluation planning occurs, the school team and you have the opportunity to change the IEP or program in some way. When children are not doing well in a school program, and the school requests reevaluation planning, parents should be prepared and anticipate in what ways the IEP may be changed, to determine whether there may be agreement. Reevaluation planning opens the doors for consideration of additional need areas, and it also opens the door for the MDT to reduce services or dismiss a student from special education or related services.

Do not sign permission for evaluations until you are convinced that you have all of the information you need, including what tests will be done, what disabilities are suspected, and the reasons for each evaluation. Consider the pros and cons of obtaining a private evaluation (see Table 5.1). Consult with an expert before signing permission if you have any doubt or questions about the process.

Common Example

Perhaps a child with a Specific Learning Disability is showing many interfering behaviors and poor social-emotional skills. The parent and MDT now suspect that the child also is a student with an emotional disturbance. Reevaluation planning means that the MDT will discuss the evaluations in all areas of suspected disability. The evaluation review will allow the school team to consider a different disability or another disability.

Preparing for the MDT Meeting

1. Know the purpose of the meeting. Know the agenda. This is required to be put in writing. Change the agenda in writing if needed.
2. Be sure the required members will be attending, as written on the meeting invitation.
3. Will you tape record the meeting? How will the meeting be documented?
4. Do you have the documents you need for the meeting, given the meeting's purpose? Or, do you need to conduct a record review before the meeting?
5. Has adequate time been scheduled for the meeting?
6. Have you discussed with your advocate the concerns you would like to share with the MDT team before the meeting?

Types of MDT/IEP Meetings

Evaluation Planning: The child will be evaluated for the first time.

Screening: Asks whether the child has a suspected disability that requires evaluation and may require special education and related services.

Reevaluation Planning: Planning for evaluations when your child already has an IEP.

Eligibility: To determine which disability or disabilities are present, and whether a child needs special education and related services.

IEP Development: After eligibility, the IEP must be developed within a certain number of days.

Periodic Review: To discuss progress and concerns, and possibly revise the IEP.

Annual Review: Discuss progress, develop a new IEP for the upcoming year, discuss Extended School Year Services; a full IEP meeting that addresses every aspect of the IEP and program.

Placement Meeting: Discuss what level of special education and related services (number of hours, place, provider, etc.) and location of services are needed.

Manifestation Determination: When a child has been removed for discipline, suspended close to or more than 10 school days, or is being recommended for expulsion, the MDT must discuss evaluations and the relationship between disability and behavior that will determine the child's placement.

Compensatory Education: When a child has not been receiving the services he is entitled to, the MDT must discuss how to make up for the lack of service.

Sample Letter From Parents: Referral for Special Education Services

Date
Principal
School Name
School Address
Sent by (e.g., fax, certified mail, e-mail)

Dear Ms. Principal,

We are writing about our son (name, date of birth). We suspect that he has an educational disability, and believe (student name) is in need of special education and related services. It is our understanding that evaluations in all areas of suspected disability will need to be completed. We understand that the multidisciplinary team needs to meet to consider this request. We are requesting that the multidisciplinary team convenes as soon as possible.

Please send us any forms that need to be completed for this formal referral for special education and related services, and inform us in writing of the process. We understand that this letter starts legal timelines. In the meantime, would you please contact us to schedule an initial meeting with your multidisciplinary team? We are interested in moving forward with this special education referral in an expedited manner.

Please contact me to confirm receipt of this information. Thank you for your consideration for (student name).

Sincerely,
Parent

Cc: (optional)
Supervisors
Special Ed. Coordinator
Advocate/Attorney

TOOLS

Sample Letter Requesting an Independent Educational Evaluation at Public Expense

Throughout our book, we advise parents that it is best practice to put concerns and requests in writing. Requesting an IEE at public expense is no different. This letter provides a template from which to write such a letter (National Dissemination Center for Children With Disabilities, 2002).

Today's Date (include month, day, and year)

Your Name
Street Address
City, State, Zip Code
Daytime telephone number

Mr. or Mrs. Principal
Street Address
City, State, Zip Code

Dear Principal,

My daughter, (child's name), is in the (X) grade, at (name of school), in (teacher's name) class. She was evaluated for special education services in (month/year) by (name of examiner). I am writing to request an Independent Educational Evaluation at public expense because I disagree with the evaluation that was conducted.

I would like this Independent Educational Evaluation at public expense to be completed as quickly as possible so that we can fully address (child's name) needs. Please respond as soon as possible, but no later than (give deadline such as 10 days). My daytime telephone number is (give your phone number). Thank you.

Sincerely,

Your name

Cc: Your child's teacher (optional)

Diagnoses and Definitions of Disabilities

Diagnoses are different from legally defined educational disabilities. This chart shows some common diagnoses and the educational disabilities to which they often correspond.

Examples of Diagnoses That Translate to:	Legal Definition of Disability
dyslexia, dysgraphia, dyscalculia, learning disorder, reading disorder, disorder of written expression, math disorder; learning disorder, not otherwise specified (NOS); nonverbal learning disorder or disability	The term Specific Learning Disability means a disorder in one or more of the basic psychological processes involved in understanding or in using language, spoken or written, which may manifest itself in the imperfect ability to listen, think, speak, read, write, spell, or do mathematical calculations. The term includes such conditions as perceptual disabilities, brain injury, minimal brain dysfunction, dyslexia, and developmental aphasia. The term does not include a learning problem that is primarily the result of visual, hearing, or motor disabilities, of mental retardation, of emotional disturbance, or of environmental, cultural, or economic disadvantage (108th Congress, 2004).
autism; pervasive developmental disorder, NOS; childhood disintegrative disorder; Rett syndrome; Asperger's syndrome	Autism means a developmental disability significantly affecting verbal and nonverbal communication and social interaction, generally evident before age 3 that adversely affects a child's educational performance. Other characteristics often associated with autism are engagement in repetitive activities and stereotyped movements, resistance to environmental change or change in daily routines, and unusual responses to sensory experiences.

Autism does not apply if a child's educational performance is adversely affected primarily because the child has an emotional disturbance. A child who manifests the characteristics of autism after age 3 could be identified as having autism (U.S. Department of Education, 2006). |

Examples of Diagnoses That Translate to:	Legal Definition of Disability
anxiety; depression; oppositional defiant disorder; mood disorder; conduct disorder; personality disorder	Emotional disturbance means a condition exhibiting one or more of the following characteristics over a long period of time and to a marked degree that adversely affects a child's educational performance: (a) an inability to learn that cannot be explained by intellectual, sensory, or health factors; (b) an inability to build or maintain satisfactory interpersonal relationships with peers and teachers; (c) inappropriate types of behavior or feelings under normal circumstances; (d) a general pervasive mood of unhappiness or depression; and (e) a tendency to develop physical symptoms or fears associated with personal or school problems. Emotional disturbance also includes schizophrenia. The term does not apply to children who are socially maladjusted, unless it is determined that they have an emotional disturbance (U.S. Department of Education, 2006).
cerebral palsy; spina bifida; use of walker, wheelchair, or other mobility device; poliomyelitis; bone tuberculosis; amputations, and fractures or burns that cause contractures	Orthopedic impairment defined as a severe orthopedic impairment that adversely impacts a child's educational performance. The term includes impairments caused by a congenital anomaly, impairments caused by disease, and impairments from other causes (U.S. Department of Education, 2006).
anxiety; Attention Deficit/Hyperactivity Disorder (ADD, ADHD); asthma; seizure disorder/epilepsy; lead poisoning; diabetes; Tourette's syndrome; sickle cell anemia; a heart condition; hemophilia; leukemia; nephritis; rheumatic fever	Other Health Impairment means having limited strength, vitality, or alertness, including a heightened alertness to environmental stimuli, that results in limited alertness with respect to the educational environment, that is due to chronic or acute health problems and adversely affects a child's educational performance (U.S. Department of Education, 2006).
Genetic disorders; Fragile X; Down's syndrome; phenylketonuria (PKU)	Mental retardation defined as "... significantly subaverage general intellectual functioning, existing concurrently with deficits in adaptive behavior and manifested during the developmental period, that adversely affects a child's educational performance" (National Dissemination Center for Children With Disabilities, 2004, p. 1).
Any eye-related problem that causes vision problems, does not include eye tracking for reading. May include congenital or injury-related conditions.	Blind or visually impaired defined as an impairment in vision that, even with correction, adversely affects a child's educational performance. The term includes both partial sight and blindness (U.S. Department of Education, 2006).

TOOLS

Examples of Diagnoses That Translate to:	Legal Definition of Disability
Any hearing loss, caused by injury or birth, with or without correction; children who wear Cochlear Implants for a variety of reasons	Deafness means a hearing impairment that is so severe that the student is impaired in processing linguistic information through hearing, with or without amplification; and adversely affects the student's educational performance (Maryland State Department of Education, 2000).
Dyspraxia, apraxia; central auditory processing disorder; articulation disorder, communication disorders, oral-motor disorders	Speech or language impairment means a communication disorder, such as stuttering, impaired articulation, a language impairment, or a voice impairment, that adversely affects a child's educational performance (U.S. Department of Education, 2006).
More than one diagnosis	Multiple disabilities means concomitant impairments (e.g., mental retardation-blindness or mental retardation-orthopedic impairment), the combination of which causes such severe educational needs that they cannot be accommodated in special education programs solely for one of the impairments. Multiple disabilities does not include deaf-blindness (108th Congress, 2004).
Any delay in any area, only applies federally to children to 9 years old. This does not apply in every state.	Developmental delay defined as children ages 3–9 experiencing developmental delays; a child who is experiencing developmental delays, as defined by the state and as measured by appropriate diagnostic instruments and procedures, in one or more of the following areas: physical development, cognitive development, communication development, social or emotional development, or adaptive development; and who, by reason thereof, needs special education and related services (IDEA, 2004).
A blow or trauma to the head that can be identified, including in utero	Traumatic brain injury means an acquired injury to the brain caused by an external physical force, resulting in total or partial functional disability or psychosocial impairment, or both, that adversely affects a child's educational performance. Traumatic brain injury applies to open or closed head injuries resulting in impairments in one or more areas, such as (but not limited to) cognition; language; memory; reasoning; perceptual, and motor abilities; physical functions; information processing; and speech. Traumatic brain injury does not apply to brain injuries that are congenital or degenerative or to brain injuries induced by birth trauma (108th Congress, 2004).

chapter 6

What Does an Advocate Need to Know About Evaluating a Child's Strengths and Needs?

This chapter explores ways to gather information about a student and discusses what information is important in the information gathering process. Information may lead to the identification of disabilities and to the development of an understanding of the child's strengths and weaknesses. When information is gathered thoroughly and properly, the advocate's in-depth understanding of the child's learning profile and of the child as a whole can be used to diagnose needs areas and prescribe effective interventions. The areas of need, with baseline data, may be translated into goals for the IEP or educational program. Accommodations, modifications, and supplementary aides and services also are clarified from information that is gathered through evaluations and other sources. Ultimately, a child's

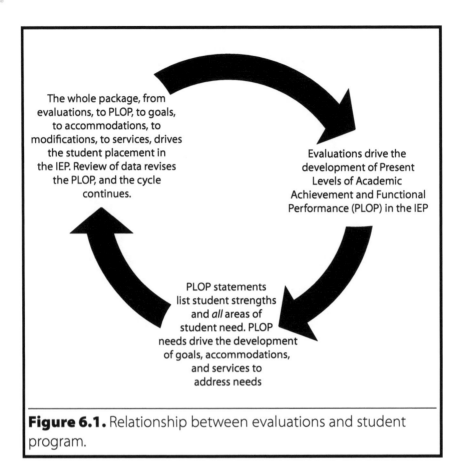

The whole package, from evaluations, to PLOP, to goals, to accommodations, to modifications, to services, drives the student placement in the IEP. Review of data revises the PLOP, and the cycle continues.

Evaluations drive the development of Present Levels of Academic Achievement and Functional Performance (PLOP) in the IEP

PLOP statements list student strengths and *all* areas of student need. PLOP needs drive the development of goals, accommodations, and services to address needs

Figure 6.1. Relationship between evaluations and student program.

Individualized Education Program is crafted with evaluation information as the foundation, or blueprint, for the plan ahead. The relationship between evaluation information and planning for the student's program is shown in Figure 6.1. It demonstrates the importance of evaluations in ensuring an accurate understanding of the student's present level of functioning.

Why Is This Important for an Advocate to Know?

Focusing on the whole child starts with consideration of the child's strengths. A student learner has many parts that interact together to positively or negatively impact school performance. The identification of strengths and gifts is valuable because the child likely will use his strengths when pursuing his career, developing hobbies, and fostering relationships. Many educational programs, however, are need-based, and tend to focus on the child's weak areas. To know when the weaknesses are or could be disabilities, it is imperative that advocates understand the typical developmental stages of child and human development.

The advocate needs to have a well-developed skills set for understanding evaluations because evaluations are the first step in developing a diagnostic-prescriptive approach to the education plan. Evaluations and their impact can change the life of a child; evaluations are used to identify disabilities and ultimately may lead to educational placement that impacts a child's future. The understanding of the child through evaluations impacts the advocate's strategy for advancing the goals set by the child's parent and school team.

The skilled advocate can provide leadership to the school team and MDT. She also may provide information related to the child's community and home functioning. Evaluation information should be gathered from the team or community surrounding the child. The advocate strives to know the school system's internal procedures so that various school system resources are used in evaluating the child's needs. When working with consultants outside the school system, the advocate is sensitive to the processes that will allow the school district to effectively use the evaluation information. Release of confidential information, explicit written consent from parents, and other processes may need to be in place. These processes should be respected and anticipated by the advocate to facilitate a working relationship with the school system.

The following gives advocates a specific list of things to know about evaluating the child's needs:

- the child's exact level of functioning based on data in all areas that impact the child, and how the child compares to the expectation of his peers, given the child's age and ability;

- the child's test scores and how to interpret them;
- the evaluations that the child needs to determine services needed;
- the strengths and areas of giftedness of the child;
- the child's behaviors and need for functional behavior assessment;
- the child's medical conditions;
- the child's culture, family system, temperament, and unique personality;
- the child's disability, characteristics of that disability, and whether there are disabilities present or suspected that have not yet been defined;
- the child's educational history and current education program;
- the child's attitude toward learning and unique personality characteristics; and
- the child's future goals and ambitions (perspectives on possible career choices and transition activities).

Developmental Stages

An effective advocate needs to understand typical development in the developmental stages of children and young adults. Children with disabilities deviate from the typical development of peers in one way or another, so understanding typical stages of development is critical to determine whether, and to what extent, the child requires specialized instruction or services to address the child's disabilities. Disabilities often are situational; a child may have a disability in the classroom, but not in the community. Careful attention to the formal and informal evaluation stage is important, because evaluations are ways of collecting this information.

Evaluations and other information only are useful if they identify and analyze educational interventions that the child needs for school success. The results are not useful unless advocates are able to understand to what extent the child is functioning where he or she needs to be based on age, grade, or ability.

Families and educators must understand the normal stages of human or child development to effectively move through the special education process. Many times, a family contacts the advocate to help them understand whether the child's struggles are normal as compared to his peers. This also applies to gifted learners and their placement in upper level courses. A child who has gifted abilities should be compared to children with similar abilities when determining her unique strengths and needs.

Obtaining Information About the Child

One general rule of thumb when gathering information about a child from the following data sources is to work with people who know and understand the child, people who work with or help the child learn and see them in many environments, and from the child himself. It is critical not to rely on only one source of information, regardless of the technique used for gathering information. Parents are the first and best teachers of children, in most circumstances. This includes foster and adoptive parents or guardians who are in a parental role. Teachers, aides, related service providers, administrators, and those in the school system who have evaluated the child are valuable sources in the school setting. At times, secretaries, building custodial staff, nursing aides, or lunchroom staff can be valuable sources of information. Professionals who see the child outside of the school day such as therapists, psychiatrists, medical doctors, babysitters, or tutors also are valued sources of information.

Evaluations

The most comprehensive way to gain information about a learner is through evaluations. Evaluation is the process of assessment, or collection of data, and the subsequent interpretation and analysis of information after it is gathered. Evaluation information can come from formal evaluation tools or from informal sources, such as classroom performance, observations, or reviewing records. An advocate is looking for current and prior evaluations to determine several things: whether sufficient information exists to develop the child's educational program; whether meaningful and adequate progress has been made in the child's program; whether disabilities have been adequately defined; and/or whether the current educational program meets the child's unique needs.

One of the best ways to unlock the secret of the student's learning profile is to read, digest, and interpret results of formal evaluation reports. An advocate must have a superior handle on how to interpret different types of statistics contained within educational records. Having a conceptual understanding about the difference between criterion-referenced, norm-referenced, or informal evaluation tools allows the advocate to correctly interpret how the results may impact the child in the classroom, and what interventions match the data findings. This skill is developed over time and as a result of reading, experiencing, and hearing about tests and their implications. As with many other facets of advocacy, the advocate must stay current and continually research the types of evaluations being used in schools and in private practice, the general trends of evaluations in school systems, and the changing beliefs of families and the practitioners from multiple disciplines who work to educate a child.

Some tests are criterion-referenced, meaning that student performance is scored based on whether the child can show or demonstrate a skill required in the curriculum, in the classroom, or in life. Teachers can administer these repeatedly over time. Criterion-referenced tests may report scores in different ways, but the best information from these types of tests is a listing of what skills the child is or is not able to do, and what type of assistance is needed for the child to perform the skill.

Other tests are formal and based on national norms. Formal evaluations are those in which the test publisher has sampled children of all ages, races, and cultures; family backgrounds; socio-economic statuses; or other factors to obtain a standard for what is *typical* for this group of children. These tests are given in very specific, standardized ways where the directions are given the same way, every child who takes the test receives the same items based on age and ability, and scores are called standardized scores. These can be given in a group or individually, but they must be given by trained examiners and in a way that is prescribed by the publisher of the test. These are formal evaluations, and the results may be reported in terms of standard scores, percentile scores, T-scores, and/or age/grade equivalents.

Most standardized tests provide either standard or scaled scores. Psychological and achievement tests are the most common types of formal standardized tests given to children in the special education process.

Formal standardized testing is used to determine:
- what disability the child has;
- whether the disability requires special education and related services, or whether the child is eligible for special education;
- progress;
- whether to dismiss or exit the child from special education;
- the child's strengths and needs; and
- whether the child needs a related service to benefit from the special education program.

There are many types of formal tests. Remember, as discussed in Chapter 5, written parent permission is required for the school system to give these tests unless the formal test is given to all students. Parents may choose not to provide informed consent until they are in agreement with the specific tests that will be given. It also is important to have regular vision and hearing testing for all children. This is critical because if hearing or vision is poor, the advocate must help the parent and MDT to rule out these factors as the causes of the student's learning problems.

Advocates must be skilled in analyzing whether adequate evaluations have been completed, or whether additional evaluations may be needed to effectively develop educational interventions. The advocate needs to know what evaluations have been done in relation to the child's current strengths and needs to determine if enough information exists to develop the child's program in a powerful and informed way. The child's strengths and needs are documented in the section of the IEP called Present Levels of Academic Achievement and Functional Performance (PLOP). That critical part of the IEP also determines the baseline or starting point for the child's measurable goals. It is imperative that evaluations are completed in every area of concern, from psychological, to educational, to assistive technology, to speech and language, and so on. This section is designed to help the advocate understand what red flags or concerns should be addressed by each type of evaluation. When an advocate learns about these red flags, the advocate is able to determine if these concerns have been evaluated by the proper members of the MDT.

Types of Evaluations

The following is a list of many of the areas evaluated by professionals from different disciplines. Although most children will not be assessed on all of these areas, this list is provided as a guide to the different areas of assessment that may be considered. This list is not exhaustive and topics listed under one discipline also may be addressed by another discipline. The purpose of the following descriptions is to provide the reader with a cursory, basic understanding of the discipline's scope of evaluation. For comprehensive information about each of these disciplines, the reader is encouraged to review the law and consult professional resources, such as Web sites maintained by the discipline's official organization.

- **Psychological:** Psychological evaluations are important for gathering a variety of information. Psychological tests can include those that assess children for:
  - cognitive/intellectual/IQ,
  - processing,
  - visual motor skills,
  - adaptive behavior,
  - attention and concentration,
  - projective or social-emotional,
  - behavior and psychopathology,
  - executive functioning, and
  - DSM-IV differential diagnoses.
- **Neuropsychological:** This type of testing includes components of the psychological evaluation but also examines other areas of brain functioning and brain-behavior relationships. It often includes assessment of executive functioning, attention, emotional factors, cognition, language use, and processing.
- **Neurological:** This type of evaluation should not be confused with a neuropsychological evaluation. A neurologist is a medical doctor who performs physical tests of the brain such as EEG, MRI, and CAT scans and utilizes a range of neurophysiologic screening procedures.
- **Psychiatric/Medical/Genetics:** A psychiatrist is a medical doctor with a specialty in psychological development and conditions. A psychiatric evaluation often includes a child/parent interview with a view to providing a differential diagnosis. Medical evaluations are conducted by physicians, and many school systems will not advertise that these evaluations are needed or available. The law is clear that a medical service can be a related service for diagnostic and evaluation purposes. Therefore, a medical professional may be a required member of the MDT.

- **Educational or Achievement:** Educational and achievement tests include those that measure a child's skills in reading, written language, math, organization, study skills, and general knowledge. Educational or achievement tests used in the IEP process to evaluate a student's eligibility for special education or for program planning are distinct from state or district assessments in that they are used to answer specific diagnostic questions about the student. Educational or achievement tools are individually administered, formal tests or data collected informally.
- **Functional Behavior Assessment (FBA):** An FBA will assess a child for interfering behaviors, organization skills, attention capabilities and deficits, work completion, and social skills. The FBA is not an individually administered test, but rather a data-collection activity performed by members of the MDT. Conducting FBAs is explored in detail later in this chapter.
- **Speech and Language:** These tests include those that measure articulation, expressive or oral language, resonance, speech sound production, receptive language or listening, pragmatic language, oral-motor skills, voice, and a child's fluency in his or her native language. See http://www.asha.org/default.htm for a complete list of areas evaluated by this discipline.
- **Audiological:** Audiological tests assess a child's hearing and auditory processing. They can determine deafness and whether the child needs hearing devices. These tests should be conducted on a regular basis. The purposes of an audiological evaluation includes determination of whether this is a needed related service. So, the evaluation may focus on auditory processing needs; the identification of children with hearing loss; determination of the range, nature, and degree of hearing loss; and the need for services such as auditory training, hearing evaluation, language habilitation, speech reading (lip reading), and speech conservation.

- **Vision:** Visual tests, which also should be conducted on a regular basis, test a child's visual acuity and visual processing. This discipline also helps evaluate the need for Braille, mobility training, and use of services or devices to support persons with a vision deficit or disability. An evaluation may focus on whether the child needs orientation and mobility related services, including teaching children how to use sensory information to travel safely in the school or community (U.S. Department of Education, 2006, p. 46761).

- **Occupational Therapy:** This related service, provided by a qualified occupational therapist, has the purpose under the law of improving, developing, or restoring functions impaired or lost through illness, injury, or deprivation; improving a child's ability to perform tasks independently; or preventing impairment through early intervention. Assessments conducted through the MDT often test a child's needs in the following areas: fine motor skills, sensory regulation, sensory integration, coordination, gross motor skills, eating or swallowing difficulties, toileting and self-care, handwriting capabilities, perception, visual processing, assistive technology, and motor skills (this list is not exhaustive).

- **Assistive Technology:** These assessments look at the hardware and software needed in the classroom or at home to help accommodate a student's learning needs. Advocates also should evaluate the training needs of staff, students, and parents, and the need for any replacement, repair, maintenance, or adaptation of equipment.

- **Physical Therapy:** Physical therapy evaluations look at the child's physical skill needs including motor skills, balance, stability, orientation, and mobility. The evaluation should help the MDT develop statements about the child's present levels of educational achievement and functional performance in the physical area, including specialized physical education, if appropriate.

- **Adaptive Physical Education:** IDEA 2004 emphasizes the importance of physical education for students with disabilities. This discipline evaluates the child's present level of academic achievement and functional performance in the physical education curriculum, and evaluates needs for special education or related services in this area. The adaptive physical education discipline may work in cooperation with other disciplines.
- **Other Evaluations:** The MDT also may want to consider evaluations in these or other areas:
  - music therapy,
  - aquatic therapy,
  - art therapy,
  - social work, and
  - Limited English Proficiency.

Formal Evaluations

Interpreting formal evaluation scores can be confounding and confusing to parents and professionals. Standard scores, scaled scores, and percentile scores are used to describe student performance compared to her same-age peers. Formal testing is the best practice for determining how a child compares to peers. There are many important terms that will help parents, advocates, and school staff to interpret the results of formal evaluations.

Standard Deviation

Standard and scaled scores assume that student performance will deviate from the exact average, or the *mean*, by a certain amount, described as the *standard deviation*. For example, if the mean is 100, and the standard deviation is 15, student performance often is described by increments of 15 points either above or below the mean, at 55, 70, 85, 100 (mean), 115, 130, and 145. Means and standard deviations will vary from test to test, but in the most commonly used tests by psychologists and special educators, the mean is 100 and the standard deviation is 15.

Standard Scores

Standard scores are the most common type of formal score discussed by the MDT. The MDT should use the description of scores provided by the publisher of the assessment tool when discussing the child's performance (when describing a standard score as an average, low average, superior, or other range score). Standard scores in the 130s and above are very superior. Less than 2% of our population scores in this range. Scores in the 120s are in the superior range. About 14% of the population falls in this category. Scores from 110–119 are in the high average range, and scores from 90 to 109 are in the average range. On the lower end, scores in the 80s are considered low average, while scores from 70–79 are considered low. Scores below 70 are more than two standard deviations below the mean, and are significantly below average (subaverage). Less than approximately 2% of the general population score in this range, while less than approximately one tenth of one percent of our population would have scores below 55, in the very low range.

Another important concept to remember when interpreting formal evaluation scores is that scores will be reported in a range, based on the publisher's statistical conversions, which vary from test to test. A child rarely will perform the same way each day and each time he is tested. This is called a *standard error of measurement*, or confidence band. So, a standard score of 90 should be seen as falling within a band of scores, for example 86–94. Let's take a look at a hypothetical example. A standard score of 88, which is in the confidence band of 84–92, actually crosses over two ranges; the score would be considered both average and low average. The child should not been seen as one number, instead, the MDT should focus on range of functioning, analyzing student performance and building the educational program based on that information.

While practitioners may use the bell curve to discuss scores in terms of standard deviation, publishers of some of the most well-used assessment tools describe ranges of scores differently, as shown in Table 6.1. For example, a standard score of 86 is in the average range, according to the bell curve. However, the same standard score of 86 is described as a low average score by pub-

Table 6.1

How Statistics Define Ranges (Bell Curve).

Score	Description	Relationship to Standard Deviation (SD)
55 and below	Very deficient	3 or more SDs below average
56–70	Low	2 SDs below average
71–85	Below average	1 SD below average
86–115	Average	Within one SD of average
116–130	Above average	1 SD above average
131–144	Superior	2 SDs above average
145 and above	Highly superior	3 SDs above average

Standard Score Descriptions Commonly Specified by Publishers:

Score	Description
69 and below	Very low
70–79	Low
80–89	Low average
90–109	Average
110–119	High average
120–129	Superior
130 and above	Very superior

lishers of many formal evaluation tools. This difference in the description of the student's functioning may make a difference in how the members of the MDT view the child's performance. Table 6.1 shows standard scores by standard deviation and the description of those scores.

Table 6.2 offers another view of the difference between range descriptions of standard scores when using the bell curve and guidelines from publishers commonly used in MDT meetings.

Formal tests may be made up of subtests, which are smaller sections of the test that focus on discrete skills. Subtests may be reported in either standard or scaled scores. Clusters of subtests then are reported together in Composite, Index, or Broad scores.

Table 6.2

Difference in Score Range Reporting

Range	According to Bell Curve	According to Publishers
Below average	84 and below	79 and below
Average range	85–115	90–109
High average, above average	116–130	110–119
Superior	Above 130	120–129

IQ tests, for example, report an overall intelligence quotient (IQ) that is comprised of different factors. It is important that the advocate understand the subtests or components that comprise a Broad, Index, or Composite Score. When there is too much variation, it is important that the advocate attend to the broad or full-scale score, but also to the strengths and weaknesses represented by the various subtest scores.

Scaled Scores

Scaled scores are used for subtests or the smaller parts of the test that are taken together to get overall scores. Scaled scores have a mean of 10, and a standard deviation of 3; scores are reported in ranges marked by increments of 3: 1, 4, 7, 10 (mean), 13, 16, 19. When discussing scaled scores, results are interpreted as follows: Exactly average is 10. Scores from 7–13 are in the average range. Scores from 14–16 are above average, and scores from 17–19 are superior. Scaled scores above 19 are highly superior, with only less than one percent of our population falling in this range. On the lower end, scores from 4–6 are below average, and scores from 1–3 are well below average. Scores below one indicate such low functioning that less than a half of a percent of our population would perform in this range. The corresponding standard scores and percentile scores are shown in Figure 6.2, a visual representation of the relationship between standard, scaled, and percentile scores.

Percentile Scores

Percentile scores correspond directly with standard and scaled scores. The exact average percentile score is 50. Well-above average percentile scores are above the 86th percentile, and highly superior scores are at or above the 98th percentile. On the lower end, well-below average scores are at or below the 14th percentile, while extremely deficient (significantly subaverage) scores are at or below the 2nd percentile. Roughly speaking, if a child is at the 60th percentile, if 100 randomly selected peers were lined up with him, about 40 of those 100 peers would perform better on the task than he did. Percentiles described in this paragraph are approximate although there is an exact formula for calculating the percentile scores. As seen in Figure 6.2, the average percentile score range is from the 25th percentile to the 75th percentile, corresponding with standard scores of 90 and 110, respectively. When interpreting percentile scores, the advocate will determine what standard score matches or corresponds by using her knowledge of the bell curve and related formal scores. Figure 6.2 is a visual representation of the bell curve with the relationship between standard, scaled, and percentile scores and description of student functioning.

Age and Grade Equivalency Scores

Advocates must use caution when reporting or discussing scores in terms of age, and especially grade, equivalents. It is best practice when discussing formal evaluation results to stick to standard, scaled, and percentile scores. The reason for this is that tests with national norms cannot take into account the differences between and among states' curriculum and testing demands. So, it is less reliable to report scores in terms of grade level. When the publishers of the test give the test to see how the average child will perform, they may assign a score to a grade level, but that has not taken into account each grade level's curriculum demand across the nation. In addition, some very small percentage of children will either score so low or so superior that the test tool is not able to calculate a grade or age equivalency. The bottom line is that

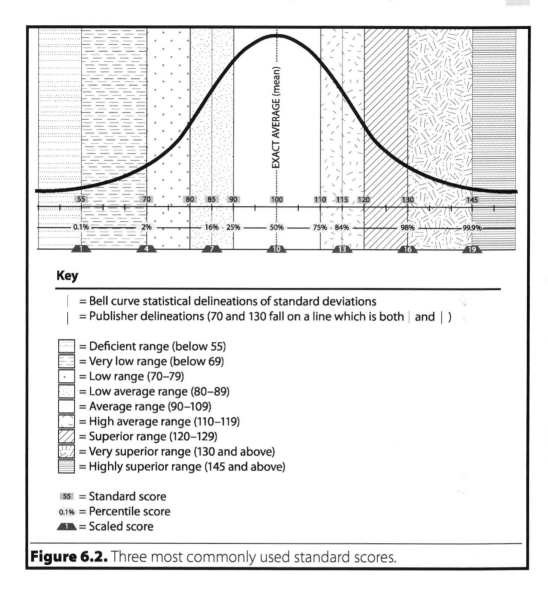

Key

| = Bell curve statistical delineations of standard deviations
| = Publisher delineations (70 and 130 fall on a line which is both | and |)

[ ] = Deficient range (below 55)
[ ] = Very low range (below 69)
[ ] = Low range (70–79)
[ ] = Low average range (80–89)
[ ] = Average range (90–109)
[ ] = High average range (110–119)
[ ] = Superior range (120–129)
[ ] = Very superior range (130 and above)
[ ] = Highly superior range (145 and above)

55 = Standard score
0.1% = Percentile score
1 = Scaled score

Figure 6.2. Three most commonly used standard scores.

discussion of formal testing should emphasize standard, scaled, and percentile scores.

T-Scores

T-scores are used less often than standard, scaled, and percentile scores, but they are common when examiners report results of rating scales. When teachers, parents, and others complete rating scales for autism, attention, behavior, adaptive, or other skills, examiners frequently report the results in terms of the T-score. A T-score's mean is 50, and the standard deviation is 10, so scores are reported in ranges delineated by 30, 40, 50 (mean), 60, 70, 80, and 90. The interesting thing about the T-score is that both very low and very high scores indicate areas of concern. One standard deviation from the mean is considered to be average: 40–60. However, the further the score is from the mean, the more the score indicates an area of concern. So, for example, scores of 30 and 70 may be equally concerning, indicating needs in the area being assessed (Green, Trimble, & Lewis, 2003).

The advocate should understand what the test requires of the child, what the numbers mean in terms of performance, what the numbers mean in relation to other tests' findings, and what the numbers mean in terms of problems in the classroom and educational interventions to address the problems.

If there are prior evaluation findings, the advocate needs to understand whether numbers can be compared to find the extent of student progress or whether the school may be giving information that cannot be compared directly to determine progress. For example, standard scores from two different tests may not be able to be directly compared if they don't statistically correlate with one another.

Generally, there are questions that an advocate must know to ask in order to obtain answers when he is not familiar with the evaluation tools in reports or those being discussed at meetings. When the advocate encounters a tool with which he is not familiar, he may want to know the purpose of the tool, the format of the task, the requirements of the task, how the student responded, and implications for programming based on test results. The test publisher often is the best source of information about the test.

Informal Evaluation Methods

Observations, record reviews, interviews, rating scales, curriculum-based measurement, portfolio reviews, work samples, functional behavior assessments, or informal reading inventories are examples of informal evaluation methods. When discussing informal evaluation results, while there may be data reported, the scores are not reported in standard scores, as they are in formal evaluations. Informal tools may describe performance in terms of narrative descriptions or nonstandard scores.

Record Reviews

Advocates need to know how educational decisions have been made and documented in a child's record. An advocate must understand the concept of Prior Written Notice—that all educational decisions must be documented in a particular way to include parent requests and the MDT's response to the parent requests (see Chapter 4). In reviewing records, then, the advocate must identify the chronology of the special education process and look for associated documents for each event in the child's educational timeline.

Parents are entitled to review and inspect their child's records, and most school systems will make copies of documents in the child's records. However, school systems are not required to make copies of the records for parents or their representatives, unless copying them is the only way the parent may review and inspect the records (Norlin, 2007).

Advocates should encourage parents to regularly review their child's records, and advocates also should review these, along with records provided by parents. Each part of the IEP process has documents associated with it. For example, evaluation stages will generate Authorization for Assessment forms, evaluation reports, and meeting minutes or prior notice of the team's decisions as a result of the evaluations. Eligibility forms may accompany evaluations if a new disability is found. Understanding the IEP process is vital when reviewing a child's records. A sample letter to request a record review is provided in the TOOLS for Chapter 11.

Advocates must look in an educational record to see whether actions have been taken in a comprehensive and timely manner. An advocate is looking for indications of progress over time and for how the school staff perceives the child, the child's progress, and his educational needs.

Interviews

Interviews can be powerful tools for gathering information. When possible, the advocate should use a consistent format for interviewing others about a child. This may include an objective measure for scoring the interview. Interviews can be informal, such as telephone calls, or formal, such as rating scales. When conducting interviews, the advocate should be aware that bias can cloud the interpretation of information, so the advocate should consider the information attained in the context of other information sources. As with any information-gathering activity, interviews should supplement other sources and types of information so that decisions are made with the use of data from multiple sources.

Advocates also should be able to develop their own interview questions based on the child's individual needs and educational program. Interviews generally should allow the responder to answer a question quantitatively and qualitatively, giving a score and an explanation. In this type of structured interview, the opportunity for bias is reduced, and persons who are being interviewed will be asked the same questions for consistency of the process of gathering information.

Conducting Effective Observations

An effective advocate is able to use observation as a primary information source. Observations can be conducted in testing settings, in discussions in an office setting, or at home. Because the advocate is focused on the educational program, the best way to conduct observations is at school. To be most effective, the observation should have a defined purpose and be conducted after at least a record review and parent interview.

Unfortunately, advocates and parents may encounter resistance from the school system when attempting to schedule and conduct observations. It may be necessary for advocates to assure administrators that no learning will be disrupted and teaching staff will not be interrupted during the observation. The advocate should comply with time and frequency limits on observations, but the advocate also should make sure that these policies are in place systemwide for all parents and advocates to prevent discriminatory practices. It is not uncommon for advocates to be accompanied by a school system monitor during observations. It is important that the observer be a "fly on the wall," with the least impact on the typical classroom routine possible. There are times when school staff invites an advocate to interact with the group and participate in the class activity or interact with the child she is observing. The advocate must use her best judgment in these situations to determine if her interaction will allow a good snapshot of classroom performance to forward the collection of necessary information.

Always ask the instructional staff whether the day was a typical day for the class and the observed student. To minimize the need to interrupt, an advocate could have these questions written with a yes or no option that can be circled or indicated by a nod, with follow-up via e-mail or phone call conducted at a later time. At times, the observation may spontaneously provide the opportunity for the advocate to informally interview staff.

To the greatest extent possible, the student should not be aware that the advocate is observing him or her. If the advocate has a relationship with the student, the student should be prepared about the purpose of the observation and should be prepared to act as he normally would on any other school day.

Rating Scales

When an advocate gives an educator or family member a questionnaire, he often is using a rating scale. Rating scales are informal tools when they are not distributed by a publisher or scored to produce standardized scores. Rating scales also can be used as a more formal part of the evaluation process, as described earlier in this chapter.

Advocates can use commercially produced rating scales or create their own. Rating scales, like interviews, should have a uniform scoring system, or rubric, with opportunities for the responder to clarify or explain answers in a narrative way.

An item that might be on a rating scale is:

Rate the child's reading level compared with typical third graders:

1 = well below average, 2 = below average, 3 = average, 4 = above average, 5 = superior

Explain the reading program that is being used:

_____

The rating scale should match the targeted information sought to the greatest extent possible. The advocate may want to determine if a certain disability exists. The rating scale would contain specific characteristics of that disability. If the advocate wants to understand classroom behavior or academic functioning, the rating scale should have target questions related to those issues. Rating scales can be used in differential diagnosis and can be standardized so that the child's performance may be compared to his peers' performance.

Portfolio Review, Curriculum-Based Measurement (CBM)

Curriculum-based measurement is a way for the classroom teacher to track progress on curriculum-based skills using data from frequent quizzes in a way that may be graphed with student participation. CBM is a best teaching practice that is data driven, visual, and very effective with many types of learners. CBM can be used for any academic skill, in conjunction with any curriculum, and even for behavior and social skills.

One of the benefits of the use of CBM is that it can be placed on the IEP as a way to measure student progress, and, when done well, it generates many student work samples, data, and graphs that are easily understood.

Portfolio evaluation is an informal analysis of student work assembled in a way that student work samples demonstrate progress, access to the curriculum, and present level of academic achievement or functional performance. The student should be involved with developing her portfolio. Technology can be used in a variety of ways with this flexible tool; student videos, PowerPoint presentations, audio recordings, and graphing software are just some of the ways technology can be used to develop student portfolios. It is prudent for the MDT to discuss how the portfolio will be used to report progress or how the portfolio will be used for planning for the student's program. As with any other tool, it is important that the portfolio is not used in isolation; the data derived from the portfolio should be considered along with other formal and informal data so that the MDT is making decisions based on multiply confirming data (TeacherVision.com, n.d.).

Functional Behavior Assessment

An advocate needs to know whether behaviors are present, and whether these behaviors are interfering in the learning of the child or other children. Behavior and discipline as they relate to the IEP process are discussed more extensively in Chapter 5. Overall, an advocate needs to help determine whether the child's behaviors rise to the level where they should be addressed in the child's IEP through a functional behavior assessment and subsequent behavior intervention plan. At times, these formal plans are not necessary for a positive reward system to be in place. A good rule of thumb is to connect behaviors to the child's IEP so that the child is well-protected under the laws that take behavior into account as related to the child's disability.

Although IDEA 2004 does not define a functional behavior assessment, there have been best practices established through study and research. The purpose of this section is to explore these best practices, which include collecting data about behaviors, forming and testing hypotheses about behaviors, and identifying the function of student behavior through data collection and the identification of antecedents and consequences to behaviors.

An FBA can be conducted for any child, whether or not the child has an educational disability. The FBA is not a test where a student sits with an examiner and does tasks or takes a test. An FBA is not performed by only one person. Instead, an FBA is a data-collection activity conducted by various members of the MDT, including parents. Because the FBA is a type of evaluation, parents may obtain an Independent Educational Evaluation (IEE) or request an IEE at public expense in this area, as described in detail in Chapter 5.

An effective FBA is completed as a team and has these components:

- properly defined target behavior;
- data regarding how often the target behavior occurs, in what settings, and under what conditions;
- an hypothesis of the reason behaviors occur; and
- interventions attempted with data to test the hypothesis for the function of (reasons for) the behavior.

There are several well-known functions of behaviors in all human beings. Students may misbehave to get attention from peers, get attention from adults, avoid tasks, obtain power and control, to regulate sensory factors or obtain stimulation, or communicate something. Overall, behaviors either get us something we want or help us avoid something we do not want.

One caution to emphasize in this process is to distinguish whether students have the skills to perform a certain behavior or whether students are not able to use the skills they have. In the case where a behavior analysis reveals that the student has a skill deficit, instruction is necessary, not reinforcement or behavior intervention. A student with autism may not have the skills to communicate feelings, so instruction or therapy may be needed. It will not matter how many times a reward is offered for this student to express his feelings because first, the skill must be developed through instruction (Fitzsimmons, 1998).

Although an FBA is the assessment that defines and supposes reasons (or functions) for a behavior, it may not specifically spell out interventions, services, and accommodations that are necessary to address interfering behaviors. Therefore, a behavior intervention plan (BIP) often accompanies the FBA. It is not appropriate for the MDT to develop the BIP without an FBA. Because the BIP provides solutions for the behavior, it is critical that the behavior is defined and data are collected before the BIP is developed. The BIP may be part of the IEP, and therefore, must be implemented as written.

The ABC method of analyzing behavior is a commonly used structure for examining behaviors. A stands for antecedent, B stands for behavior, and C stands for consequence. Behaviors are reinforced by consequences and may be caused by or worsened by antecedents. Let's look at a situation that provides an example of behaviors reinforced by consequences.

Common Example

Sampson is in third grade. His teacher begins the morning routine every Monday through Thursday with a warm-up on the overhead. In the warm-up, students must copy a paragraph from the overhead and correct five spelling, punctuation, or grammatical errors in the paragraph. The teacher tells Sampson's parents that he has difficulty in the morning, and has been sent to the office for talking to other students and walking around the classroom. Because the teacher has started to send Sampson to the guidance counselor in the morning, this behavior has only gotten worse. The teacher tells the guidance counselor and the administration at the school that she believes that Sampson's medication for his ADHD is not working in the morning. When the MDT develops the FBA, the members examine these behaviors more closely, and find out that Sampson is unable to read or understand the warm-up paragraphs due to his learning disability in the area of reading a written language. He has been acting out in an effort to avoid the work and because of his desire to visit the counselor.

In the example above, the antecedent to Sampson's behavior is the presentation of frustrating academic material. Talking to other students and walking around the classroom is the behavior that's followed by a consequence of Sampson being able to leave the classroom and see the guidance counselor, who he likes very much. The consequence of the behavior in this case is actually reinforcing. Because the function of Sampson's behavior is avoiding work that is too difficult, being able to leave the classroom and talk with the guidance counselor is a reward. If the MDT had not conducted the FBA to get an understanding of Sampson's behavior, it may appear that Sampson simply is being disrespectful. The MDT develops the BIP and revises the IEP to make sure that teachers give Sampson academic material that he is able to complete successfully, and list trips to see the guidance counselor as rewards given only after Sampson completes his work.

Although it is considered best practice to conduct a functional behavior assessment to address interfering behaviors, or behaviors that impact the student's ability to progress in and access the curriculum, there are times an FBA is required by law. An FBA is required when students violate a code of conduct and the MDT determines that the behavior *was* a manifestation of the child's disability. Also, an FBA, being a type of evaluation, must be considered by the MDT at parent request: Because the FBA is a type of assessment, the MDT must consider a parent request for this assessment. Parents may request an IEE related to the FBA (see IEE and evaluation sections).

The results of the FBA are used to develop the behavior intervention plan (BIP). Data gathered in the process of conducting the FBA should include known rewards the child responds to, possible antecedents or precursors to behavior, and interventions that have been attempted. BIPs should not be developed before the FBA is conducted. Positive behavior supports, accommodations, interventions, and other aspects of the BIP should consider the function of the student behavior, which may change over time. A student wants to "get" something, "avoid" something, or "escape" something, so he behaves in a certain way. Behavior can be seen as communication. The development of the BIP should be a team effort, and the team should use data to determine how to manipulate the antecedents and consequences in the school setting. Replacement behaviors should be directly taught, along with coping skills, so there is an instructional piece of the BIP that should work in tandem with the IEP, or stand alone as a guide to instruction if the child does not have an IEP (Center for Effective Collaboration and Practice, 2001).

Using Technology

With the ever-increasing use of technology in our society, audiotaping or videotaping is readily available. Advocates who are concerned about homework time or reading material for homework may ask a parent to audiotape or videotape the child during reading at home or during homework time. Video feedback is becoming more widely used both as information sources and for shaping student behavior.

Evaluations When the Child Has an IEP in Place

The advocate needs to know the information from many sources about a child as the information relates to the parts of an existing IEP, including:

- identifying information;
- background information;
- student strengths and goals for the future;
- parental concerns about the program;
- present level of school achievement and functional performance: strengths and needs based on classroom and testing information;
- goals, either in place or needed;
- accommodations, modifications, and aides and services needed for progress; and
- placement: to what extent is the child currently in a setting with peers without disabilities, and/or to what extent should the child receive services with students without disabilities?

Defining the Suspected or Known Disability

While conducting observations and interviews and gathering information, advocates need to listen and look for information related to a known or suspected disability. There are patterns of learning and behaviors that are common to each disability category and disabling condition. Whereas Chapter 4 describes conditions that may translate into disabilities, this section more practically describes behaviors and learning patterns that may be associated with known or suspected disabilities. Advocates must remember that even though a condition exists, it does not automatically equate to a disability that requires special education and related services through an IEP or 504 Plan (see Chapter 4). The following are some practical descriptions of disabilities advocates must understand in order to recognize red flags of disabling conditions. Advocates should know the exact legal definitions of disabilities and be able to spot the defining characteristics of each one.

The advocate uses the different definitions of disabilities and his knowledge of various disability categories in the evaluation planning process. It is important to understand the criteria and definitions for each category of disability, so that the evaluations will reveal the correct and desired information needed to determine whether a disability exists, and whether the child requires special education and related services. The advocate defines possible disabilities and strives to assure the evaluations are conducted in a way that may be useful in planning for the child and determining his or her present levels of performance, academic achievement, and functional performance in the classroom.

The following sections describe the most common disabling conditions. It is meant to supplement the legal definitions of each disability, which are provided as a tool at the end of Chapter 5. Chapter 5 legally defines the disabilities, and this section discusses the disabilities as they relate to evaluation of the child's needs, including the red flags or indications with which an advocate is familiar to guide the evaluation planning and educational programming for the child. It is important to note that evaluations for an individual child should not be limited to just a narrow disability classification but should examine all suspected areas of impact and all suspected disabilities. For example, a student who is suspected of having a Specific Learning Disability also may have issues that lead the MDT to recommend a speech and language or occupational therapy evaluation.

Problem

Different disabilities may share common characteristics, so parents and school personnel may see the presence of the characteristic in different ways. Parents and school personnel may interpret the same evaluation information differently.

Common Example

An 8-year-old has been diagnosed with Asperger's syndrome through the evaluation process. He shows social skills deficits and sensory defensiveness, which makes him anxious in the school setting, sometimes leading to meltdowns in the cafeteria. The parent sees these areas of deficit as related to autism, whereas the school system sees the needs related to an emotional disturbance.

Specific Learning Disability

Specific Learning Disability (SLD) is characterized under IDEA 2004 by an underlying psychological processing disorder and presents academic difficulty in one or more specific areas such as writing, reading, listening, speaking, or doing mathematics. Red flags of a processing problem can include uneven performance across academic areas such as differences in the ability to speak versus write a paragraph, or the ability to understand and complete tasks.

Advocates must further understand how a particular state defines the disability; in the case of SLDs, the federal law does allow states to define the disability based on different standards. It used to be that the MDT would test a child's IQ and test a child's academic performance to determine if there was a mathematically determined significant difference between the two. Utilizing this discrepancy model is no longer a requirement for determining the presence of a SLD. Federal regulations now encourage the use of the Response to Intervention process or the finding of a pattern that is indicative of a learning disability. For this and other disabilities, the advocate must understand how the disability is defined, how it is legally determined, and what red flags may be raised to point to possible disabling conditions.

Types of evaluations to consider include: psychological (cognitive, processing); educational (all areas); and required classroom observation.

Emotional Disturbance

Emotional disturbance is characterized by one or more of the following:

- an inability to learn that is not explained by sensory or heath issues,
- unusual or inappropriate thoughts or feelings under normal circumstances,
- a pervasive sadness or depression,
- physical complaints or fears associated with emotional conditions (somatization), and
- an inability to form and maintain interpersonal relationships.

Emotional disturbance includes schizophrenia and may or may not include students who are socially maladjusted. Based on this understanding of the disability, the advocate should be able to discern whether social problems are a result of an emotional disturbance or whether the child is having social and emotional difficulty for other reasons.

Under this definition, students may be socially maladjusted and also have an emotional disturbance. But, the MDT also may deny the child services under IDEA because the student is said to be socially maladjusted, without having an emotional disturbance. There is no diagnosis or criteria defined for social maladjustment. We advise the MDT and parent to clearly define social maladjustment, especially if the MDT is using it as an exclusionary criteria, denying IDEA eligibility. The other hot topic under this area relates to whether attendance can be considered by the MDT as the impact of the disability, making the student eligible for special education services. Attendance and other nonacademic areas must be addressed by the MDT. A student who is not attending school because of his emotional condition can be determined to be a student with an emotional disturbance who requires special education and related services.

Types of evaluations to consider include: cognitive, projective, behavior rating scales, depression scales, social and behavioral measures, and functional behavior assessments.

Other Health Impairment

Other Health Impairment is the disability category for ADHD and other medical conditions like epilepsy or Tourette's disorder. It means that a student's strength, vitality, and alertness are limited in the classroom, and that there may be oversensitivity to environmental distractions. Children with Other Health Impairments often have trouble with the area of executive functioning, as well. They also may require ongoing medical monitoring or even emergency health procedures.

Types of evaluations to consider include: psychological (attention, concentration, cognitive, rating scales), educational, medical (when appropriate), functional behavior assessments, neurological testing, and genetics testing.

Executive Functioning

Executive functioning is not a federally defined disability; it is a set of self-regulatory functions that exist for any child with or without a disability. Executive functioning is more than attention, more than organization, and more than task completion, but it can affect all three of these areas and more. Dr. Martha Denckla (1994) identified the major areas of executive functioning as initiating, sustaining, inhibiting, and shifting. In simple terms, initiating means beginning a task, sustaining refers to staying on task and completion of tasks, inhibiting refers to blocking out other distracting thoughts or actions that are not directly related to the task, and shifting means moving from one part of the task to another or leaving one task entirely to move to another (Silverman & Weinfeld, 2007). Executive functioning can be evaluated and listed as an area of need on the IEP. Therefore, it can be addressed by goals on the IEP, and services may be provided in this area that impacts many children regardless of their disability.

Autism

Autism significantly affects verbal and nonverbal communication and social interaction, but it does not include emotional disturbance. It is characterized by poor social reciprocity, resistance to changes in routine or making transitions, repetitive or stereotyped movements, and unusual responses to sensory experiences. This category includes all five of the pervasive developmental disorders: Pervasive Developmental Disorder–Not Otherwise Specified (PDD, NOS); Asperger's syndrome, autism, Rett syndrome, and childhood disintegrative disorder. PDD, NOS and Asperger's syndrome are characterized by general intelligence in the average to superior range, no delay of language before age 3, having narrow topics of interest, and preoccupation with small parts of objects (Silverman & Weinfeld, 2007). Children eligible under IDEA 2004 in the category of autism have diverse needs. Although these children will share some characteristics, this is a broad category that is rapidly growing as we learn more about how to diagnose and distinguish the types of pervasive developmental disorders.

Types of evaluations to consider include: psychological as appropriate, rating scales, educational evaluation, sensory processing, functional behavior assessment, consultation or observation by specialists, communication evaluation (speech and language evaluation), and adaptive behavior evaluation.

Speech or Language Impairment

Speech or language impairment is an articulation, stuttering, or other language disorder that adversely affects educational performance. Children with a speech or language impairment who are eligible under IDEA 2004 will receive special education and related services in the areas that are affected by the speech and language impairment. The American Speech-Language-Hearing Association (ASHA) provides certification called the Certificate of Clinical Competence in audiology or speech and language pathology for the related service providers in school districts and for persons in private practice. A child does not have to be eligible with a speech or language impairments under IDEA 2004 in order to qualify for speech or language related services. This is one of the disability categories where the name of the disability (speech or language impairment) is the same as the related service for which any child with a disability may qualify (speech or language therapy services). In other words, a child with autism or a Specific Learning Disability may receive speech and language therapy as a related service without being categorized as a child with a speech or language impairment.

Types of evaluations to consider include: psychological, speech and language, and educational.

Mental Retardation

Mental retardation means that three areas are significantly below average (generally defined by more than two standard deviations below the mean or standard score of 70 or below): (1) IQ or cognitive ability; (2) academic achievement; and (3) adaptive behavior (daily living skills such as eating, dressing, communicating for functional reasons, and use of transportation). Children with mental retardation may have difficulty with functional skills, daily living, memory, acquiring new knowledge, understanding consequences of actions, or understanding high-level concepts. Children with mental retardation can do well in school, and more postsecondary options are being developed for them. Community colleges now have programs for persons with mental retardation. Parents sometimes resist the classification of mental retardation because of the perceived social stigma of the disability. However, if the child is diagnosed accurately and provided with the appropriate education, persons with mental retardation are able to be participating and important members of their communities.

Types of evaluations to consider include: adaptive functioning evaluation (social skills, communication, daily living skills), psychological (cognitive), and educational evaluations.

Other less frequently occurring disabilities include:

- **Traumatic Brain Injury:** A blow or trauma to the head that is caused by an external force, not related to a problem at birth, that impacts functioning in one or more areas. Types of evaluations to consider include: psychological, educational, functional behavior assessment, speech and language, and evaluation of other related services as appropriate.

- **Orthopedic Impairment:** Students who have a physical challenge caused by birth defects or amputations or other causes. It includes children with a wide range of other physical impairments. Types of evaluations to consider include: orientation and mobility evaluation, physical therapy, occupational therapy, psychological (adaptive), educational, and adaptive physical education evaluations.

- **Developmental Delay:** A federally recognized disability, this only applies to students up to age 9, and it is not recognized by all states. It applies to children who have more than a 25% delay in one or more areas, who may not yet be identified with another disability due to age or developmental stages. Types of evaluations to consider include: educational, speech and language, occupational therapy, motor evaluation, physical therapy, psychological (adaptive), and social or emotional evaluations.

- **Multiple Disability:** This has become one of the least understood categories. In some states, the use of this category is being discouraged to the extent that MDTs may tell parents that the team must select only one disability. As discussed in Chapter 5, identification with a multiple disability continues to be one of the legally recognized federal disability conditions. This means that a child has more than one disability at the same time, both of which combine to cause such impact that the child cannot be accommodated for only one disability.

Advocates understand these disabling conditions in order to identify or pick up on the sets of learning behaviors that distinguish each one. There are factors that may overlap disabilities such as sensory integration, language needs, executive functioning, behavioral difficulties, or fine or gross motor concerns. For example, a child with a Specific Learning Disability also may have sensory or fine motor needs, requiring a related service by an occupational therapist. To complicate the disabling conditions' definitions, children may present with a number of factors that are ancillary to their primary disability, factors that may require a service related to their special education program.

Culture

Overall, students cannot be penalized for having cultural differences, and specifically, cultural differences cannot cause disabilities. In many of the definitions of disabilities, this is called a *rule out* factor. School teams must not provide special education for students if the student weaknesses are primarily due to cultural factors. The MDT should consider and discuss when applicable the learning and evaluation needs of students with Limited English Proficiency, immigration issues, economic privation factors, and issues of minority overrepresentation.

Student Attitude, Acceptance, and Advocacy

An advocate needs to know the student's level of awareness in relation to accepting his or her learning style, disability, abilities, and behavior, so that developing these skills can be built into the child's educational program.

Self-determination (Field & Hoffman, 2002) is a lifelong process that includes these stages: knowing yourself, valuing yourself, planning to reach goals, acting upon those plans, and learning from the experience. It is never too early to start teaching children to know and value their own strengths and weaknesses. This is the first stage of the ability to understand one's self and advocate for our needs. Even elementary-aged students are able to tell a trusted adult what works for them, what they like, or how they can best be supported in the classroom. By the time students are in high school, with very few exceptions, students should be participating in their own IEP process, attending meetings, and speaking up in classes about their need for accommodation or services. Although supports for young adults with disabilities are available at the college level, college students with disabilities are expected to speak up for their own learning needs; college professors likely will not approach a student to offer an accommodation. This is true for undergraduate, graduate, and postgraduate level programs.

In a general sense, students in late elementary school are able to understand that everyone learns differently, and that they have an individual learning plan. The advocate may evaluate the child's skills in the area of concern by conducting observations or testing the child. The child may begin to request accommodations and alterations when provided with a list or menu of selections, as appropriate. It may be useful to use a visual form with icons to promote this type of self-advocacy skill.

The advocate may prepare the middle or early high school student for advocacy through the student's educational program, and through those to whom the child is already connected or acquainted. Counseling groups or other support groups along with opportunities for the student to be successful in the school environment are ways that the advocate helps the family prepare the child for self-advocacy (for a self-advocacy worksheet, see the TOOLS section). The middle school student may understand the concept of the IEP related to curriculum goals about the community and laws. The student generally is able to understand and be involved with the development of his 504 Plan or IEP by the end of the eighth grade. When the student will attend his meetings, it is usually a good idea to prepare him and limit the time that he participates depending on the topics and agenda.

Starting at age 16, the child is formally invited to her own IEP meetings so that the MDT may consider her preferences and interests. Although the student's attendance at the IEP meeting is not mandatory, advocates who know how to successfully involve the high school student in his own educational program will be the most successful in preparing the student for self-advocacy. The high school student who is not involved and in agreement with her IEP and overall educational program will not be invested in making the educational program succeed. The advocate may meet with the young adult student at home, in the community, at the advocate's office, or at another mutually agreeable place. The advocate is interested in the level to which the student is able to articulate plans for his future after high school, whether the plans are appropriate, and how to tailor the transition section of or the overall IEP into a document that the student understands and agrees to.

Students who reach the age of majority before being exited from special education are to be considered an independent adult. At least one year before turning the age of majority for the state, the child must be informed about the rights that will be transferred to her for educational decision making. There are processes to delay or stop this process, so that the parent maintains the educational rights if the student is not capable of understanding the implications of his authority or is not in a position where he may maintain the rights for educational decision making.

Students in college after exiting IDEA services likely may be eligible to receive accommodation through the 504 or other plan, in collaboration with the college or university student support office. There are advocates who specialize in college consulting for students entering college or attending college or a university as a postsecondary school option.

Medical Issues and Medication

The advocate must understand medical issues, if present, of the child and how they may impact the child's learning. In this area, it may be important for the advocate to be in touch with the child's treating medical staff, including physicians, psychiatrists, or other providers. At times, families may have elected to use alternative medicines or practices. Side effects can impact school performance, and there may be a need for medical services or a medical plan at school. For children with seizure activity or disorders, or with other medical emergencies, a written plan may be important. Overall, the physical health and profile of the child is critical to see the child as a whole learner and to address issues that may be impacting the child's school day.

Medical services, nursing services, medication services, psychiatric services, and other medically based services may be contained in the IEP as discussed in Chapter 5. The need for services should be tied to the child's education. The courts have considered the issue of whether residential placement is medically necessary, whether medical services are required for educational reasons, and what components of the child's IEP are necessary for the child to get meaningful benefit from her education program.

In our view, medical professionals should discuss medical issues as part of the MDT. Ideally, the MDT may include a medical professional who is qualified to review and approve evaluation information, provide treatment, report progress, and be part of the multiple disciplines serving children with medical needs, including Other Health Impairments and physical impairments.

Tip for School Personnel

Instead of discussing medication with parents, find a written way to share information with the prescribing physician that will be distributed to and from one medical member of the MDT. That member should be able to understand implications of the medical condition and be able to participate in the IEP or 504 Plan process. Avoid telling parents to go to the doctor for a diagnosis of Attention Deficit/Hyperactivity Disorder. Teachers should avoid discussing medication or medical concerns without the expertise of a medical professional from the MDT. It is the school district's responsibility to have a medical professional represented in the MDT.

How the School Team Sees the Child

The advocate needs to know how the school team views the child, the child's strengths, and learning challenges. This is important especially in relation to how the parents view the child and his learning strengths and needs. Although more will be discussed in Chapter 7 about parent attitudes and perceptions, it is important in relation to the information needed about the child, as well. More often than not, a parent is contacting and retaining an advocate because of some concern. It is not unusual that the parents and school staff see the child in different lights. Home and school environments also have different demands, so it often is the case that the child appears different in the different environments. There can be different perceptions of the child in different classes within the school day, as well. A child may excel in math or music and these teachers may view the child differently from teachers in subjects where the child is not as proficient. Although teacher and parent perception are not to be viewed as absolute, perceptions are important for the advocate to understand related to student learning, behavior, gifts and talents, or other aspects of the child in different environments.

It is important for advocates to understand how staff members view the child's peer interaction, academic achievement levels, motivation for learning, problem-solving abilities, ability to recover and regroup after problems, or resiliency, among other factors. This can point an advocate to identify and capitalize on student strengths, identify appropriate behavior supports, or help to plan for and implement specialized instructional programs or remedial interventions.

How the school team views the child can be impacted by how the school team members view the parent. At times, when interpersonal interactions are challenged by strong feelings or miscommunications, the advocate can be a facilitator of communication, listening to parent concerns and communicating to the members of the MDT in a way that is productive and neutral.

Curriculum Demand and Assessment

As noted in Chapter 5, the IEP should clearly spell out the child's curriculum and types of assessments the child receives. Basically, there are three options for the curriculum the child is receiving: (1) general curriculum that leads to a high school diploma; (2) alternate, functional life skills curriculum that leads to a Certificate of Attendance (no diploma); and (3) tiers of curricula in-between these options, depending on the state. An advocate needs to know the type of curriculum recommended for the child and be able to determine whether the correct selection has been made in an appropriate time period.

No Child Left Behind and IDEA 2004 work in tandem to ensure that only the smallest percentage of children are receiving an alternate curriculum paired with alternate assessments. Many states have guidelines about when this decision should be made. Generally speaking, it is not appropriate for the MDT to determine that a child should be removed from the general education curriculum until the child has demonstrated the inability to successfully acquire the credits toward graduation, unless a child has been in the functional life skills curriculum all along, including in elementary school. In any case, the child's IEP should reflect the child's individual needs for instruction supplementing whatever curriculum the child receives.

We have found that the pressure placed on schools for good performance on state and district tests has increased the tendency of the MDT to remove children from the general education curriculum at too early an age. If the MDT and parent agree to remove the child from the general education curriculum and agree to alternate assessments, regardless of whether the child is placed in a functional life skills program, the child may not be counted in the scores that calculate whether schools have made Adequate Yearly Progress (AYP). Removing a child from the scores that are counted unfortunately may provide the motivation for some school districts to make the decision about removing the child from his participation in the general education curriculum. When evaluating a child's needs, the advocate must consider the appropriate curriculum for the child, and therefore, which evaluations will adequately gauge the child's access to the general education curriculum. Access to the curriculum must be determined individually by the MDT for the child, and state guidelines should be consulted before removing the child from the general education curriculum.

Interventions, Educational Progress, and Services

An advocate needs to know what interventions have been in place in the school setting, and outside of school to effectively plan for a child's success. When the child with autism has been provided with one-to-one instruction through applied behavior analysis (ABA), the advocate may conclude that more intensive services are required, when compared with a child with autism who had not demonstrated the need for the same type of service. Similarly, the advocate may plan differently for a child with a learning disability due to dyslexia who has received daily reading instruction compared with a child with a learning disability who has not received a specialized reading program.

An advocate also needs to understand the child's educational program during the school day. This requires collaboration with school staff, observation of the school program, and review of the documents that drive the school program. If the Read Naturally program has been in place for 6 months and evaluations show that the child has regressed, the advocate would use the information about the response to the current interventions to make educational decisions, and perhaps to guide the school team and parent to different methodologies through the IEP process.

Private Providers

An advocate should be aware of services provided outside the school day or privately provided by parents to supplement the school program, because the advocate may not wish to repeat effective or ineffective interventions, and responses to privately provided interventions can be used for educational decision making. A child's level of performance in school may be better than it otherwise would have been because of the extra supports provided by the parents. School teams should consider what the student's performance would be without these extra interventions when making decisions about whether the student qualifies for or needs certain services (WrightsLaw.com, n.d.).

Common questions that occur related to private providers include:

- **Why does the private provider make recommendations that the school team does not agree with?** Private providers are not bound by the criteria for providing services through the IEP process. Related services such as counseling, speech and language therapy, parent training, or any other number of services may not be necessary for a child to benefit from his special education program. A parent could hire a private counselor for her child who recommends that the child receive the same type of services during the school day through the IEP. But, this has to be considered by the MDT in the context of the IEP. The MDT must first consider whether an evaluation in a particular area is warranted, then perhaps conduct an evaluation to determine the child's need for counseling. Then, the MDT would consider the child's strengths and needs or PLOP to potentially develop an IEP annual goal. Then, the MDT would be in the position to respond to the parent request for counseling. Private providers may provide services to anyone who is able to pay, whereas IDEA services under the IEP are provided based on the child's unique needs as documented by the child's IEP. Tutoring is an interesting example. Under NCLB, some children may be eligible for tutoring at public expense, based on test scores and the needs as defined by the state. Tutoring can be provided through an IEP. If public funds are used for services, there are entrance or eligibility requirements that must be met. On the other hand, any parent who can pay is able to secure tutoring on a private basis.

- **To what extent has the private provider been doing the job of the school system?** Sometimes, parents provide private services because the school system has refused to provide services or because the parent has not asked for services. A common example occurs when parents pay for a private reading program. The advocate and MDT must determine whether this type of service should be provided at public expense to either supplement or replace the private services. If a private service overlaps the needs on the IEP, there must be close collaboration between providers so that instruction is provided in a productive and beneficial manner. Parents then must decide whether to continue to supplement the school program with private services.

- **Is the private service benefiting the child? Does the child have the ability to use the skills learned in the private sessions at school?** When parents are providing private services, the advocate should be able to determine the efficacy of the services for the school program. Sometimes children have difficulty using strategies and skills learned in settings other than the school setting and with peers other than peers in the classroom. The advocate needs to know how well the child is able use lessons learned in private settings.

- **To what extent has the private provider been in communication with the school staff, teacher, and/or similar discipline on the MDT?** If private services are being provided, the advocate should encourage collaboration between private providers and school-based personnel to assure smooth delivery, consistent educational approaches, and communication with the team.

- **Have the attempted interventions been scientifically sound, researched, and peer reviewed to the greatest extent possible?** The concept of scientifically sound, research-based, and peer-reviewed intervention is explained in Chapter 4 because it is part of what the advocate needs to know about the law. Private providers should use these practices and be able to justify the use of interventions based on evaluation information.

Evaluating a child's strengths and needs is the most important aspect of the advocate's participation in the child's education. Evaluation may lead to the identification of the disability, which can be a life-altering decision by the MDT. Evaluation information provides the starting point that allows progress to be measured. Evaluation and curriculum are two sides of a coin; education without evaluation is meaningless.

Problem

Parents are not aware of how to interpret standard scores or percentile ranks, or how to track data. Parents do not know which evaluations to request to target an area of concern. Parents know their child best, but don't understand why the school system sees their child differently. Parents who are vocal and express disagreements more overtly are barred from visiting classrooms or conducting observations. Parents do not know what information to request from the classroom teachers. Parents need experts to help them, but cannot afford the cost.

Common Situation/Example

The parent sees her 6-year-old child's hyperactive behavior, and notices attention concerns, but believes that her son is "just a normal boy. At the parent-teacher conference, the first-grade teacher shares the concern that the attention problems are impacting the child's ability to follow the curriculum and complete work. A parent wants to know how much progress her child has made, or whether the reading difficulties she observes in her child are common for other children of the same age.

What the Law Says

The school system or education agency shall provide written notice to the parent of a student with a disability before the school system or education agency proposes or refuses to initiate or change the identification, evaluation, or educational placement of the student or the provision of FAPE to the student. There is no law about parent visitation or observation. The policy for this will vary from district to district. It usually is up to the administrator to determine whether an observer disrupts instruction, resulting in disallowing observation. There is no legal rule about prevention of observation because of confidentiality.

Tips for Parents

When you are asking for a service, be sure the need area is listed in the section of the IEP concerning Present Levels of Academic Achievement and Functional Performance (PLOP). If there is no data or information for the area you are requesting, give the school system permission to do an evaluation, or get a private evaluation in the area of concern.

If the county is barring you or limiting you from observing or visiting the classroom, get an objective observer or professional to do the observation or visit for you. Observe and visit the classroom regularly. Do not use the observation times as a time to talk with staff; do not disrupt instruction during a visit. Be a fly on the wall, as invisible as possible. Always ask if the visit or observation showed you a typical snapshot of your child.

Document everything, and assure that your documentation is filed in your child's confidential educational record. Review your child's record and get copies of all documents you do not have in your possession. Remember this is a legal process, and if it did not happen in *writing*, it did not happen! If the school system wants to charge you for copies at the going average rate, try not to fight that battle, if you can afford it. Pay the school and think of it as a donation.

Implications for the School System / Tips to Avoid the Problem

Treat parents as the consumers they are. Parents' public money pays for the education of their children. Avoid inconsistent implementation of visitation or observation policies, especially for parents who are more vocal or who have hired an advocate. Have the observation/visitation policy ready for all parents, in writing, and require all parents (cooperative or uncooperative) to adhere to the written policy, to avoid discrimination.

Making the Most of Tutors or Outside Therapy

Ensure collaboration with the teaching staff. Ensure that the school and tutors are teaching the same strategies, process, or methods for tasks. Develop a checklist for school staff to document whether the strategies or interventions are being used or generalized in the school setting.

Sample Checklist

Our child, _____, sees a private speech and language pathologist twice per week for _____ (language therapy and social skills). The speech and language pathologist wants to know how our child is using skills at school learned in these therapy sessions. We would appreciate if you would return this to us weekly, so we can communicate with our private provider.

Skill of the Week: Turning to face the speaker while returning a greeting

Scale: 1 = Uses independently; 2 = Uses with prompts; 3 = Does not use

Monday	Tuesday	Wednesday	Thursday	Friday
Reading	Reading	Reading	Reading	Reading
1 2 3	1 2 3	1 2 3	1 2 3	1 2 3
Math	Computers	Media	PE	Math
1 2 3	1 2 3	1 2 3	1 2 3	1 2 3
Science	Social Studies	Science	Social Studies	Science
1 2 3	1 2 3	1 2 3	1 2 3	1 2 3

Determining Readability Level of Schoolwork

Want to determine the readability level of your child's school-work? Evaluate your child's reading and writing levels by following the steps below.

1. Scan or type in several 100-word passages (or passages of shorter length if needed) into a Microsoft Word document. You also can have your child type or write the passage.
2. Configure the options in Word spelling and grammar check to "Check Readability" or "Calculate Readability Statistics."
3. Click the grammar and spelling check to get the grade level at which the passage is written or at what grade level your child is writing. This is called the readability level.
4. Utilize the information below and determine the readability level of text.

Your child is reading independently if he is able to read 98–100% of the words correctly, and answer at least 90% of comprehension questions correctly. Your child is reading at the frustration level if he is unable to read at least 90% of the words aloud and cannot answer at least 50% of comprehension questions correctly.

The chart below shows different tasks appropriate at different reading levels.

Independent Level Activities	Instructional Level Activities	Frustration Level Activities
Homework	Classroom activities with teacher assistance	None, very few
Directions on worksheet		At times, reading aloud to child
Work with parent help	Textbooks	
Leisure reading		

TOOLS

Self-Advocacy: What Defines Me as a Successful Learner

This worksheet can be used with students ready to take part in the advocacy process to help them influence their educational program.

Who I am (strengths and needs):

_____

_____

_____

_____

_____

What I need (adaptations and accommodations):

_____

_____

_____

_____

_____

Which tools work for me (interventions and strategies)?

_____

_____

_____

_____

_____

How to get what I need to succeed:

_____

_____

_____

_____

_____

chapter 7

What Does an Advocate Need to Know to Work Effectively With the Parents and Family?

W h e n   a n   a d v o c a t e helps a family to obtain appropriate services for their child, she forms a special relationship with one or more of the child's parents. Although there are situations where it is the school staff or a related service provider that first identifies the need for new or different services, more often it is the child's parents who bring this issue to the attention of the school. How the parents approach the issues surrounding advocacy for their child will depend on their view of the child's strengths and needs, the structure of the family system itself, the child's educational history, what the parents may have learned from experts outside of the school, and their own "baggage" from their personal history.

Some parents may not be at a point of acceptance of their child's disability and may still be mourning the loss of their ideal picture of their child. A parent may have struggled in school and may see reflections of himself in his child. Another factor in the family's reaction to the special education process is the level of family knowledge and understanding about special education law and process. A parent who is more knowledgeable about the law and process may have different concerns than the parent who is just learning about the process. All of these issues will impact the parent's view of and participation in the process of advocating for his or her child.

Why Is This Important for an Advocate to Know?

In order to effectively stand up for the child, the advocate must have a thorough understanding of the parents and the entire family. Each child has become who he is both as a result of the characteristics that he may have inherited from his biological parents and from the impact of the environment that has shaped him. By gathering information from the parent about the family constellation and history, about her perceptions of the child's educational history, about her experience in dealing with schools, about her own individual history as a student, and about her own view of the strengths and needs of her child, the advocate not only will learn about the child, he will, just as importantly, learn about the prejudices and feelings that the parent is bringing to the process. This baggage will be especially important as the parent and advocate interact with school personnel in an effort to secure appropriate services for the child.

Family System

In order to fully understand the child, the advocate must understand the current family system within which the child lives, as well as the history of the child's family system. The advocate will want to know if the child's biological parents are different than the parents who are the current guardians. Knowing any relevant information about the biological parents that may predict or explain the child's strengths and needs is extremely helpful to the advocate. If the child had been adopted, the advocate also will want to be aware of any issues that may be specific to the child's previous living conditions and/or adjustment to his new family. Equally important is an understanding of the opportunities and stressors that exist in the current family system. These opportunities may include services and experiences that the family provides for the child. Stressors may include mental or physical health issues or economic stressors that currently are being experienced or have been experienced by a parent or a sibling. Stressors also will include significant traumatic events that have influenced the life of the child, such as serious illnesses or deaths of family members.

It is crucial for the advocate to understand whether there are other adults who are influential in the child's life and who may have different perspectives on the child and family, whether they live with the child or not. For example, the father and the mother may have very different viewpoints about the strengths and needs of the child and very different desired outcomes for the advocacy process. This issue may be complicated even further if the parents are separated or divorced. The advocate must be aware of the custody situation and understand which of the parents has the legal rights and responsibility for educational decision making. The advocate is responsible for making data-driven educational decisions. Doing so will help the advocate avoid being put in the middle of a battle between the parents that can only take the focus away from where it belongs, on the child.

Advocates and school system personnel will encounter a variety of family systems, some that function very well and others that are clearly dysfunctional. It is the job of the advocate to find a way to help the family to understand its child's needs, as well as to allow the advocate to work in the child's best interest. It may be difficult for the advocate to publicly acknowledge to the school system that she may fully understand the difficulties a family may have created in their communication with school staff. Although it would be ideal if those communication problems could be solved, the advocate's priority is to help the child get an appropriate education.

Family systems have been studied since the 1960s, allowing a greater understanding of how families operate and ways to work with families based on family characteristics. The research has focused on characteristics that are shared by families that are well-balanced. These characteristics can impact how the advocate works with each family. Families have different levels of flexibility and different levels of cohesion, or togetherness. When a family is highly flexible, it can be chaotic, lack leadership, inconsistently discipline children, or experience change often. When the family is low on the flexibility scale, it can be rigid, authoritarian, and too strict with discipline, and everything often remains the same, with little change. The family is balanced when it is somewhere in the middle of those extremes.

When the family is too low on cohesion, or there is too little togetherness, the family becomes disengaged, with members being highly independent with little loyalty and focusing on their own needs instead of those of the group. At the other extreme, a family can be too connected or enmeshed. If the family is enmeshed, the family members are highly dependent on one another, decisions may not be made without the family, and members may not share information if it affects the closeness of the family. The unbalanced families fall at the extremes of both flexibility and cohesion scales (Olson, 1999). An advocate who has an awareness of how the family functions will be better able to work with the family in the best interest of the child.

The advocate must strike a balance between gathering information about the family and keeping the focus on the child. The advocate will want to gently steer conversations with the parent back to issues that directly impact the child's educational functioning. The advocate will provide an opportunity for a parent to express the variety of emotions that she is experiencing and complaints she wants to have addressed, before helping the parent focus on attainable action steps. It is our experience that this can be helpful to the parent, as it provides both a needed release and a sounding board for him or her. It also is our experience that this is helpful to the school, so that parental concerns (when communicated) have been refined, are clear, and are directly connected with the special education process.

Identifying Information and Desired Outcomes

Many advocates find it useful to develop some type of form (see the TOOLS at the end of this chapter) that provides a place for parents to give all of the identifying information about the child such as current school, grade, date of birth, and parents' contact information. Either as part of the same form or as an additional form, it may be helpful to have parents state the desired outcomes that they are hoping to achieve as a result of working with the advocate. We believe that it is crucial to emphasize to parents at the onset and throughout the process that desired outcomes may change as the advocate gathers more information about the student through reviewing records, observing the student, and consulting with school staff and outside service providers.

Sometimes the parent comes with an expectation that the advocate should achieve unrealistic or inappropriate outcomes. This should be expected. After all, the parent is hiring an advocate because he needs help with the process that includes the identification of appropriates outcomes. The advocate should emphasize that she is not a "hired gun," contracted to achieve a predetermined outcome for the child, but instead is a "hired expert." The difference is that the professional, unbiased advocate will form an independent expert opinion about what is in the best interest of the child based on information gathered and the advocate's expertise. Although the advocate will not automatically seek the outcome that the parent initially identifies, she will rely heavily on the parent's intimate knowledge of his own child.

The parent's opinions about the desired outcomes for his child are often very well-founded because the parent is an expert about his own child's strengths and needs, as well as the child's educational history. In addition, knowing what the current desired outcomes may be will alert the advocate to possible options that may or may not be appropriate for the child. If and when the advocate finds that the parent's desired outcomes are not in sync with the advocate's expert opinion about what the child needs, it is crucial that the advocate has an honest discussion with the parent about why the parent's desired outcomes should change. We have found that when there is good, honest, open communication between the parent and advocate and where the expectation that desired outcomes may change over time has been discussed from the onset, there are very few times when the parent does not accept the change in outcomes that the advocate may suggest. However, in the rare cases that the advocate and parent cannot agree on the desired outcome, it may be necessary for the advocate to withdraw from his work on behalf of the child.

In summary, it is helpful for the parents to be able to articulate the outcomes that they desire and for the advocate to understand and to take those possible outcomes into consideration. It is at least equally important for the parents to understand that the advocate will be providing them with an expert opinion, after she has had the opportunity to gather all of the appropriate information about the child, and that this expert opinion may lead to a change in the desired outcomes. It also is crucial to remember that there often is not just one desired outcome that is appropriate for the child. For example, although placement in a private special education school may seem to be the best outcome for the child in question, other appropriate outcomes may include obtaining additional services within the child's neighborhood school or in an alternative public school placement.

Educational History and Concerns

Parents are uniquely qualified to provide information about their child's educational history. Learning is a lifelong journey. It takes place before a child enters school and, once a child has entered school, happens not only within the walls of the school building but also at home and in the community, before and after the school day. Parents will be able to provide the full history of their son or daughter's strengths and learning needs and how these needs and strengths have developed or failed to develop over the years. Parents will know when their child has functioned at her best and, with help from the advocate as he interviews them, be able to describe the characteristics of the teachers and the learning situations that have created the best educational environments for their children. Conversely, parents will be able to describe the educational environments that were not productive or were, perhaps, even harmful for their child.

As part of this history, a parent will be able to share his perceptions of how his child has responded to interactions with other teachers or outside service providers in the community. He also will be able to share the information that has been reported to him in the past through the formal or informal assessments of psychologists, educators, doctors, speech and language pathologists, occupational therapists, physical therapists, or other specialists. All of this information will help the advocate develop a picture of the strengths, weaknesses, and learning style of the child that will, in turn, help her match the child with the most productive learning environment. The concerns that are expressed by the parents will give the advocate clues about issues that need to be further explored to determine the exact scope and nature of the problem, as well as the possible solutions.

Checking Your Baggage

Parents come into the process with their own baggage that can greatly influence their interactions with the school system. This baggage may be the result of their own previous difficulties as students, their own feelings about whether their strength or gifts were adequately addressed, and the unresolved anger they may still carry over their perceptions of their own education. The baggage may be the result of interactions they have had with the school system or other authorities in the past as they have attempted to get what they believe to be appropriate services for their family members. The baggage may be a result of their own cultural views of their role vis-à-vis the role of the authorities. They may not believe it is appropriate for them to question the decision making of the professionals, or they may believe that the only way to get anything done is through direct confrontation.

Any and all of these beliefs can be counterproductive. It is part of the role of the advocate to get parents to set aside the perceptions that are not productive in getting services in the current situation and to turn the focus back to the child in question and how to get him or her what he or she needs. It also is crucial to remember that the overall goal should be to gradually move children from dependence to independence. The advocate should help parents to see that while some additional adaptations, accommodations, services, or placements may be exactly what the child needs at this time, others may be too restrictive and may not provide the child with the appropriate level of challenge and opportunity to develop self-sufficiency.

Problem

A parent feels that her child is not making educational progress and she, the parent, is not being heard by the school.

The family has alienated the school system personnel and the school system has responded by closing down channels of communication.

Common Situation/Examples

Parents feel that the school is not developing their child's strengths or that the school is not adequately addressing their child's needs. Parents feel that the school environment is having harmful effects on their child. Parents feel that they are not able to be a partner in decision making for their child at school. The school feels that parents are making unreasonable demands and/or are communicating in a disrespectful manner.

What the Law Says

IDEA 2004 requires steps that must be taken to ensure parental participation as equal partners in the IEP process. Wright and Wright (2005), utilizing the code of federal regulations as their source, have defined parental involvement as being when "parents play an integral role in their child's learning, are encouraged to be actively involved in their child's education at school, are full partners in their child's education, are included in decision making about their child's education" (p. 156).

Parent is defined in federal law, as follows:

> (23) PARENT.—The term 'parent' means—
> (A) a natural, adoptive, or foster parent of a child (unless a foster parent is prohibited by State law from serving as a parent);
> (B) a guardian (but not the State if the child is a ward of the State);
> (C) an individual acting in the place of a natural or adoptive parent (including a grandparent, stepparent, or other relative) with whom the child lives, or an individual who is legally responsible for the child's welfare; or
> (D) except as used in sections 615(b)(2) and 639(a)(5), an individual assigned under either of those sections to be a surrogate parent. (IDEA, 2004, p. 11)

Tips for Parents

Parents should strive to keep the child at the center of the conversation. They should request and expect regular communication with school staff. They should engage in active listening, demonstrating that they have truly heard the opinion of the school staff, even when they disagree. They should strive to find school staff members who are acting in their child's best interests and form alliances with them. They should identify and celebrate their child's strengths, as well as identify and name the challenges. They should insist on making measurable plans and agreeing on how they will be evaluated and when follow up will take place. Finally, they should maintain focus on the overarching principle of moving children from dependence to independence (Lawrence-Lightfoot, 2003).

Implications for the School System/ Tips to Avoid the Problem

Schools should proactively work with parents and engage them as true partners in the process of seeking appropriate educational services for their child. Schools should recognize that parents have information about who their children are and what works best for them educationally, which is crucial to the educational planning for the individual child. Schools should be willing to "think outside the box," in order to come up with solutions that may have not been tried before. Schools should find ways to make meetings less intimidating for parents. Schools should recognize that parents may come to meetings with baggage based on previous interactions with schools or other authorities and work to help them to see that the current home-school partnership will be more productive.

TOOLS

Outcomes and Identifying Information

Child's Name: _____ DOB: _____

Current Grade:_____

Parent's Name(s):_____

Address: _____

_____

Phone: Home: _____ Work:_____

Cell:_____ Fax: _____

E-mail: _____

Parent Interview Questions

1. Tell us about your child's family, both those that he lives with and other significant family members.
2. What are you child's strengths?
3. What are your child's weaknesses?
4. What concerns do you have about your child's education?
5. Tell us about significant events in your child's educational history.
6. What are your goals for your child's education?
7. What has been your experience in working with your child's school to try to get appropriate services?
8. Who are the people at school who have your child's best interest at heart?

With the understanding that desired outcomes may change over time, please state your current goal(s) in retaining these advocacy services:

_____

_____

_____

chapter 8

What Does an Advocate Need to Know About the School System, School, and Classroom?

An advocate must be an expert on what services, resources, and programs are available in the local school system and how they are accessed. Every child is entitled to a free appropriate public education. However, exactly what FAPE will look like in any given school system will vary, not only on the basis of what the child needs and the law says, but also on the basis of the educational options the local public system has to offer. Every child should have access to appropriately rigorous instruction. Gifted instruction opportunities also will vary based on the options the local public school system has to offer.

Ideally, every parent will easily and completely understand all of the services, resources, and programs that the local school system has to offer. The reality is that the information often is kept in different offices and by different staff members in the school system. School system staff is not always forthcoming about all of the options; money to pay for these options is limited and there may be an effort to reserve certain options or resources or programs for only the "most deserving" of students. Procedures for accessing the programs also may be complicated and involve both written and unwritten rules.

In order to have a full understanding of what should be happening in the local schools, the advocate must know the school system's policies regarding all aspects of the student's day, the roles and responsibilities of the various staff within the school system, and an in-depth knowledge of the special education and gifted education services and programs.

Why Is This Important for an Advocate to Know?

In previous chapters, information has been presented regarding the need for advocates to thoroughly understand the child and the law. When an advocate understands the child, she will be able to work toward ensuring that the child receives the educational services and programs that are needed. Understanding the law will empower the advocate to understand the types of services and programs to which the child may be legally entitled.

The advocate also must understand what services are possible for the student in his local public school classroom; what special classrooms or programs are possible in his local public school; what services or programs are available outside of his local public school, yet within his local school system; and what services and programs are available beyond the local public school system. A thorough understanding of what is and isn't possible for the child gives the advocate the knowledge that is crucial in working toward achievable goals, while communicating to parents and school staff that he is an expert, not only about the child and the law, but also on the possible outcomes available for the student.

This chapter will focus on the services and programs that may be available within the local public school system.

Learning About the Local School System and Individual School

Each school system will have a range of services and programs available to all students, as well as more specialized services for special education students, and possibly some greater opportunities to challenge highly able or gifted learners. Most school systems attempt to inform parents about their programs and policies. This information is provided to the public through publications, Web sites, and informational meetings. There are typically at least four levels where information is available:

- the local school,
- the local school system,
- the state department of education, and
- the United States Department of Education.

Parents and advocates are encouraged to look at all of these levels for information about programs and services that may be available to children, as well as policies that may affect children's daily life in the classroom.

Unfortunately, the literature that is available and the information that is posted on Web sites may not always fully disclose all of the information that the parents may need to know. Even when the information does exist somewhere it may be very difficult to find. An effective advocate must be at least part detective, asking numerous questions about policies and programs in both informal and formal conversations with teachers, specialists, and administrators. Some suggested questions include:

- What might happen if a child's needs are not being met in the classroom?
- Are there any special resources in this school that can provide help or extra challenge for a child?

- Are there any special groups that meet in the school to address students' special strengths or weaknesses?
- Are there other special programs in the school district for students who have exceptional strengths or weaknesses?
- Where are the special programs located?
- How does one get referred to or qualify for that service or program?
- Who might I talk to in order to find out more about that service or program?

An advocate always will be looking for new and current information by asking each person with whom they interact similar questions that may provide them with new leads to new sources of information. An advocate should not assume that information that is received from one source at one time, even if it is an authoritative source, is the final answer. Policies and procedures are always being modified and always changing.

An advocate knows that an initial rejection is not necessarily the last word. There usually are appeal processes. One of the parents who we have worked with tells the story of having her child finally accepted into a wonderful public school program for twice-exceptional students on the third try. She was able to accomplish this because she took on the role of persistently advocating for her own son. Unfortunately, many parents assume that there is nothing that they can do other than accept the first decision to turn down services or the decision that special services will not even be considered.

With the advent of the Internet, there is a tremendous amount of information about our schools available online. In addition to Web sites, there are many electronic mailing lists that post valuable announcements for their members, and whose members are available to answer questions posed by others on the list. While we urge that any information that is offered via this source be verified in other ways, this does not diminish the value of this virtual community for keeping one another informed.

There are other more traditional parent and community sources of information, as well. Parent and special interest advocacy groups often operate Web sites and electronic mailing lists and conduct meetings featuring knowledgeable guest speakers. For example, there are many local chapters of the Learning Disabilities Association, as well as CHADD (Children and Adults with Attention Deficit/Hyperactivity Disorder). In addition, every school system is required to have in place a parent information center that provides information about legal rights and resources at no cost to parents. Additional information about parent advocacy groups will be presented in Chapter 12.

Specific Information Needed Regarding the Local School and School System

An advocate will want to understand both the policies and procedures governing the life of students during the school day. These policies and procedures will include curriculum and instruction, behavior and counseling, special education, gifted education, and parent participation. The advocate not only should seek out information about these policies and procedures by talking to authorities and specialists, but it is crucial that the advocate read the policies and procedures for himself. It is not unusual for an advocate to find that he may be the only person at the school meeting who has actually read the law, procedure, or policy. Others may be basing their decision on what they have been told about the law, procedure, or policy without seeing for themselves what it says.

Similarly, the advocate must be familiar with the special services, classes, and programs that the school or school system offers. Knowing the names or the acronyms that are used for these services in the local school system will greatly facilitate the process of getting the information that she is seeking. It is not enough to know that the classes exist. The advocate must have recently seen the service, class, or program in action to truly know how it is functioning. These services, classes, and programs are dependent on the staff leading them, as well as the students who have been placed in the group. A service, class, or program may look totally different from one year to the next or even from one point of the year to the next depending upon the staff and the students that are involved.

Understanding the Services, Special Classes, and Programs in the Local Public School System

Most school systems offer a continuum of services beginning with services in the typical classroom, moving on to services offered to fewer students but still within the local school, and then, sometimes, moving on to services in special classes that exist in only a few regionally located schools, and finally, to services in special programs that only exist in one or very few locations in the school district. These services and programs may include both those that are provided for students with special needs, as well as those that are provided for students with special strengths.

At the school level, these services include counselors, reading specialists, math specialists, technology experts, special educators, or gifted specialists coming into the classroom to work with selected individual students or groups. These same service providers also may offer special voluntary pull-out groups before or after school, at lunch time, or during the school day. It is crucial that advocates understand the roles that each of these service providers plays at the local school, as well as in the school system as a whole. At one school, a speech language pathologist may only deliver services to students who have severe speech needs identified on their IEP. At another school, the speech language pathologist may co-lead a social skills group for "at-risk" students who have not and may never be identified for special education. At one school, the school psychologist may be used only to perform evaluations for students who are suspected of having a disability, while at another school the school psychologist may give counseling intervention to all students who are in need. At schools where services are already being provided, the IEP team may be more likely to agree to provide the service in question. However, it is crucial to remember that the individual child's needs, rather than what programs already exist at the individual school, should drive what services will be provided.

At some point, through procedures that the local school may have in place, a student may be formally referred to receive one of these special services either in or outside of the classroom (see Road Map, p. 22). For some students whose needs or strengths may require services that exceed what is available at the home school, the local school system may place them in a special classroom outside their home school at a regionally located school. This may happen as part of the special education process for students with an IEP or as part of an application or selection process for gifted students. For special education students, the special classes may be comprised of students who have a similar disability, such as a learning disability, emotional disturbance, or autism spectrum disorder. In some school districts, these special classes may be noncategorical or crosscategorical and may contain students with a variety of disabilities. For gifted students, the special classes may be magnet programs that select the most highly qualified applicants or special "signature" programs that focus on a specific topic or specialty, such as computer technology or the performing arts. Students may apply for the signature program and be selected either by chance or on a space-available basis.

Similarly, the local school district may operate an entire school that is only for special education students or dedicated solely to gifted students. Some local school systems also have "alternative" or last chance schools for students who have not been successful in the typical school environment for any of a variety of reasons. Many local school systems also have vocational programs where students can spend part of their day learning a trade such as automotive technology or one of the construction trades. Although vocational programs were primarily thought of in the past as being for students who did not have the ability to handle a more rigorous academic program, many academically able college-bound students are now seeing the benefits of having vocational experience in addition to their traditional academic courses.

Understanding the Roles and Responsibilities of the School Staff

Chapters 4 and 5 describe in detail the special education procedures, as well as the roles of school personnel within those procedures, as required by law. Although federal and state law defines the special education process, the process for making other decisions about service or programming for students is not as well-defined. Schools and school systems may have their own internal policies about who is present at these non-IEP meetings. In our experience, it is typical and considered best practice for the classroom teacher and parent to be part of all decision-making meetings about the student. Often the principal or grade-level administrator (team leader or assistant principal) will lead the meeting. Other participants in the meeting may include the counselor, a gifted specialist, a reading or math specialist, the school nurse, or a special educator.

It is crucial that the advocate understand who will be participating in the meeting and what perspective the individuals may bring to the meeting. These perspectives may be colored by the individual's own personal philosophy or by the philosophy or policy of their specialty. For example, in many school districts affected by a national shortage of speech/language pathologists, the speech pathologist on the team may have a bias toward not identifying students as needing services. On the other hand, a gifted specialist who has been trained in identifying and working with gifted students with disabilities may be more likely than an untrained gifted specialist to identify for gifted services the student who is verbally gifted, but can't write effectively.

Procedures for Identifying Students for the Special Services, Classrooms, and Schools Available Within the Local School System

Even though special education, federal, and state law provides guidelines for procedures, there will be variance in how those procedures are interpreted by local school systems. The advocate must be aware of these local procedures. Some school systems will have a separate eligibility team to consider whether or not the student qualifies for special education before the school-based IEP team develops the student's Individualized Education Program. Some school systems have a two-tier system for IEP decisions, whereby the local school must refer an IEP case to a central IEP team to look at systemwide options if the child's needs cannot be met within the school. We believe that some of these local practices do not comply with the spirit of IDEA. However, advocates need to fully understand the procedures as they currently exist in each locality to effectively navigate that system on behalf of the client.

Beyond the realm of special education, there is even more variety in how local school systems make decisions about special services, classrooms, and schools. The advocate must be familiar with these processes so that he can guide the parents through these decisions and help to get the appropriate outcome for the student. For example, placement in gifted programs involves initial decision making at the school level, but also may include several levels of possible appeal to district-level committees and boards.

Problem

The parent doesn't know about the possibilities within her own school system or, if aware of the possibilities, she doesn't know how to access those services, special classrooms, or placements for her child.

Common Situation/Examples

Parents feel that their child is not making adequate progress in his or her current classroom. They are not aware that their local school district has a program that is designed for exactly the need that their child is currently experiencing. No one at the school is making them aware of this special program or the steps that will be necessary for their child to be placed in the program.

Parents feel that their child is not being challenged appropriately. They are not aware that their current school has a special pull-out program that will provide the appropriate level of challenge for their child. The staff member at the school who runs the accelerated program is not aware that their child may be a good fit for the program.

What the Law Says

Both the No Child Left Behind legislation and IDEA 2004 impact what the advocate needs to know about the school system, school, and classroom. For all of the negative criticism about NCLB, it has made some specific information about the quality of the local school and the school system available to parents and advocates. School systems are required to publish test scores showing whether or not students in a variety of groups including special education students, students from a variety of specific racial groups, limited English speakers, and economically disadvantaged students are making Adequate Yearly Progress (AYP). In addition, school systems are required to provide information regarding whether their teachers have met state qualification and licensing criteria, as well as the qualifications of any paraprofessional who may be serving the child (NCLB, 2001).

Regarding the special education laws, school systems are required to have a continuum of alternative placements to meet the needs of children with disabilities for special education services. Each public agency must ensure that instruction in regular classes, special classes, special schools, home instruction, and instruction in hospitals and institutions is available (IDEA 2004, Sections 300.115 & 300.38). Schools also are required to provide parents with procedural safeguards informing them of special education processes and their rights of appeal (U.S. Department of Education, 2006).

Finally, school systems are required to provide parents with information about school system services and procedure through parent information centers (U.S. Department of Education, 2006).

Tips for Parents

Parents need to educate themselves about the options within their local school system, as well as the procedures that are used to access those varied options. Parents should gather this information by reading school system publications, attending informational meetings, reading information posted on a variety of educational Web sites, attending advocacy group meetings, participating in electronic mailing lists, and questioning school staff as well as other parents. Parents may find it valuable to have an educational advocate help them to understand their options, as well as the process for accessing those options.

Implications for the School System/ Tips to Avoid the Problem

We understand the motivation for school staff to not always be forthcoming with information about the variety of programs that may be available for students. They may not want to raise the parents' expectations by telling them about a program or service that they personally don't feel is appropriate for the student. They may not want to open the "floodgates" of having a deluge of parents asking for or demanding certain services and programs.

However, the benefits of being transparent about the options (as well as how these options are accessed) outweigh the harm. Openly sharing this information with parents will create a climate of trust and lead to more honest communication that could only serve to have everyone acting as more of a team in the child's best interest.

Questions to Ask School Staff and Other Parents

1. What might happen if a child's needs are not being met in the classroom?
2. Are there any special resources in this school that can provide help for a child?
3. Are there any special resources in this school that may provide extra challenge for a child who is ready for that?
4. Are there any special groups that meet in the school to address students' special strengths?
5. Are there any special groups that meet in the school to address students' weaknesses?
6. Are there other special programs in the school district for students who have exceptional strengths?
7. Are there other special programs in the school district for students who have significant weaknesses?
8. Where are the special programs located?
9. How does one get referred to or qualify for that service or program?
10. Who might I talk to in order to find out more about that service or program?
11. What are the procedures for appealing a decision that my child is not appropriate for a service or program?

chapter 9

What Does an Advocate Need to Know About Educational Options Beyond the Standard Public School Offerings?

In Chapter 8, we discussed the wide variety of educational options that may be available in the local school system. Yet, for some of our students, none of these options may be a good fit at the present time. For these students, we must look outside of the school system for the educational alternative that provides them with a free and appropriate public education. For other students, their parents may choose to look outside of the school system even if there is a free and appropriate alternative within the school system. In these cases the advocate may be helping parents to find the best possible placement for the child rather than the adequate placement the public school system has offered. Educational options beyond the standard public school system offerings include day and residential private special education programs, day and boarding private schools that are not special education certified, and the option of homeschooling.

Why Is This Important for an Advocate to Know?

To be an effective advocate, one must know all of the possible educational options that may be appropriate for the student in question. When there is not a public school placement that can provide FAPE, then the public school system may be required to fund the child's placement in a private special educational placement. The advocate must have an understanding of which private placements may be a good match for the student, whether or not they are certified by the State Department of Education as an approved special education placement, and whether the local school district is likely to approve funding for such a placement. The advocate must not only know about the schools in question, but must thoroughly understand the process of working with the local school district to access appropriate funding for these private placements.

There also will be times when the funding of the private special education placement by the school district may not be possible, yet a placement in a private program is still in the best interests of the child and the parents are either able to fund the program themselves or get financial aid through another source or through the private school itself. The advocate must be familiar with all of the private school placements that may be a good match for the student whom he serves, even those placements that are not eligible for funding by the local school district. An advocate also should be able to assist those parents who may choose the option of homeschooling to follow the procedures that will allow the homeschooling to become approved by the local school district so that parents are in compliance with the local attendance laws.

Characteristics of Day and Residential School Programs

The advocate constantly must be up-to-date about the characteristics of the day and residential private educational placements that may be available to the students for whom she is seeking an educational placement. The characteristics of a school that the advocate must be aware of include:

- the defined mission;
- the types of disabilities served;
- the age or grade range;
- the cost of the school;
- whether it is certified to accept public funding and how often this occurs;
- whether it accepts private funding;
- the types of related services provided;
- the types of methodologies employed in order to teach the skills that may be a deficit for the student in question;
- the curriculum used and how it may be enriched and accelerated as appropriate to challenge the student in his area of strengths;
- the availability of adaptations and accommodations, including technology;
- the climate of the school, including systems in place for staff training and communication;
- the system of case management used, including how communication between school and home is structured;
- the extracurricular offerings that may be available; and
- the transitional services that are in place.

We will discuss each of these characteristics below.

In order to learn about the characteristics of an individual school, the advocate will employ a combination of strategies. There is no substitute for frequently visiting the schools, engaging in discussions with key staff, and actually observing in the classroom. Schools constantly are changing based on both their staff and the students that they serve. An observation that took place a year ago may not provide accurate information about what the school currently looks like. The advocate also will want to read the school's Web site information, as well as other publications, as these will offer important information about the school's vision and mission, and signal new directions in its curriculum, methodologies, and services. An advocate must keep up ongoing relationships with the admissions directors of each school. These relationships will facilitate honest, open discussions about whether the student in question is really a good fit for this particular school. Finally, an advocate will need to depend on other parents and professionals to share information about the characteristics of the school. It is virtually impossible to be current on all of the school options that may be available to a student at any given time. When an advocate does not have current information about a particular school, he may need to turn to his network of professionals for the needed information.

Characteristics of Schools

As the advocate looks at a school, she should consider the following characteristics.

- **Mission of the school:** Each school should have an articulated mission that gives the reader a good idea of how it sees itself. Although this mission may sometimes be more ideal than real, it will still give the advocate an idea of whether the student in question fits into the school's stated purposes.
- **The types of disabilities served:** The advocate must determine if the types of disabilities or challenges currently experienced by the student in question are the types that can be addressed effectively by the school. Even when the school is not a special education certified school, there must still be a determination as to whether it will adequately address and/or accommodate for the student's weaknesses.

- **The age or grade range served:** It is crucial not only that the advocate know whether the student in question currently fits into the age or grade range that the school serves, but also for how many years into the future this may be an appropriate placement. Sometimes it may be preferable to choose a school that just focuses on the challenges that a specific age range represents, while at other times it may be more desirable to know that once accepted at the school, the student will be able to remain there for years to come.

- **The cost of the school:** Particularly when the parents will be paying for the school themselves, it will be important to know whether the cost of the school is affordable for them. Part of determining this cost will be to explore whether there may be scholarships or other financial aid readily available.

- **Whether it is certified to accept public funding and how often this occurs:** Schools certified by the State Department of Education as appropriate special education settings for students who have a certain disability will be eligible for funding from the local school district. It is crucial that the advocate is aware of an individual school's eligibility for public funding so that his clients can consider whether or not they will pursue obtaining this funding from the local school district. There also will be cases when the local school district decides that it cannot meet the student's needs in a public setting and allows the parents to provide names of schools that would be acceptable to the parents and that are special education certified.

- **Whether it accepts private funding:** Some private schools will only accept public funding, while most others will accept payment directly from parents. In the case of a school that only accepts public funding, parents will not be able to directly apply to this school. Instead, it will be up to the local school system to make the application. An advocate may be able to communicate with this type of school even though the school officially may not be able to interface with the family.

- **The types of related services provided:** Most special education certified schools will have related services available as part of the school day. These services may include speech and language, occupational therapy, physical therapy, and/or psychological services, as well as other services. Sometimes these services are included in the cost of the school and provided to all students. More typically, they are offered as needed and at an additional cost to students who are identified as needing the specific service. Sometimes the services are offered by in-house staff, while at other schools the services are provided by specialists who come into the school on an individual contract basis to work with identified students.

- **The types of methodologies employed in order to teach the skills that may be a deficit for the student:** Schools have specific methodologies that are used by their teachers to instruct students who may have had difficulty learning to read, write, do mathematics, or perform well with a variety of other related skills such as social skills, organizational skills, coping skills, and study skills. It is important not only to know if the methodologies are research based, but also to know what system is in place for determining which students will be taught using which methodology, and how the students will be assessed to determine the effectiveness of the approach. An advocate will want to see that the school determines the appropriate methodology for the student based not on the teacher's favorites, but on what the individual student needs.

- **The curriculum used and how it may be enriched and accelerated as appropriate to challenge the student in his areas of strength:** It is important for the advocate to know whether the private school is using an established curriculum and whether or not teachers will typically differentiate lessons so that they are appropriately challenging for students who may have gifts or strengths in a particular area.

- **The availability of adaptations and accommodations, including technology:** The advocate will want to be familiar with how teachers will adapt lessons to teach to the strengths of learners, as well as how they utilize accommodations to remove the obstacles that individual students may face that affect performing at their best. Computers and educational software programs provide many outstanding opportunities to circumvent learning difficulties. The advocate will want to see that state of the art technology is in the classrooms, that teachers know how to use it, and that the students are given the training and the access to these adaptations and accommodations.

- **The climate of the school, including systems in place for staff training and communication:** Although it is hard to measure the climate of the school, visits to the school will give the advocate a feel for the morale of the staff, the rapport between staff and students, and the students' "joy of learning" in the school in question. It is our experience that schools in which ongoing training and good communication between all of the stakeholders occurs are schools likely to have a good climate. Although some parts of the school climate are hard to quantify, the systems that are in place for ongoing training and staff-to-staff communication can be analyzed readily.

- **The system of case management used, including how communication between school and home is structured:** It is crucial that there is one staff member who is in charge of the individual student's program and is the focal point for communication between the staff, the student, and the home. An advocate can look for evidence that systems are in place to facilitate effective case management.

- **The extracurricular offerings that may be available:** Many students will thrive at school, not solely because of what happens academically but also because of what happens outside of the classroom. The advocate will want to examine the athletics and arts programs and clubs that will be offered and see if they are a good match for the interests and talents of the student in question.

- **The transitional services that are in place:** A good school will have a plan in place for the day that the student leaves. For some students this may mean leaving for a different special education school or to participate in classes and/or activities in their neighborhood school. For other students this may mean moving on to postsecondary opportunities. The advocate should take a close look at how students are prepared in advance for the move to the next school environment and how that transition is facilitated to ensure success.

Day and Boarding Private Schools That Are Not Special Education Certified

Even when a student has special education needs, there may be a private school that is not special education certified, but still can do an excellent job of meeting the individual student's needs. The advocate will need to take special care to research these schools, using the methods described above to discover whether the school's mission, curriculum, methodologies, and services are a good match for the student in question. The advocate will want to know whether the school in question has been successful with a student or students who have had a profile of strengths and needs similar to that of the current student in question. Ideally, the advocate will want to observe students with similar profiles who currently may be served in the school that is under consideration. The advocate will want to explore how special services may be provided within the school or if the school may allow parents to bring in their own special services during the school day. Private schools that are not special education certified, yet may meet the needs of special education students, could include some traditional independent schools, some wilderness programs, some religious schools, some talent-based schools, and some last chance schools, such as military style schools.

As a general rule, an IEP team will consider placement in a special education certified school. Some states are exceptions to this general rule, so it is crucial that advocates check on the regulations in their own state. Parents and advocates also will want to know whether the school they are considering has been approved or licensed by the state. Each state maintains a list of schools that are approved or licensed. This list distinguishes which schools are approved to serve students with disabilities and which are approved to served general education students.

Only the local school system is required to evaluate children and develop IEPs. This means that only a public school system can develop a legally binding IEP for children attending private, parochial, religious, or independent schools. Private schools may develop other types of school plans, but they are unable to develop a legally binding IEP.

Day and Residential Private Special Education Programs

Parents and advocates will want to be aware of the wide variety of private special education programs that may meet the needs of the child in question. These programs include private special education day schools that specialize in specific disabilities and private residential schools. As mentioned before, there usually is a list of state-approved schools for serving students with various disabilities. Advocates should have knowledge of the current schools that are on that list.

For schools that are special education schools, goals and objectives may be developed and evaluations may be completed, but the special education schools must involve the local school system in order to have the child's Individualized Education Program in place, including funding for the services in the child's plan. When a local school system agrees to and funds the special education private school placement, it is the local school system, not the private school, that is legally responsible for overseeing the implementation of the child's special education program. The overarching responsibility for providing FAPE, regardless of where the student is placed, rests with the public school system.

Homeschooling

There are times when homeschooling may be the most desirable educational alternative. Often this happens when parents, with the help of the advocate, determine that there is more harm than good resulting from continuing to attend a school placement outside of the home. In some cases this may be a short-term solution while a suitable school placement is located. In other situations, the parents and advocate may agree that homeschooling is the available program that best meets the child's needs for the long term. These situations may include a parent who doesn't feel that her child's gifted needs are being addressed adequately in the public school system. Some parents also may feel it is desirable for their children to be provided with the religious education that is not available in local public or private schools.

When a decision to homeschool is made, the advocate will need to be familiar with the local school district's rules as they apply to this decision. Parents will have to register their homeschooling plan with the local school district or become affiliated with a licensed school program. They will have to demonstrate that they are using an appropriate curriculum and they will have to make themselves available for periodic meetings with school personnel to evaluate the efficacy of the homeschool program. The advocate can help the parents comply with these regulations by making parents aware of approved homeschooling curricula and by helping parents to understand and comply with the rules surrounding their decision. The advocate also may help the parent of a special education student to access some special education and/or related services through a service plan as described in Chapter 5.

Homeschooling a child with special needs requires a great deal of thought and preparation. Parents may not have the expertise that is required to teach a student with disabilities. The advocate can help the parent to connect with professionals in the community who can help provide the needed expertise. Another concern is that homeschooling may not offer the social opportunities that are crucial to help the child develop. The advocate can help parents to connect with homeschooling communities so that the student can have the opportunity for appropriate social interaction and cooperative group learning. Although there are many good proactive reasons for homeschooling, we believe that parents should not make the decision to homeschool in reaction to a dispute with the public school, thereby relinquishing some of their child's rights to educational opportunities.

Charter Schools

Some states have moved ahead with developing a variety of charter schools to answer parents' call for school options beyond the public school system. A charter school is a publicly funded elementary or secondary school that has "been freed from some of the rules, regulations and statutes that apply to other public schools, in exchange for some type of accountability for producing certain results, which are set forth in each charter school's charter" (National Education Association, n.d., ¶ 1). Some charter schools are able to work as if they are their own school system. In this case, the charter school is its own Local Education Agency under the state and has the legal authority to develop IEPs and provide special education and related services.

The Process for Getting Private Placements Approved by the Local School District

Some private school placements will qualify to be funded by the local school district. The advocate must be familiar with the procedures of the local school district for getting the student approved for this funding. In Chapters 4 and 5, the special education processes are described, including how they apply to both students who are already in private placements and those students who are currently in public school placement but for whom FAPE is not being provided. The IEP team process, with the parent's input, will make a decision about when the child requires a private placement.

In some cases, it only will be as a result of a due process hearing or court proceeding that the private school placement may be funded. In these cases the advocate may work with a special education attorney to make the case that FAPE is not being provided in the public school system.

A unilateral placement occurs when parents disagree with the public school system, and as a result, select a private school and send their child there at their own expense. The parents are said to have made a unilateral placement because the placement was one-sided, or selected by the parent. The parents are paying for the school, tuition, and services, while still participating in the IEP process with the local school system.

When the local school system offers parents a placement as a result of the IEP process described in Chapter 5, and the parents disagree with the school system and plan to seek tuition reimbursement for a parent-selected placement, specific procedures apply. Parent must provide written notice that formally rejects the public placement, spells out the parent's concerns, describes how the private school will meet the child's needs, and states the parent's intention to enroll the child in the private school at public expense. The notice is to be provided at the most recent IEP meeting or 10 business days before removing the student from the public school (see TOOLS at the end of this chapter for a sample letter). Parents must reject the public program and prevail at a due process hearing or other dispute process in order to receive reimbursement for the tuition. Although the student will attend a private school, parents also must keep the child enrolled in the local school system in order to hold the school system accountable to provide FAPE.

Problem

Parents don't know about their school options outside of the public school system and if they do know about them, don't know how to access them or whether they may qualify for funding from the local public school district.

Common Situation/Examples

Parents feel that their child is not making adequate progress in his current public or private school. They are not aware that there are other private schools that would be an excellent match for their child's strengths and needs. They need help in finding a match between their child and the private school options.

Parents have found a private school that is an appropriate match for their child's needs. They need help in determining if this placement qualifies for funding from the local school district and they need help in navigating the process to secure that funding.

What the Law Says

IDEA 2004 makes it clear that each school district is to provide a continuum of services, including access to and funding for private special education programs, if that is what is required to provide the individual student with FAPE. The law also requires that local school districts find the students who are attending private schools in their school district and offer them appropriate services.

Tips for Parents

Parents need to educate themselves about the options that are available beyond public schools. This includes private schools that are certified as providers of special education for specific disabilities, as well as private schools that are not certified to provide special education but do a good job of meeting the needs of students with special challenges.

Parents who may wish to consider homeschooling will need to educate themselves about finding an appropriate curriculum, the support of appropriate professionals, the appropriate opportunities for socialization and cooperative learning, and the rules and regulations that are involved in choosing this educational alternative.

Implications for the School System/ Tips to Avoid the Problem

School personnel may not want to discuss private options for fear of being perceived as encouraging parents to take those options. We believe, however, that there is a middle ground whereby school personnel can refer parents to resources that provide information about which private schools currently are being funded by the local school system, as well as which schools could be funded. It also would be helpful for school system personnel to clearly provide parents with the information that describes exactly what process(es) they need to go through in order to get funding for a full-time placement. By being open and honest about this information, we believe that school systems can help create an environment of trust and help to avoid becoming adversaries with parents who are struggling to find the most appropriate educational match for their children.

Web Resources

http://www.independentschools.com/usa
A Web site with list of independent schools by state.

http://www.nais.org
A link to the National Association of Independent Schools.

http://www.napsec.org
A Web site listing nationally recognized special education schools.

http://www.homeschool.com
A Web site providing various resource and information related to homeschooling.

http://www.americanhomeschoolassociation.org
A Web site with frequently asked questions and resources related to homeschooling.

What to Look for in a Private School Placement

Use this form to gather information about the private schools that you may be considering.

Mission of the school: _____

The types of disabilities served: _____

The age or grade range served: _____

The cost of the school: _____

Whether or not it is certified to accept public funding and how often this occurs: _____

Whether or not it accepts private funding: _____

The types of related services provided: _____

The types of methodologies that the school employs in order to teach the skills that may be a deficit for the student: _____

The curriculum used and how it may be enriched and accelerated as appropriate to challenge the student in his area of strengths: _____

Available options, including technology: _____

The climate of the school, including the systems in place for staff training and communication: _____

The system of case management that is used, including how communication between school and home is structured: _____

The extracurricular offerings that may be available: _____

The transition services that are in place: _____

Sample Unilateral Placement Letter

Date
Principal
School Address

Dear Ms. Principal,

I am writing to let you know that we are formally rejecting the proposed placement for our daughter, (*child's name*), and to let you know of our plans to unilaterally place (*child's name*) at the (*school name*) School for the (*year*) school year. She will begin school there on (*give date at least 10 business days in the future*).

(*school system name*) has recommended (*school name*) with (*describe services*). We have observed (*school name and program or class name*). We continue to believe that the (*school and program name*) is not appropriate. Our reasons for not believing the proposed placement is appropriate are as follows: (*describe reasons*). At the most recent IEP meeting, on (*date*), we informed the team that we did not believe the placement is appropriate.

We have decided to place (*child's name*) at our own expense at the (*school name*) School, located at (*school address*). (*School name*) is able to provide (*give reasons for enrolling in the private school*). After much consideration and consultation with those who know (*child's name*)'s needs, we believe that (*school name*) School will provide the education that (*child's name*) requires. We are requesting that (*school system*) support this placement by funding her education at the (*school name*) School.

Thank you for your consideration for (*child's name*)'s education. Please do not hesitate to contact us for any reason.

Sincerely,
(*Parent's name*)

Copy to (optional):

chapter 10

What Does an Advocate Need to Know About the Dynamics of School Meetings?

The advocate must be prepared for the IEP meeting. She must know the child, the child's family, the school program, and the current concerns of school staff and family, as well as have a plan in mind for the types of requests she will make in the upcoming meeting. Just like a family system, the school team is comprised of individuals who, by working together, form a system. Each part of the system works independently and then must work together to accomplish effective educational planning and programming for the child.

In order to ensure a successful experience, the advocate needs to know how to understand and interpret group dynamics, how to use effective techniques such as caucusing, how to successfully navigate around and with individual personalities, how to gauge alliances, when to invite additional members to the process, and how to take on and use others' perspectives about the child. Team members have specific roles and titles. They come to the table with different perspectives and experiences that influence their attitudes when working with families and children with disabilities. These varying perspectives can impact decision making of individuals, and therefore, also impact the decisions of the multidisciplinary team. When one part of the team or system is not working efficiently or one or more members control the power in meetings, the advocate must be able to respond and adjust her approach to effectively work with the multidisciplinary team.

An effective advocate acknowledges others' accomplishments; uses techniques before, during, and after meetings to accomplish predetermined goals; and adjusts her presentation to impact the dynamics of school meetings.

Why Is This Important for an Advocate to Know?

Even the most skilled and prepared advocate will not be able to communicate effectively with the multidisciplinary team if the dynamics of the school meetings are not anticipated carefully. The consequences can be severe: trust between parents and school team members are lost, time is wasted until the next meeting is scheduled, and in the meantime, further communication break-downs are likely. So, it is important for the advocate to know the school's resources, the school system, the law, the child and family, and the dynamics of the school meetings such that her actions on behalf of the child are intentional and purposeful, accomplishing forward moving actions from the school team and parent.

As much as school personnel may love children, and enjoy working with them, they most likely will not jeopardize their jobs to stand up for children if it means disagreeing with their colleagues and/or supervisors. A school district's system of organization is designed to maintain order, and at times, ensure that the school system is protected from uncomfortable situations and legal actions by parents. It is absolutely critical that advocates are sensitive to the dynamics of school meetings and use the interactions between and among team members in a manner that is best for the child whom they represent.

Understand and Interpret Group Dynamics

Tuckman identified the stages of small-group development in 1965. In 1977, he added a fifth stage, adjourning. The stages (Tuckman & Jensen, 1977) include:

1. **Forming:** Where the participants are polite, and defer to each other, but not much work gets accomplished.
2. **Storming:** Where the group members confront each other even if conflict develops and start to accomplish group tasks.
3. **Norming:** Where the members gain trust and create a cohesive group that produces better results.
4. **Performing:** Where the group is finalized, cohesive, and productive.
5. **Adjourning:** Where the group disengages after completing tasks and its individuals reflect on their accomplishments. There also may be a sense of loss felt by group members.

Regardless of the theory of group dynamics adhered to, the advocate needs to understand that different groups are in different stages of development.

The members of the MDT are usually a tight-knit group whose members know each other well because they meet on a regular basis. They are aware of the other members' thoughts about a particular issue, child, family, or advocate. An advocate entering an already-formed group does not have the opportunity to become part of the group dynamic, except with sporadic participation in the IEP process. The advocate must quickly gauge the group and jump into the role of facilitator, participant, leader, and expert consultant at the same time. Further, the advocate also can become the group's agent of change, a role in which the advocate attempts to break into and alter processes, procedures, paradigms, or attitudes that have been solidified over time. The advocate's role is challenging, but with proper care and attention to the group's dynamic synergy, he can be a powerful and productive member of the MDT.

Personalities and Titles

Parents and advocates must read written meeting invitations carefully. Written invitations to the IEP process received by parents a specified number of days prior to the meeting inform them of the participants in the upcoming MDT meeting and the purpose of the meeting. The purpose and participants of the meeting will set the stage for part of the meeting dynamics.

If an advocate attends the meeting, it is not unusual for the school system to respond by making sure a supervisor or director is in attendance. However, the supervisory member or director who is not usually housed in the school full-time may not be the most powerful member of the team. The principal or administrator, if present, may not be the most powerful member of the MDT. Although titles are important to recognize, a title may not dictate the level of decision-making power of the individual. MDTs are supposed to be teams that come to a consensus. Depending on the issue at hand, comments made by the staff most familiar to the student may hold more weight than a comment by a supervisor or administrator. For example, if the IEP is being developed and the general educator at the meeting comments that the child's IEP cannot be implemented in her classroom, her comment can lead to a placement decision by the team that includes a special education environment or special education support in the general classroom.

The advocate understands which members of the MDT are required members, as discussed in Chapter 4, so the advocate also should understand why members who are not required may be invited to participate. It is critical that the advocate understand MDT members' roles and titles to understand the group fully. If this information can be gathered prior to the meeting, less time during the meeting will be spent on sorting out which members play which roles.

Finding Allies

The advocate and family usually are not part of the daily and regular communication between the members of the MDT, so when the family and advocate find an ally who is willing to communicate more freely, it is important to utilize him or her in the most effective way possible, without causing division on the team. Sometimes, a member of the team will actually refer a family to an advocate "off the record" to help them forward a cause.

An advocate should understand that when a school system team member requests that the discussion is off the record it means that the advocate will not bring up the conversation or share the source of the information. However, it also means that the team member is willing to give information to the advocate that he may not otherwise have, and this should be protected so that the relationship is preserved. The members may call the advocate or pull a parent aside to request a call from the advocate. Team members may even write anonymous, typed letters to the advocate or parent with cryptic messages about things to look for that have negatively impacted the child's performance or interactions and events of which the advocate would otherwise likely not be aware.

At times, members of the team are concerned about how the other members will view them. These members approach the advocate off the record or outside of the IEP meeting so that information can be shared in a way that protects the member from scrutiny. The advocate should work through sensitive issues to retain integrity and a good working relationship with the team on behalf of the child.

Communicating and Caucusing

The rules for effective communication in the MDT meeting are the same as the rules for general effective communication. A powerful tool called *reflective listening* can help break down barriers of communication. In reflective listening, the listener first seeks to understand the speaker, before trying to speak or be heard. Often, the advocate starts with, "So, what I hear you saying is . . . ," or "I am hearing you say that . . . ." If the advocate has effectively heard what is said, the speaker will usually respond very positively as in, "Yes, that is what I am trying to say!" This allows the speaker to be heard such that the advocate's response is relevant and well-taken.

Communication can break down when there is too much attention paid to small details that do not impact the child during a meeting. Communication of concerns is more valid when attached to a written document. Preparation and organization of documents facilitates communication in the MDT meeting.

At times, parents and advocates or school system personnel need to take a break during a meeting. This technique of caucusing can be an effective and powerful tool, or it may further deteriorate negotiations. To ask for a caucus, the advocate tells the team that the client needs a break to discuss the proposal or to clarify the client's understanding of the issues. The timing of the caucus is important. When the advocate and parent leave the room or separate from the rest of the group, the school personnel can solidify their stance against the parent request. If the caucus is taken too early, when another caucus is needed, the breaks can disrupt the flow of communication and become prohibitive. However, a caucus may provide a valuable break in the action of a meeting so that power players at the table can have conversations with the team to facilitate the parent request or to brainstorm counteroffers or alternative solutions without the parent present. While it is critical that parents participate in all meetings about their child, allowing the school or parent team to caucus during a meeting can positively impact group dynamics.

Alliances

An advocate needs to understand that certain members of the MDT may have formed alliances with or against the parent before the meeting. Other team members may or may not be aware of these alliances. Interpreting nonverbal communication, interacting with the MDT as much as possible outside of the meeting, and networking in the school community (online, in person, through written materials) are all effective ways of understanding the alliances within the group dynamics. The effective advocate does her homework and collaborates with as many professionals as possible as part of observation, data collection, review of work samples, and other methods noted in Chapter 6.

In the meeting, the advocate should be keenly attuned to verbal and nonverbal communications by the various members of the MDT. A 1972 study by Albert Mehrabian found that only 7% of the emotional meaning of a message is communicated through direct verbal talking; 38% of communication is based in "paralanguage" or the use of the voice; and a majority, or 55%, of communication is nonverbal through the use of body language, facial expressions, posture, and gestures (see Figure 10.1). If the advocate is in tune with the MDT members' verbal, paraverbal, and nonverbal communications, she can get clues to allies in the meeting, agreement or disagreement before a word is spoken, and may be able to gauge the group dynamic in a way that allows the advocate to adjust his presentation, method, information, or communication style. More on nonverbal communication can be found in the TOOLS section of this chapter.

Once an ally is identified, it is important to build consensus in the group. This may be accomplished best over more than one

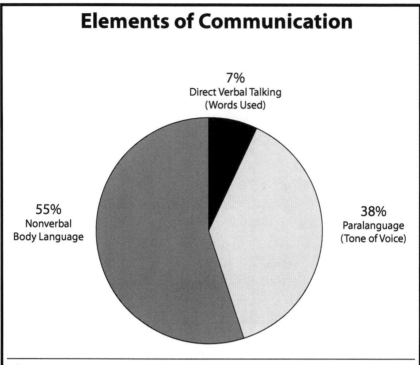

Figure 10.1. The elements of communication as posited by Mehrabian (1972).

meeting, and with interactions between meetings. The parent is usually the front-line communicator with the members of the MDT, so the communication between the parent and advocate is critical. A parent has a good sense of her allies in the group, and advocates should build on those relationships.

In the meeting, seating position may be somewhat important. People are more likely to talk to those across from them when seated in a circle. Much of the time, the MDT members already have secured their positions at the table, and parents or advocates are assigned a seat. Other times, the meeting is crowded into a small room and not everyone can be seated at the table. Because these factors send messages to and from parents, advocates, and school teams, the advocate may select to change the seating, and request a different position at the table. Having eye contact and being close to certain people at a meeting can make a difference in forming and interpreting alliances during the MDT meeting.

In particularly difficult situations where there has been conflict, finger pointing or accusations of blame, or other heated disagreements, the advocate may have to work simply to establish a relationship of trust and communication with the school team. In these situations, it is almost impossible to accomplish anything without authentic communication, goal setting, and acknowledgement of past problems with a commitment to move forward in the best interest of the child.

Perspectives, Diversity, and Bias

People of varying backgrounds, cultures, socioeconomic status, religions, and races have viewed people with disabilities differently for many generations. Of course, there is much diversity about attitude toward people with disabilities within and between groups, as well. These differences may impact group dynamics in MDT meetings. Members of the MDT may hold certain beliefs about a particular culture, and parents may hold beliefs about education or educational institutions. Ways of communicating concern or expressing requests may vary and impact school meetings. Different uses of tone and volume of voice, nonverbal communication differences, or differences in ways of speaking can be misinterpreted during meetings. It is important to reflectively listen, repeat your understanding of what is communicated, and use other various communication tools to assure understanding.

Throughout recorded history, the behavior and appearance of people with disabilities have caused misunderstanding and stereotyping. Many disabilities are "invisible," and attitudes have shifted considerably toward individuals with disabilities. Celebrities and other famous, successful individuals have shared their experiences and challenges with their own or family members' disabilities; this shared knowledge allows the public to shift its perspectives about individuals with differences in learning. However, there is still bias and bigotry toward individuals with disabilities. There is an achievement gap between races and overrepresentation of various racial groups in certain disability categories. These issues are at play in meetings where MDT members and family members come together to accomplish the goal of educational planning. It is critical to be aware of these factors and to constantly evaluate to what extent these factors play a part in the dynamics of meetings. A successful advocate will seek and strive to understand these differences, create a culture of respect in meetings, and keep the child's needs in the forefront of the meeting.

Language and Interpreters

Parents who are not English proficient, who are deaf or hard of hearing, or who do not communicate in the modality used in meetings may require an interpreter. The school system must provide this service when requested. The presence of the interpreter can cause the meeting to be longer than usual. MDT members should speak directly to the parent to show respect for him or her, instead of speaking to the interpreter. The interpreter's role is not for decision making or giving opinions. Sometimes, a parent will want to bring a friend to interpret, but this is not ideal; the school system should secure interpreters.

School systems often have bilingual assessment offices that contain professionals who understand diverse cultural issues and languages. These participants may be very helpful. Written materials also may need to be translated into a parent's native language. It is critical that parents receive and understand their rights in their native language or mode of communication. Of course, diverse family language issues can impact the dynamics of meetings. It is important to keep in mind that communication of trust, openness, and respect frequently can be nonverbal, and that language barriers can be overcome when parents are seen as equal partners, even when language differences are present.

Inviting Others

A parent may invite anyone for support and anyone with special expertise to the MDT meeting. When a parent includes an advocate in the IEP process, we believe that the parent should make sure that the advocate is trained, knowledgeable, and professional in her role. An untrained, angry advocate can destroy the dynamics of school meetings, and leave the parent with little credibility in the eyes of the MDT members. Inviting extended family members can be a good idea if the family members have something to contribute and understand the purpose of the meeting. Inviting attorneys to the MDT meeting can alter meeting dynamics. If the parent is represented by an attorney, it is likely that the school system also will be represented by an attorney. If the school system is represented at the meeting by an attorney, and parents are without legal counsel, parents should reschedule the meeting at a later time and bring an attorney who specializes in special education law.

Advocates will invite others who privately provide services to children as needed. A private speech and language pathologist, for example, can attend a meeting to address the student's present levels of achievement and functional performance, goals, or services. The advocate understands that this private provider will be most productive in the meeting when the school system's commensurate professional attends the meeting. In this case, the advocate would schedule the MDT meeting at a time when the school system's speech and language pathologist could attend, so that the private and public professionals at the table are matched together.

The more participants in the MDT, the harder it is to schedule the meeting, and the longer the meeting will be. However, the more relevant participants in the meeting, the more that generally can be accomplished.

Involving the Child

Involving the child in the IEP process can be a positive way to help the child develop self-advocacy and self-awareness skills, allow the child to help make educational decisions, and bring the child into the IEP process. However, based on the age and maturity of the child, the decision to have the child participate should be made carefully on an individual basis. There is nothing in the law requiring the child's participation, except when that child turns 18 years old, and becomes a legal adult with the capacity to make decisions. Many schools formally invite the child to participate at 16, but this is not required. At 18 years of age, the young adult is able to give permission for his own services or evaluations or even dismiss himself from special education services, assuming no actions have been taken to prevent his rights to be transferred based on his inability to make decisions as an adult.

For high school students, their participation in the IEP process often is appropriate, especially if they are college-bound or will need accommodation in the workplace or college setting. After students exit from IDEA services and no longer have an IEP, accommodations are still possible through a 504 Plan, but the young adult will need to take charge of advocating for these accommodations by approaching college professors or employers. So, it makes sense for these students to understand the IEP process to foster independence in securing accommodation or special services, to the extent possible and appropriate given the student's disability and other factors. Starting at age 14, or earlier if appropriate, the MDT must plan for the child's transition from school to work or for college or activities after high school. The MDT may wish to interview the child about his interest areas and strengths to help with transition planning. This can be done in the MDT meeting or in a private meeting with a school professional. The child's presence is never required; the law does not require a child to be present, but it encourages the older child's input into the IEP process.

For young children, the decision to have them in a meeting should be carefully considered by all parties. Sometimes, school personnel or parents want to have a child participate in the meeting to have the child say something about the educational program. This can be productive, but it also can be a way for parents or school personnel to prove a point, and this is at times not in the best interest of the child. It also may not be in the best interest of children of any age to hear the results of evaluations in the way they are presented at meetings. Much of the time, it is possible for students to meet privately with one or more of the MDT members to get or give information. Very young children who know their parents are coming to school for a meeting may want to take part. Let them greet the MDT and say something about how they like school and then return to class. There are many options for partial or full participation by the child. It may be very helpful for the MDT members in the IEP meetings to hear from a student whether an accommodation is helpful or get input from the child at the meeting about his educational program. The important point is that parents should not feel pressure to have the child attend a meeting.

Tape Recording the Meetings, Participating by Phone, and Using Technology

Tape recording of meetings has some obvious benefits. However, tape recording meetings sometimes changes the dynamics of school meetings. Table 10.1 provides some advantages and disadvantages of creating audiotapes of school meetings.

Parent or advocate participation by phone also changes the dynamics of school meetings. Participation by phone means that the advocate must attend carefully to the tone of voice, use of words, and direct verbal communication, relying on the school team for consideration of social graces like unintentional inter-

Table 10.1

Advantages and Disadvantages of Taping Meetings

Advantages of Tape Recording	Disadvantages of Tape Recording
Tapes can be transcribed for a written record of the meeting.	Transcription services can be expensive and time consuming.
School personnel may want to get concerns on the record more if on tape.	School personnel may refuse to talk on tape or will not bring up issues on tape.
Parents feel empowered.	Staff may be intimidated.
Content is verifiable.	Parents may become upset on tape.
Time may be managed better.	Meetings may start late while staff locates equipment.

rupting. Participation by phone may mean that the advocate must ask unnecessary questions such as, "Is it my turn, or were you finished?" that do not occur at face-to-face meetings. Phone meetings tend to be longer for that reason. The person on the phone may be at a disadvantage for meetings in which the issues on the agenda are complex, contentious, or longstanding. In addition, the advocate who participates by phone has a harder time seeing allies and is less able to interpret nonverbal communication. Sometimes, phone participation is the only feasible option or makes sense because of the nature of schedules or the agenda for the meetings.

School systems may not be on the cutting edge of technology application for parent participation through videoconferencing. There may be a time in the near future where that and other technologies are being used to facilitate parent participation in meetings. Schools and school systems respond differently to the use of e-mail, Web-based information and services, use of faxing, text messaging, and blogging. In some states, a software-generated statewide IEP is being used with the intention of projecting the IEP on a screen at every meeting. This changes the meeting dynamics, as staff members may be unable to make changes to the IEP due to software glitches or the onscreen IEP forces members to look at a blurry screen, instead of at each other. Some schools are able to save the IEP to a CD for parents and others say this action is prohibited.

Advocates should understand that, without a uniform written policy, these differences may be a function of school resources, knowledge of staff use of technology, or simply resistance to novel ways of communicating. At times, school systems tell parents that a certain use of technology is not allowed, citing confidentiality or restrictions on public information. This is not the case. Unfortunately, school meeting dynamics can include efforts to keep parents in the dark about certain information. Technology changes quickly and advancements will impact the dynamics of school meetings. Advocates must be on the forefront of any possible way to use technology to advance parent participation, and ultimately, child success.

Advocates Acknowledge Others and Use Praise

Just as advocates expect school staff to use praise effectively and to acknowledge parent and child accomplishments, advocates should use praise effectively during MDT meetings. Authentically acknowledging others for a specific accomplishment, following through on an action step, or applauding work well done can positively impact meeting dynamics. Appreciation for the MDT members should be shown as often as possible in a genuine manner. Openly acknowledging that at times the meeting dynamics are difficult may also "clear the air." Advocates can appreciate and praise the MDT members, even when disagreements exist.

Making Requests

Because most parents working with an advocate have at least one complaint about the education of their child, it is important that advocates learn how to translate complaints into requests that will move the IEP process forward in the best interest of the child. Meeting dynamics shift when advocates make requests, not complaints. Much of what an advocate ultimately does with the school team is make requests after providing or collecting information that would justify the requests. Requests can relate to any stage of the IEP process, from evaluation to program implementation.

In understanding the dynamics of the MDT meetings, the advocate must understand her own attitude toward the idea of making requests and her own feelings about possible reactions to requests. Consider a salesperson and how many requests he makes that customers purchase his vacuum cleaners. Time after time, the salesperson is emphatically told "no" with a door slammed in his face, yet he does not stop selling vacuum cleaners; the most successful salespersons have a relationship with the word "no" that most people do not share. They hear "no" and think of the possibilities for getting a "yes." The advocate and the salesperson share this phenomenon.

An advocate who understands the dynamics of school meetings understands that requests have three possible responses: *yes, no,* or a *counteroffer.* An advocate must persist and carefully discern the request being made and the accompanying reaction. A skilled advocate will understand how to make a counteroffer based on the data or will collect information that will allow the team to reexplore the question or issue at hand. A school system may need to decline a parent request in order to grant another request. An advocate who understands the dynamics of school meetings will persist despite experiencing resistance or refusal. The advocate will explore the causes for the reactions from the school team members, continue to find ways to persist depending on the dynamics of the school meetings, and keep the goal in focus on behalf of the child.

Table 10.2

Possible Reasons for School Resistance

What Advocates May Hear:	Actual Reason for Resistance:
We don't provide that in this county; We've never done that before; That is not possible.	Money, resources
We are not clear; What is that?; I am confused; How do we do that?	Lack of information, lack of training
We don't have information that it is a need area; What data support that request?; The evaluations we have don't show that.	Lack of sufficient data to support the request
Most parents are satisfied with what we do; That is not feasible; That is not necessary.	Belief that the parents are never satisfied; if more is given, more will be requested
Parents want what's best, but we don't have an obligation to provide the best, only what's appropriate.	Interpretation of "appropriate"; interpretation of "meaningful progress"
We can't consider that here; Those decisions aren't made by this team; You'll have to ask . . .	Legal counsel, supervisor pressure, not required members, attempt to avoid

Understand the Root Cause of Resistance by the Team

There are reasons that the MDT or school system may be resisting an advocate's requests. Understanding which reasons are at play will allow the advocate to negotiate or take action steps to address the concerns.

Possible reasons for school system resistance to advocate requests include those listed in Table 10.2.

Problem/Common Situations/Examples

As the advocate, parent, or MDT member from the school system, you know the child, are familiar with the educational program, and are ready for the MDT meeting. But, personality conflicts are so intrusive that nothing seems to get done at the MDT meeting. Most of the meeting time seems to be spent talking about things that really are not important for educational planning. Instead of talking about data, progress, and goals, the MDT seems to be arguing about who did what and when. The meeting dynamics are breaking down, and the child is not at the center of the conversation. Although everyone at the meeting seems to want what is best for the child, the members leave the meeting frustrated, annoyed, and generally in an uncooperative mood. The communication between the school and parents between meetings deteriorates. Have the MDT members paid adequate attention to the dynamics of the school meetings?

What the Law Says

Parents are equal partners of the school team. There is nothing in the law that states that a student or child is a required team member, but after age 14, the school team should get input from the child regarding transition planning (see transition section of Chapter 5). Parents are allowed to tape record meetings. School systems are encouraged to find alternate ways for parents to participate in school meetings such as by telephone or in locations such as the home that are convenient for parents. Lack of resources or money for these alternatives is never an excuse for the school system not to provide services.

Tips for Parents/Advocates

Give off-the-record information to school system personnel when possible to reciprocate sharing of information that may not normally be shared in the IEP meeting. Get to meetings early and make time to stay after the meeting, or give a cell phone or private number to the IEP team members so they can contact you if needed. Have a child attend only part of the school meetings to allow the child to experience the meetings in a positive way. Consider carefully beforehand to what extent the child should participate. If you are going to tape record a meeting, let the team know in advance. Attend to and get professional help for red flag statements that signal discriminatory practices in the school system (e.g., "We just don't do that in Smith County"). Know that sometimes, school system personnel feel as though they are being interrogated or as though advocates and parents are trying to "trap" them into saying something at a meeting. Although this may signal a problem with the educational program, effectively working with dynamics of meetings may provide an opening to more effective communication.

Implications for the School System/ Tips to Avoid the Problem

For team members who are problematic, secure training or other interventions to address the lack of knowledge or interpersonal skills if the deficiency causes problems that are unnecessarily burdensome for the team. Acknowledge when there are "weak links" in the chain of communication or follow through. Admit breakdowns and find solutions to problems. Insist on time during the day for the MDT to collaborate, share resources, get training, and plan for solutions to problems. Do not assume that your way is the only way or even the correct way. Adhere to the same policies for every family; do not make up rules that pertain to only one family or only families who work with advocates. Meet frequently with parents and treat parents and advocates as equal partners to develop trust and communication. Have a functioning tape recorder, plenty of tapes, batteries, and other technology tools handy in case parents tape record meetings. As a matter of course, have a speakerphone available at all times for the school meetings.

Check Yourself!

- Become a great listener. Learn how to reflectively listen, then speak.
- Think of ways that the school team and parents feel they are winning.
- Set goals, but don't be married to them.
- Be aware of "paralanguage," gestures, facial expressions, and nonverbal communication.
- Manage time in meetings well; focus on what is important.
- Take a caucus or break at appropriate times.
- Use humor when you can, in a respectful way.
- Remember issues of culture, race, and diversity are always at play.
- Celebrate privately or publicly, depending on the circumstances.

Time Management Tips

- Set an agenda for the meeting, including time to spend on each item.
- Put in writing your priorities for items to be discussed in the meeting.
- Insist that the meetings start on time, call ahead to determine if the meeting is delayed.
- Set a time limit for the meeting.

Ways to Praise

- Be specific, tell the person how he or she positively impacted you or your child.
- Link the praise to the IEP when possible.
- Praise, if possible, before making a request based on a complaint: "Mr. Smith, thank you for calling the evaluation office on Tuesday. I appreciated the way you followed through on what you said you were going to do." or "Ms. Jones, my son came home excited that he could do his homework. It means a lot when you take the time to modify the assignments for him and attend to his IEP in that way."

Nonverbal Gestures and Their Meanings

Note. Information adapted from Coping.org (n.d.)

Openness, Confidence:
- open hands, palms up
- eye contact
- smile, leaning forward, relaxed
- standing straight, feet slightly apart, shoulders squared

Cooperation, Readiness:
- a person moves closer to another
- open arms or hands (palms out)
- smile
- eye contact

Indifference, Boredom:
- leg over arm of chair
- rhythmic drumming, tapping
- glancing at exit
- yawning
- fidgeting or rocking

Evaluation, Interest:
- leaning forward (positive) and leaning back (negative)
- head tilted
- sucking on tip of pencil or earpiece of glasses indicates wish for nourishment in form of more information
- arched eyebrows

Doubt:
- pacing
- eyes closed
- brow furrowed
- frown

Suspicion, Secretiveness:
- folded arms
- moving away from another
- lack of eye contact
- frown
- scrunching in with head down
- throat clearing

Need for Reassurance:
- clenched hands with thumbs rubbing
- stroking arms
- cuticle picking
- sucking on pen, glasses, etc.

Anxiety:
- nail biting
- sighing
- hand wringing
- rapid, twitchy movements
- lips quivering
- chewing on things

Frustration, Anger:
- making fists
- hands on hips
- stomping
- lips pressed together, jaw muscles tight
- clenched hands with white knuckles
- hostile stare

Defensiveness:
- hands in pocket
- clenched hands
- folded arms (can be reinforced by making fists)
- body twisted away, moving away, sitting back
- looking at door

Self-Control, Inner Conflict:

- hand holding wrist or arm
- suppressed gestures or displacement activities such as fist clenched and hidden in pocket
- hand to mouth in astonishment or fear (suppressed scream)
- blowing nose and coughing (disguised tears)

Dominating:

- elevating self, like standing when others are sitting
- taking a different posture than others in a group, especially hands behind head
- loud voice or low voice carefully enunciated
- standing or walking with hands behind back and chin up

Superior, Subordinate:

- can violate the subordinate's space, and can express doubt, evaluation, domineering gestures
- more likely to signify self–control, anxiety, defensiveness gesture clusters
- putting feet on desk

Professional:

- taking notes
- leaning forward
- eye contact
- index finger to lip to restrain from interrupting

What Does an Advocate Do to Ensure Effective Implementation and Evaluate Efficacy of Individual Student Plans?

This chapter focuses on understanding how the advocate helps to ensure the correct implementation of the individual student plan, but further, how the advocate strives to ensure that the overall program is appropriate. Evaluation and monitoring is the process of providing information about the overall educational program as related to the child's IEP. Data are collected about the efficacy of a program and about the various parts of the program that should be systematically defined and evaluated. Evaluation and monitoring is a critical stage after the development of plans that address the child's strengths and needs. When a child's education is at issue, this stage takes on special significance.

After the educational program is developed on paper, the program must be implemented as soon as possible. There is, at times, a difference between implementing the IEP to the letter, and providing an appropriate educational program. Because the IEP can be revised, it is important for the advocate to have intimate knowledge about how the plan has changed over time and whether the plan is written in a way that monitoring is possible.

IEP and overall program evaluation is a critical step in formulation of effective plans. A good evaluation plan changes the knowledge base of the providers. The conclusions reached as a result of an evaluation should be reported, analyzed, and disseminated, should affect change in both the child's school day and overall school plan, and may even affect how school systems operate.

Why Is This Important for an Advocate to Know?

The first thing that the advocate can do to help ensure the effective implementation of the plan is to make sure the present levels of performance are specific and detail the child's current academic strengths and weaknesses using data as the baseline or starting point for the goals. Then the advocate should ensure that the goals on the IEP are written using specific condition statements, measurable and observable behaviors, and clear mastery criteria. The IEP goals and accommodations sections should include methods for evaluation or ways that data will be collected.

In monitoring the implementation of the program, the advocate should ensure that the evaluation methods match the behavior or skill to be evaluated, are specific, and yield data in written form to be shared with the parent and the MDT. The advocate also must understand the importance and implications of accommodations, modifications, and supplementary aides and services and the different interpretations of ways these can be provided. Because there are aspects of the Individualized Education Program document and of the educational program in "real life" that cannot be captured in the IEP document, the advocate also must attend to the documentation of decisions made by the IEP team through the prior written notices, important documentation of MDT decisions, and responses to parent requests.

The IEP and overall educational program must afford the child access to his curriculum and the ability to progress to preserve the child's right to a free appropriate public education (FAPE). The advocate often hears parents' concerns that the program they agreed to in the MDT meeting is not being implemented. If this is true, and the child is suffering educational losses because of it, the advocate needs to know what actions can be taken to assure the program is implemented and effective. Because it is not uncommon for the programs to be implemented over a 12-month period that may encompass parts of two different school years, the practice of monitoring the program implementation can be complicated by staff turnover from year to year.

This chapter explores action steps that may be taken to monitor and evaluate the implementation of the educational program. Advocates who are able to use these tools effectively are in a better position to determine whether a program meets a child's needs.

Assure all Providers Are Informed About Their Responsibilities

One of the first things that the advocate will do to help ensure the effective implementation of the child's program is to be sure that all staff involved with the child's education have the correct document (IEP, 504, or other plan), and that all staff members understand their specific responsibilities when implementing the plan. Each regular teacher, special education teacher, related service provider, and any other person implementing the plan should know his specific responsibilities for the implementation of the plan, and understand the specific interventions in the document.

If this does not occur, it is unlikely that there will be effective implementation of the plan.

Evaluating Student Progress and Educational Program

Conducting evaluations is one of the best ways to collect data to determine whether students are progressing or whether the program is working. Student progress, educational benefit of the education program, and effective implementation of the program are concepts that often are subject to opinion and interpretation. A parent may believe that the child is not making enough progress or that a program is not adequately monitored or effectively implemented. An advocate understands that evaluation information is the foundation, cornerstone, or blueprint on which to build an effective educational program. Classroom information is being more heavily emphasized by the MDT, based on NCLB and the reauthorized IDEA; what used to be called present levels of performance are now called present levels of academic achievement and functional performance.

Present Levels of Academic Achievement and Functional Performance (PLOP)

The importance of the development of the child's present levels of academic achievement and functional performance has been stressed in other sections and will be reiterated here because the implications are vast for children whose IEPs do not contain adequate PLOP statements. To illustrate the importance of the crafting of the PLOP statements, the starting points or baseline for the IEP, contemplate the following examples in relation to how the child's progress will be measured:

- Inadequate PLOP statement: "Student reads below grade level."
- Adequate PLOP statement: "Student comprehends expository text at an instructional level of 3.6, third grade, sixth month."

In the first example, the PLOP statement does not provide a baseline or data-driven foundation for goal development. Even if the child continues to read below grade level, the evaluators of the IEP and reading program will be unable to determine whether the program is effective. In the next example, the IEP goals are written with the instructional level of the child's reading defined adequately so progress can be measured specifically.

If we do not know from where we begin, we are not able to determine whether the end point demonstrates any, some, or meaningful progress for a child. Adequate, data-driven, comprehensive PLOP statements for every area that impacts a child's performance are critical for the monitoring of the child's IEP and assurance of effective implementation of the IEP. Without a clearly defined, data-driven starting point, effective implementation of the educational program is not possible.

Goals, Including Observable Behavior, Mastery Criteria, Method of Evaluation, and Timeframe

In order for the advocate to effectively monitor and evaluate an educational program, the IEP must contain annual goals that are observable and measurable and define the academic or social behavior. There also are overall goals of the educational program as defined by the school system or individual schools. In striving to ensure the implementation of the IEP and educational program, it is important that IEP, classroom, schoolwide, and school system goals are articulated and written in a way that evaluation of their success can take place.

The IEP contains defined goals based on baseline data, but it also contains how the goals will be measured or what tools will be used to evaluate progress. If the IEP contains goals in the area of phonemic awareness and reading comprehension, then a reading program should be in place to address the goals. Taking this example further, the IEP would contain a way to evaluate or measure student progress, such as an informal reading inventory or a teacher-made, curriculum-based probe. Therefore, in monitoring the implementation of the IEP, the advocate will require the results of those predefined evaluation tools in order to assure that the educational program is being effectively implemented. The IEP also spells out what tests the child will take, how often they should be taken, and under what circumstances. The vast majority of students with disabilities will take the standard state and districtwide tests that their nondisabled peers take.

The advocate also should closely attend to the services defined in the IEP. Services that need to be evaluated can include tutoring, any type of related service, or any special education service. How the advocate evaluates implementation can relate to start dates and frequency and duration of services, all of which are required to be specifically documented in the IEP. When the school is not providing services in the IEP, the advocate may request compensatory education services and the child's educational program may not be appropriate. This should be determined on an individual basis.

Advocates must strive to assure that services are specified on the IEP in terms of how often, how long, for what purpose the services are provided, whether the service will be delivered in the general education environment or in a separate environment, and who is responsible for providing the service. Specifically defining each of these required aspects will allow the IEP to be implemented in the manner intended by the MDT and parent, and will allow the efficacy of the services to be monitored and evaluated. The IEP services are defined by the goals, the way the goals are measured, and what accommodations and modifications are necessary for the goals and program to be implemented. The way the IEP goals are written and how the services are provided determines how the curriculum will be delivered to the child on a daily basis.

Accommodations

Another important factor that the advocate must consider when evaluating the implementation of an IEP and educational program is the nature and type of accommodations necessary for the child. In the IEP, the accommodations, modifications, and supplementary aides and services are listed, along with how often and when they should be provided. Accommodations are to be provided by all teachers, paraprofessionals, related service providers, or anyone else the child sees in the course of a school day. There may be confusion about gray areas in the implementation of necessary accommodations; however, clarity can be provided in the IEP or 504 Plan documents. Testing accommodations should be used in the classroom and vice versa.

When an advocate evaluates the use of accommodations, many factors should be considered, including the age of the child; the child's ability and present levels of achievement and functional performance (PLOP); the sensitivity with which the teaching staff implements the accommodation; the need for the accommodations in every setting; the supports and services the child receives; the intention or purpose of the accommodation; and how the child perceives the accommodation. Accommodations can change the way the state views test results and the way students respond to the test items or the way students respond to content in the classroom. Response accommodations such as use of use of writing software with read-aloud and word prediction capability will change the way a student responds to a writing prompt, for example.

It is important for the advocate to understand the nuances of the provision of accommodation. Students should not be made to request accommodations or be separated from peers in order to receive accommodations. Also, it is important that the child's progress, present levels of academic achievement and functional performance, and goals are considered in the context of the accommodations being provided. There is case law emerging that requires more specific accommodations to be listed in the child's IEP. How the accommodations are used should be clear and precisely stated in the child's IEP.

For example, if a child has a "read aloud" accommodation, the IEP or 504 Plan should specify under what conditions this accommodation is to be provided. An experienced advocate would not consider that this accommodation is appropriate during reading instruction where independent reading decoding skills are being taught. In addition, the accommodation can change how the MDT members view progress, especially when parents express concern about progress in skill areas that are being accommodated. If the child receives a dictation accommodation for written assignments (the child speaks an answer to be written down by the adult), the parent may express concern that written language skills are not being taught. The MDT members may believe that it is not necessary to teach the skill directly, if the accommodation allows the child to access the curriculum and progress. Similarly, a parent may express concern that a child is not making meaningful progress in reading because all text is read to the child.

To ensure the successful implementation of the IEP, 504 Plan, or educational program, the advocate must evaluate how the accommodations are in place, whether they are effective, and whether any accommodation is needed that is not in place. It is important for teachers to think about the goal of each lesson in determining which accommodations may be appropriate. For many lessons, demonstrating understanding of the concept is the goal, so we will want to provide the accommodations that allow a student to do her best work. There will be times when the goal, however, is to demonstrate the specific skill that may be impacted by the student's disability. In these cases it may be important to see how the student performs without the benefit of his accommodations. The Adaptations and Accommodations Checklist on p. 39 provides the best practices and guiding principles for providing appropriate adaptations and accommodations for students to ensure access to instruction.

Behavior Interventions

Like accommodations, behavior interventions can influence the school day, the way information is presented, the way students respond to classroom tasks, and a variety of other important aspects of a child's educational program. In helping to ensure that the child's IEP and educational program is in place as intended by the MDT, the advocate must consider necessary behavioral interventions and positive behavioral supports; the behavior intervention plan, if developed, becomes part of the student's IEP or 504 Plan. If the BIP is already developed, it is important to evaluate the interventions, whether they are being provided effectively, and whether additional supports or revisions to the plan may be necessary (see Chapters 5 and 6 for a more complete discussion of behavior).

Response to Homework and Long-Term, Independent Assignments

Part of the advocate's evaluation of the educational program relates to the ability of the child to complete homework as expected, with or without modifications or accommodations. Because IDEA 2004 calls for increased parental participation and specifies parent training as a possible related service, the advocate should assure that necessary supports are included in the child's IEP and overall educational program. If a parent is spending well beyond the expected time for homework, homework is impacting family systems and the child's ability to function during the school day, or if homework time is more like a battlefield, the advocate may utilize this information as part of the evaluation of the overall educational program. The MDT can and should consider all portions of the school day including homework time and the interventions the parents are using before and after the school day as affecting the educational program.

Related Services Logs

An advocate may recommend that the child's service providers complete logs of sessions or time spent with the child, including which goals were addressed in sessions with teaching staff or related service providers. Some states require this practice, while others may resist this request. Generally, when there is resistance to such a request, the advocate may need to investigate the situation further to determine the root cause of the resistance. It is not unreasonable for the IEP to call for progress reporting *more* often than is typically used with the child's nondisabled peers. This type of log is available, but parents may not be aware to request them. Many times, this type of log shows up in evidence at a due process hearing to determine whether a child may be entitled to compensatory education services.

Gather and Chart Data

To realistically request in a powerful manner work samples, curriculum-based measurement, or assessment probes or samples, portfolios, checklists, behavior charting, data from the classroom, or other work products, the advocate should ensure that these are written into the IEP as ways that progress will be measured. Work samples should accurately match goals and goals' mastery criteria should be written to conform to the type of skill being evaluated. Mastery criteria shows how well the behavior or skill should be achieved. The evaluation procedure used to collect data should be appropriate for the components of the annual goal.

When teacher observation is being used as a data source for measuring student progress, there should be actual data that is collected and is shared with the MDT. For example, if an observation yields a statement that the child is attending better in the classroom, data should be provided to support the opinion statement. At times, the IEP is so vague, the advocate cannot adequately collect data from sources without revision to the written IEP plan. When compiling the data, it is a great technique to graph the information visually with, for example, a pie graph for types of behaviors documented or a line graph to show progress. Another good source of information, especially for older students, is the agenda or planner that is used to record assignments or grades. The MDT may review the planner to understand the student's needs in the area of organization by collecting data regarding how accurately homework assignments are recorded.

Depending on the way data is collected as recorded in the annual goals, different types of data collection may be necessary. If the goal is to compose a five-sentence paragraph and edit the paragraph by finding and correcting 95% of errors on the computer, the work sample should reflect stages of the writing process and the final product. If the annual goal is to complete and turn in 4 of 5 assignments, there should be in place a reproducible monitoring checklist or form to demonstrate degree of progress toward the goal. The general and often inappropriate way that the MDT thinks about mastery criteria is with 80% accuracy. Many skills are not appropriately measured by percent accuracy, so the advocate should introduce rigor to the process of identifying ways to measure annual goals so that the IEP and program may be effectively evaluated. Instead of writing "the student will spell words with 80% accuracy," the MDT should consider "the student will correctly spell words in her writing with 25% improvement over baseline, as measured by work samples."

Documentation of Accommodation

How will the advocate monitor the implementation of the IEP or program without being in the classroom on a daily basis?

How will parents understand the ways that accommodations help their children? One answer may be to request that work samples include the accommodations, modifications, supports, and services provided in order for the child to complete a task. As a simple example, on the top of a math worksheet a handwritten C could mean that the child used the calculator to complete the worksheet. The amount of extra time could be documented on the assignment, test, or task. Checklists and other monitoring tools may be developed by advocates in conjunction with parents and school staff. To make this process more binding and effective, however, the advocate will need to ensure that the tool used for monitoring progress is added to the IEP itself as part of the measurement of the objective.

Request Schedules and Conduct Observations

Most advocates will agree that seeing the IEP and program in action is one of the best ways to assure and understand the implementation of the paper documents. To conduct effective observations in the context of ensuring the implementation of the IEP and program, the advocate will require the written weekly schedule, with times, subjects, teacher or provider names, and special or related service times specified. The advocate, as described in other chapters, should be skilled in conducting observations to determine whether the implementation of the IEP and educational program is meeting the child's needs or needs revisions. When the advocate observes a program that is being proposed for the child where the child does not currently attend school, he will need to analyze whether that program can effectively implement the IEP and provide an appropriate program.

Unfortunately, some districts have told parents and advocates that they are not allowed to observe proposed programs, usually citing confidentiality as a reason. This practice may be discriminatory and may require that attorneys be involved. In general, an effective advocate understands that if a policy or regulation or practice is not in place the same way from school to school or district to district, there may be a question of whether the policy has legal basis, and whether it has the effect of hampering the exercise of legal rights. In this case, legal counsel may need to be consulted. More unfortunately, some school districts have attempted to limit the advocate's and parents' observation of their own children in a school setting. The district may cite classroom disruption or confidentiality as reasons. Often, more vocal and dissatisfied parents are subject to this practice. We have found that school districts do not uniformly enforce observation policies, calling into question possible bias against parents or efforts to shroud information from parents. This greatly contributes to the breakdown of trust between schools and families, which should be prevented by open access to information needed to determine whether a school program is effective or appropriate.

Observations of the child's program or the proposed program should take into account every aspect of the child's IEP and the intentions of the MDT in developing the program. Because not every aspect of a program can be written into the IEP, it is critical that the advocate understand the intention of the MDT when developing the IEP to determine whether a program is in place. For example, the IEP may not specify the Wilson Reading Program, but that reading program may be in the Prior Written Notice as the program that is supposed to be in place. Advocates must consider the written document and the intention of the services when observing or evaluating program implementation.

Defining Qualification of Program Providers

No Child Left Behind in conjunction with IDEA requires that all teachers are highly qualified. For years before this, provisionally certified teachers, teachers uncertified in content areas, and those certified in special education only were able to teach a wide range of subjects without special expertise.

NCLB emphasizes the importance of the impact of teacher quality on student achievement. It makes sense that a highly qualified provider would more effectively implement an IEP or educational program, and states have adopted ways of determining how all teachers will meet this criterion. It may be the case that students who are not receiving services by a highly qualified or certified provider, may be entitled to compensatory education services, as determined by an MDT IEP team or dispute proceeding. The IEP also includes service providers, so the advocate knows to evaluate the educational program and IEP implementation based on the personnel of the MDT who are providing services and who are responsible for the effective implementation of the education program. By the end of the 2005–2006 school year, all teachers should have reached the status of a Highly Qualified Teacher (NCLB, 2001).

What Makes a Special Education Teacher Highly Qualified?

IDEA acknowledges that special education teachers should take different steps to become highly qualified based on the subjects that they teach. There are, therefore, different requirements for different categories of teachers, based on experience and teaching assignment.

All special education teachers (regardless of experience or subject taught) need to hold:

1. a state special education certification or license that has not had any lapse or waiver on an "emergency, temporary, or provisional basis" (National Education Association, n.d., ¶ 1), *and*
2. at least a bachelor's degree.

For special education teachers who are teaching in elementary school, where students are removed from the general education curriculum and are taking alternate assessments, the teacher must meet:

1. above criteria for all special education teachers, and
2. NCLB requirements for an elementary school teacher by passing a test of basic skills in multiple core subjects (the test counts if it is taken as part of the licensing requirement).

Special education teachers who are teaching in middle, junior high, or high school, where students are removed from the general education curriculum and are taking alternate assessments, must:

1. meet the above criteria for all special education teachers, *and*
2. have "subject matter knowledge appropriate to the level of instruction being provided, as determined by the state, needed to effectively teach to those standards" (National Education Association, n.d., ¶ 2).

For special education teachers teaching two or more core academic subjects (core academic subjects are English, reading/language arts, mathematics, science, foreign languages, civics and government, economics, arts, history, and geography), the Highly Qualified Teacher must:

1. meet all above criteria for special education teachers, *and*
2. demonstrate competence in each subject taught by passing a state test or going through the state to meet the High Objective Uniform State Standard of Evaluation (HOUSSE) of the state.

The HOUSSE process is different for each state. Each state allows a High Objective Uniform State Standard of Evaluation as a way of demonstrating competence in core subject areas.

If the special education teacher is a *new* teacher, she has 2 years to:

1. meet above criteria for all special education teachers,
2. be highly qualified in one core area, and

3. demonstrate competency in other core subjects she teaches, or go through the state HOUSSE.

Some special educators do not provide core content instruction; these special education teachers provide consultation to core teachers, such as coteaching in general education classes or providing behavior supports to students with disabilities. These teachers are exempt from the subject matter requirements. They must still meet the criteria listed above and required of all teachers (National Education Association, n.d.). States must report the progress being made for all teachers in the qualifying process. Go to your state Web site to understand the Highly Qualified Teacher requirements for HOUSSE criteria.

Know When Training Will Make a Difference

Advocates suggest and conduct training for parents and staff to help ensure the implementation of an effective educational program. Advocates need to be skilled in identifying the type of training needed to improve the educational program and even in conducting training of parents or school staff. There are times that the structure of a program is correct, the program has appropriately skilled professionals to deliver the program, and all the foundations are in place, but the program just needs a little training for the implementation of the child's IEP. In these cases, the IEP should be revised to document the type of collaboration, training, or consultation needed for the staff. The advocate can attend the trainings, observe the program before and after the training, and be involved with the training on many levels.

However, there are times that training is just not enough. The advocate should work with the school team, resource personnel within the school system, and parents to determine if this is the case. If training is not the issue, and the program needs to be changed, the advocate will know to meet with the MDT, revise the IEP as needed, and strive for a change of placement when appropriate. The change may be from one class to another within a school or increasing of services within the same school or a change of placement may occur to another school. Overall, the advocate needs to know how long to wait for a program to make changes that work and how feasible it may be for changes to take place. Ultimately, if the program needs to be changed, the advocate will be satisfied that all measures were taken to make a program work, including training, before seeking to change a child's placement or program. In some cases, it may be immediately apparent that the program needs to be changed, and other times, it may take many meetings and much collaboration to reach this conclusion.

Hold Periodic Review Meetings

A periodic review is a type of IEP meeting held by the MDT. Advocates and parents may request a periodic review at any time. There is no limit on the number of IEP meetings or periodic reviews that can be requested. Periodic reviews are one effective way of getting all providers to the MDT table to discuss the implementation of the child's IEP and program.

An advocate will strive to hold periodic reviews so that the MDT has an opportunity to respond to parent concerns in a more formal and organized way, in which the outcome of the meeting is required to be documented by law through the prior written notice procedures. This is effective, especially when the advocate has concerns or believes that the program is not being effectively implemented and needs changes that cannot be more effectively accomplished by informal collaboration.

Review Your Child's Records

Parents have a right to inspect and view their child's records. Because the school system should be giving parents copies of all written materials and correspondence, parents likely will have a great deal of information to share with the advocate. Some families keep records better than others. Many parents who seek advocacy services are not aware of the importance and implications of all of the papers and documents in the child's records or even those that are given to parents at the MDT meetings. Parents often will say, "Well, it was just the meeting invitation, so I threw it away after I responded I would attend." A parent may not realize that the invitation contains the purpose of the meeting (which is highly relevant) or that it documents required members of the MDT. A record review may provide some surprising and interesting information to help with the implementation of the child's IEP and educational program. Staff may have documented behavior, lack of progress, concerns, or correspondence with others including parents. Periodically reviewing your child's record is a good idea in general, but it is an imperative step when parents do not believe the educational program and IEP are being implemented correctly.

Get Help From Supervisors, Specific Departments in the Local Education Agency, or the State

The MDT members at the local school often do not have the power or authority to respond to, reject, or grant parents' requests. An effective advocate knows that it is important to pull into the process supervisors and other resources from the local school system who usually represent the central office of the local Board of Education. For example, many school systems have autism specialists, assistive technology specialists, placement specialists, reading specialists, functional life skills curriculum specialists, and behavior specialists, among others. Requesting assistance from these high-level positions, especially from personnel located in the compliance or legal offices, has its pros and cons.

Often, these specialists will bring into the school resources, training, technical support, or assistance for the MDT to implement the child's IEP or educational program. At other times, staff members in these higher positions can frustrate the parents because they can try to remove services or revise the program in a different way from the original design in order to prove that the program can be implemented. Being aware of the roles and thinking of these individuals is important in determining from whom to request assistance in IEP implementation.

Know What Constitutes Meaningful Progress

When evaluating the effective implementation of the IEP or overall school program, the advocate must be aware of how much progress constitutes meaningful progress. This is a critical question that must be answered in order to determine if the child is receiving FAPE. Although all likely will agree that children should get meaningful benefit from the program, parents and school districts may have different interpretations of what this means. The terms *meaningful* and *benefit* are not specifically defined in the law, and this is confusing to parents who often have different ideas about how these concepts apply to their own children.

Often, parents believe that the program is not working for their child because the child is not progressing academically, is regressing behaviorally, or is not making adequate progress in general. While a parent believes with all of her heart that the program is not effective and is convinced that the child's progress is not *meaningful*, the school system staff also may be absolutely convinced that the program is adequate and providing benefit for the child. Both sides may be equally passionate about their respective positions. It is important for the advocate to evaluate as objectively as possible whether the child benefits from the program and whether meaningful progress is being made. Additionally, the advocate must analyze the extent to which the child is getting *access* to the curriculum, despite program or IEP deficiencies.

Many administrative law judges, hearing officers, and judges have heard cases about meaningful progress in due process hearings or in higher courts. The most commonly cited case, the *Board of Education of the Hendrick Hudson Central School District v. Rowley* (1982), asks and to some extent, answers this question: How do we determine whether a student is receiving sufficient educational benefit? The answer is: Has the state complied with IDEA, and is the IEP "reasonably calculated" to enable the child to receive educational benefit? Since 1982, many courts have heard this argument, and there is still much confusion and a variety of interpretations for the question of how an advocate determines whether the program or IEP is implemented and written in a way that the child is receiving FAPE. In another case, *Polk v. Central Susquehanna Intermediate Unit 16* (1988), the court ruled that the IEP should be crafted in a way "likely to produce progress, not regression or trivial educational advancement." In *Doe v. Smith* (1988), the court ruled that educational benefit should be more than minimal, citing parts of the Polk case.

One recent case, *J. L., M. L., and K. L. v. Mercer Island School District* (2006), overturned a lower court decision, saying that the IEP was not crafted in a way that the child would benefit, and therefore, awarded parents tuition for the child's private placement. This important case defines new standards for FAPE to "ensure that [students] have the skills and knowledge necessary to enable [them] to meet developmental goals and to be prepared to lead productive, independent adult lives, to the maximum extent possible" (Wrightslaw.com, 2007b, ¶ 37).

An advocate needs to be aware that this is an ongoing question that is not answered easily by comparing test scores year to year, analyzing whether annual goals are being achieved, or even examining progress on the IEP. It is a complex question that local schools and parents feel equally passionate about, and that ultimately may have to be answered by the courts. This issue will continue to be very important and determined in part by the legal process because educational benefit and meaningful progress are the two of the ultimate goals for providing students with FAPE.

Compensatory Education Services

When the school system has not implemented the IEP or educational program, and the child has suffered as a result, the child likely is entitled to compensatory education services. The amount, type, and provider of these services—designed to make up for the past where the services have not been provided— usually are decided by the MDT with the parents' input. The advocate can assure implementation of the IEP and program by helping parents request that prior deficiencies are corrected and that the school has a plan to prevent this from occurring. There are times, however, that lack of following or implementing the IEP is so severe and causes so much harm to the child, that no amount of compensatory services could make up for it. In these rare cases, the child's placement likely should change, in addition to providing compensatory education services. When the MDT refuses to consider a parent's request for compensatory education services, or when the MDT refuses any action or there is a disagreement, it may be necessary for advocates to ultimately advise parents about their options for dispute (see Chapter 4).

To effectively monitor the child's education program, and participate in the evaluation of student progress, the advocate contemplates multiple facets of the child's program. Whether the advocate advises the parent to request additional evaluations, attend periodic reviews, submit a complaint, or do any of the action steps described in this chapter, the focus of evaluating the program should be on the program's ability to provide the child with a free appropriate public education.

Problem/Common Situations/Examples

A parent believes that the child is not allowed to use the calculator, even though that accommodation is listed in his plan. The teacher tells the parent that she cannot give a calculator to the child, based on school system policy.

Parents are not sure who is providing speech and language services now that the speech and language pathologist is out on maternity leave.

When the child sits down at home to study for the unit test, there are no copies of notes or teacher notes in the child's binder, despite the assisted note-taking accommodation in the 504 Plan or IEP.

An eighth-grade student has the accommodation of extended time for tests and assignments. In order to receive extended time, according to the teachers, she must request it, and come in after school or lunch to have the accommodation.

A child with an IEP has goals and objectives for phonemic awareness, reading fluency, decoding, and reading comprehension, but he is not receiving a special reading program in a small class setting.

The child's IEP calls for 15 hours per week of special education service. The parents believed that the child would be taught by a highly qualified special educator in a small class as in the previous year. At Back to School Night, the parents realize that a paraprofessional is providing special education service in the regular classroom, yet they are told that the IEP is being followed.

A parent finds many documents in the child's records that he has not seen before, but when he asks for a copy of the documents, the school system says that each page will cost 25 cents to copy. The local copy store charges 7 cents per copy.

What the Law Says

Compensatory services may be a way to remedy a situation where services have not been provided per the child's IEP. Compensatory services may be ordered by the state or independent hearing officer. However, compensatory services also may be discussed by the MDT. There is no set rule to guide the MDT regarding the length or amount of compensatory services. If the parent disagrees with the amount or nature of the compensatory services, she can dispute that issue using one or more of the processes described in Chapter 4.

How often does progress have to be reported? At least as often as the disabled child's nondisabled counterparts receive progress reports. Most of the time, this corresponds with general education report cards. The MDT must determine how often progress will be reported.

IDEA requires "public agencies to ensure that each regular teacher, special education teacher, related services provider, and any other service provider who is responsible for the implementation of a child's IEP, is informed of his or her specific responsibilities related to implementing the child's IEP and the specific accommodations, modifications, and supports that must be provided for the child in accordance with the child's IEP." (U.S. Department of Education, 2006, p. 46544).

Can parents be charged for copies? Some school districts do not make this an issue, but for those that try to charge parents for copies of the child's records, the going "market rate" should be passed on to the parent, not an inflated copying rate.

Tips for Parents

Use the IEP as a guide for the nature and amount of compensatory services you request to remedy services that have not been provided.

Tape record meetings and transcribe the tapes, referring to the discussion to recall how the team designed the program. Collect data and document your data collection. Do research and read and study about your areas of concern. Talk with your child's providers frequently and be involved in the school community. Get help for your own areas of weakness (take a note taker to the meeting if you have trouble taking notes, for example). Understand the impact of your emotions on your ability to objectively monitor the school program.

Do not accept general statements in the IEP when it comes to how often and how long services will be provided or who (what discipline) will provide the service. Request compensatory education services in writing when you believe the IEP has not been implemented and document the effect of the IEP not being implemented on your child.

Do not overhelp with homework or do your child's long-term assignments by providing accommodations that are not being used in the classroom. For example, do not type or write for your child at home unless that accommodation is in place at school.

If the purpose of the periodic review meeting is to review progress, and the MDT is unable or unwilling to produce data, do not continue with the meeting only based on oral reporting. Instead, spend time at the meeting defining the behaviors and skills expected in the annual goals, including the mastery criteria and how progress will be measured (evaluation methods).

Get familiar with scanning documents so you can save them on a hard drive or disk. Save and organize every paper you receive from the school system. Periodically copy your child's work and homework. Keep good and thorough records.

When conducting observations, do not talk with staff, disrupt the learning process, or cause a distraction in any way. Do not chat at the back of the room, or interact with your child unless you get specific agreement by the teaching staff. The way that the school can prevent your observations is to document that they cause a disruption to the learning environment. Learn to be a "fly on the wall" when observing classrooms.

Implications for the School System/ Tips to Avoid the Problem

Avoid general language in the IEP. Always provide parents with written notice before implementing a change in the IEP or educational program. Develop trust with parents by acknowledging their concerns, instead of making statements that the IEP is being followed to the letter of the law. Make efforts to put into place services and educational programs that have been shown to work based on scientific methods and peer-reviewed research to the greatest extent possible. Modify homework and independent projects to the child's instructional or independent level, so that parents are not forced to overhelp the child. Take into account the parentally provided supports the child receives in the context of the child's age and developmental level when considering how to revise the educational program. Come to meetings with ample work samples, data that matches annual goals, and data in a visually clear and understandable way for parents.

Consider carefully notes and documents you place in the child's confidential folder. These may have ramifications for the child's progress, placement, or for the provision of FAPE.

Explain to parents and advocates the policies and procedures for conducting observations. Attempts to thwart observations make parents feel that the school has something to hide. Treat parents like the consumers they are; assume the customer is right and attend to customer service.

Resource

http://www.nichcy.org/enews/foundations/stafftraining.asp

A wonderful resource for staff development related to many different areas of special needs advocacy including: ADHD; behavior, including functional behavior assessments and behavior intervention plans; learning disabilities; proficiency; science; social-emotional competence; reading; and assistive technology.

How Do You Know if Your Child's Teacher Is Highly Qualified?

Guidelines for Writing a Parent's Right-to-Know Letter

- List all names of teachers and staff you would like information about and include the subjects they teach.
- Address the letter to the administrator.
- Ask:
    - whether the teacher met state qualifications and certification requirements for the grade level and subject he or she is teaching,
    - whether the teacher received an emergency or conditional certificate through which state qualifications were waived,
    - what undergraduate or graduate degrees the teacher holds, including graduate certificates and additional degrees, and major(s) or area(s) of concentration,
    - whether your child is being taught by an aide or paraprofessional, and
    - the qualifications of the aide or paraprofessional.

Write a Letter Requesting Your Child's Records

Today's Date (include month, day, and year)
Mrs. Principal
Street Address
City, State, Zip Code

Dear Principal,

I would like to review my child's confidential records. His full name, birth date, ID number (*if applicable*) and grade are below (*list these*).

Please let me know the proper process for making an appointment to review my child's records, so that I am able to review the records at a time when the complete file is available. I will need copies of all or part of the record, so I would like to review them on a day when I will be able to leave with the copies I require. Thank you for your consideration. I look forward to hearing from you by (*give date*).

Sincerely,
Your name

Note. Adapted from National Dissemination Center for Children With Disabilities, 2002.

Homework Checklist for Parents

Evaluate your child's independent ability to complete homework by discussing the following questions with the teacher or in the MDT meeting.

- How long does the school expect your child to work on homework overall and by subject?
- Is the modification of homework specifically spelled out on the IEP?
- Are you providing accommodations while working on homework (e.g., writing for your child, reading to your child) that are not being used in the classroom?
- Is your child misbehaving during homework time? What is the cause or function of the misbehavior—homework is too difficult, time for homework needs adjusting, location and structure for homework time needs adjusting?
- Have you considered a peer tutor or older child or other tutor to remove any power struggle around homework time?
- Does your child know what the homework expectation is, and is there an effective way for him to record the homework?
- Does your child need an extra set of texts at home or online texts to help manage materials?
- Does the child's homework reflect his own work, and show his skill level to the teacher?

chapter 12 How Can Parents Organize Into Groups and Effectively Advocate for Their Children?

Public advocacy groups take a systemic and organized approach to raising public awareness about the special needs of exceptional children and work to enact policies and laws that affect the quality and range of programs and services available for these children. Public advocacy for children with disabilities and those with exceptional gifts and talents operates at the national, state, and local level. Advocacy groups include professional organizations and their state affiliates, as well as local school system parent advocacy groups.

There are other opportunities outside of organized groups to be involved in public advocacy. These include serving on educational task forces, commissions, and even the local school PTA. Any venue that provides a public forum to discuss education is an opportunity for the advocate to raise awareness about the needs of exceptional children. This chapter will prepare the advocate to find these opportunities, become involved, or start a new local advocacy group.

Why Is This Important for the Advocate to Know?

Although the advocate's role is to support an individual child, the extent and quality of the programs and services available to that child largely depends on public advocacy. Therefore, the advocate must become informed and involved in speaking out in a public forum.

As presented in Chapter 4, laws and local polices are enacted to protect children from discrimination and to ensure equal educational opportunities regardless of disability. The history of special education law had its roots in Civil Rights litigation over the concept of "separate but equal." The Civil Rights litigation opened the door for parents of disabled children to advocate for the rights of their children, and this advocacy was largely responsible for the first enactment of the Elementary and Secondary Education Act (ESEA) in 1965. This act not only provides the funding for educational resources and support but also for *parental involvement and promotion.* A wise and forward-thinking move on the part the advocates!

National Advocacy Groups

Based on this cause and effect relationship of public advocacy, legislation, and appropriate educational services for children, most professional organizations have active public advocacy agendas. The National Education Association (NEA), the largest professional organization for educators with more than 3 million members, hosts a "Legislative Action Center" on its Web site with legislative updates, a search engine to find your representatives in Congress, and links to their voting records (accessible at http://www.nea. org/lac). The NEA's Legislative Action Center also contains tips for writing to your legislators, writing effective letters to the editor, and rules for successful lobbying (available at http://www.nea.org/ lac/getinvolved.html). Although the NEA offers membership only to educators, its Web site offers numerous resources for parents, and the NEA has collaborated with the Parent Teacher Association (PTA) to develop Parent Guides on numerous topics (visit http:// www.nea.org/parents/parent-guides.html).

The Parent Teacher Association is the nation's largest volunteer child advocacy organization with the mission to be "a powerful voice for all children." The PTA considers that an important part of that mission is to speak before governmental bodies and other organizations. The PTA Web site provides parents with a wealth of information for local advocacy, including a PTA Grassroots Lobbying Toolkit (available at http://www.pta.org/advocacy) with tips on developing a message, working with lawmakers, and more. The PTA also provides local chapters with information about how to host a nonpartisan candidates' forum without violating their nonprofit status.

While the PTA is the voice for every child, other profes-sional organizations target the needs of exceptional children. Organizations such as the Council for Exceptional Children (CEC), the National Association for Gifted Children (NAGC), and the National Center for Learning Disabilities (NCLD) have federal advocacy goals and provide support for local advocacy groups.

The Council for Exceptional Children describes itself as "the recognized leader in advocacy for special education policy" (CEC, 2007, ¶ 2). The CEC credits its public advocacy as cru-cial in developing the Education for All Handicapped Children Act of 1975 (PL 94-142). Its policy manual (available at http:// www.cec.sped.org/Content/NavigationMenu/PolicyAdvocacy/ CECPolicyResources/cecpol.pdf) states that "all persons con-cerned about the education of children and youth with exception-alities must initiate and maintain efforts to ensure that appropriate public policy is adopted, fully implemented, and enforced" (CEC, 1997, p. 3). The CEC works to improve public policy at all levels of government, and its Web site lists weekly government policy updates, contact information for state affiliate organizations, and support for local advocacy groups, and suggests venues for individuals to publicly argue the cause of exceptional children.

Similarly, the National Association for Gifted Children (NAGC) mission states that "we support and develop policies and practices that encourage and respond to the diverse expressions of gifts and talents in children and youth" (NAGC, 2005, ¶ 2), and the NAGC strategic plan has a goal for legislative advocacy and policy development with a corresponding subcommittee. The NAGC Web site publishes an extensive Advocacy Toolkit designed for state and local advocates in gifted education. There are tools for communicating your message to the media and elected officials, and tips for starting a local advocacy group. In addition, NAGC publishes the biannual *State of the States* report with data collected from the Council of State Directors of Programs for the Gifted (CSDPG). This report (available for a fee online at http://www.nagc.org) gives a snapshot of how programs are regulated, implemented, and funded in each state.

There are many other national advocacy groups that also are doing important work on behalf of exceptional children. These groups included the Council of Parent Attorneys and Advocates, Inc. (COPAA); National Association of Parents with Children in Special Education; and Wrightslaw. This list is far from exhaustive and does not include any of the many wonderful advocacy groups that speak for exceptional children with specific categories of disability, such as learning disabilities or autism.

State Affiliates

National professional organizations such as NAGC and CEC partner with state affiliate groups that share the parent organization's mission and goals and pay its membership dues. Most of these affiliates are organized and led by parents and community members. Typically, the affiliate develops a constitution and bylaws (a sample is included in the TOOLS section at the end of this chapter) and applies to the Internal Revenue Service (IRS) for nonprofit status. State affiliate organizations take an active role in educating the public, as well as in grassroots lobbying.

State affiliates often sponsor conferences and other educational events, and their Web sites can provide a wealth of information and links. Large states may have several local affiliate groups that operate in different geographic regions. It is not beyond the reach of a small group of well-organized advocates to start a state advocacy group.

Other Public Advocacy Venues

Many local school systems have special education and gifted education advocacy groups modeled after their parent organizations at the state and national levels. If your local school system does not have a group, there are tips for starting one included later in this chapter. However, even if the local affiliate group is not up and running yet, there are other groups currently operating in which you can begin your advocacy efforts now.

One option is to seek membership on an existing state advisory council. IDEA 2004 requires that states maintain a special education advisory panel that has broad stakeholder representation. The special rule pertaining to this advisory panel states, "a majority of members of the panel shall be individuals with disabilities or parents of children with disabilities . . ." (108th Congress, p. 43). The members are appointed by their state's governor or designee. The panel has the responsibility to advise the state educational agency on any unmet educational needs of children with disabilities within the state, to assist the state in developing appropriate policies for the coordination of services, and to comment publicly on the proposed rules and regulations. Many local school districts have similar advisory panels for the purpose of providing policy guidance to the district. Parents and representatives of advocacy groups can exert a powerful influence on the implementation of special education policy by serving on these groups.

Some states also maintain similar advisory councils for gifted and talented education. The council may be required by state regulation or may operate at the discretion of the state superintendent of schools. A sample framework for a state advisory panel is included in the TOOLS section of this chapter.

Educational task forces and committees provide another opportunity to speak on behalf of the needs of exceptional children. State and local boards of education typically create task forces to study issues before making a decision that will create systemic change. These task forces or study committees seek a broad representation of viewpoints and provide the advocate a forum to speak to the impact of the change on the targeted group. Similarly, state and local governments often create commissions to study an issue and develop recommendations before enacting legislation. The advocate should look for these opportunities that may come through invitation or application.

Some local school systems have standing committees, such as a curriculum committee, that review and approve materials, such as a new reading series. This is another crucial opportunity for the advocate to ensure that the needs of exceptional children are discussed and addressed.

Local and state boards of education also have a time for public comment at their meetings. Typically, these comments are timed and speakers must sign up in advance. However, at most of these meetings the advocate has about 3 minutes of undivided attention from policy makers in which to inform and persuade for change.

Whether or not a local school has a parent advocacy group for exceptional children, it is likely to have a Parent Teacher Association. One of the PTA's core values is *inclusivity*, which means that your views are welcome. Some PTAs create Special Education and Gifted and Talented Education liaison positions on their local boards and other systems have separate Special Education PTAs.

Although there are benefits in collective action, do not underestimate the power of a single voice. If you are not able to become involved in any of these groups, you can go it alone. Through the wealth of information available from the national organizations, you can write letters to the editors of your local paper, and you can write your elected officials. Both of these venues are effective in getting the message out to the public and decision makers.

How to Start a Local Parent Advocacy Group

Regardless of federal and state legislation, the availability and quality of the programs and services for exceptional children depends largely on local school system funding and policies. Public advocacy is essential to maintain and increase funding and support for special needs students. A local parent advocacy group is recommended.

There is some difference between an advisory group and an advocacy group. An advisory group usually is appointed by the school superintendent, and, in a sense, is a watchdog for the program. Advisory groups often originate from task force recommendations for monitoring and quality assurance.

The advisory council has an overlapping function with an advocacy group, but there are differences. The advisory council is appointed by and serves at the pleasure of the superintendent. It typically has membership that represents a diverse range of experts from outside the field of education, as well as experts in the field. This is advantageous as it brings in outsiders, but also creates a large learning curve for the members who sometimes lack commitment if they do not see a practical application for their particular areas of expertise.

An advantage of the advisory council is that the council has a formal function to give advice, and typically has regular communication with the superintendent regarding program issues and needs. The parent advocacy group, however, can be started without the official seal and sanction of the school superintendent.

Because all school systems have parent involvement goals, from the standpoint of the school system, the administration should welcome an advocacy group that can lobby for the local funding and policies that are needed to increase support and improve services. Advocacy groups often can present to legislators the plight of the special needs child in ways that the school system cannot.

Both advocacy groups and advisory councils must develop a mission statement, goals, and organizational framework. Advocacy groups can start small with just a few parents and one or two goals for the year. These goals should focus on becoming better informed about the programs and services that are available in the system and educating the public about the needs of exceptional children.

The small advocacy group can begin to build membership and influence by creating a simple Web site that posts the goals and activities for the year, contact information, and links to the state and national organizations. Once the group builds membership, it can begin an electronic mailing list to disseminate information about group activities and legislative updates. Some advocacy groups have created Google groups where members can post information and discuss issues. These groups have a minimal cost and require a Webmaster to coordinate their activities.

In addition, the advocacy group can create a simple tri-fold brochure that can be widely circulated in schools and the community. Schools typically have parent newsletters and can include an information blurb that the advocacy group supplies. One school system created a Parent Mobile, a converted school bus that travels to different neighborhoods, parking at shopping centers and libraries as an outreach to parents who may not typically visit schools. The Parent Mobile was always looking for print information to disseminate; something like this would be a good opportunity to advertise your group's presence. Schools and school systems traditionally have information booths at community fairs and festivals. Public libraries also have information tables and news boards, as do grocery stores.

All of us act as advocates when we express our point of view wherever we live, work, and play. Advocates for the needs of exceptional children have many opportunities to speak on their behalf outside of organized advocacy groups. Advocates can and do make a powerful difference.

Problem

A major challenge for parent advocacy groups is maintaining an active membership. This challenge is exacerbated by a secondary problem: a lack of a focused agenda for the group. When the group's meetings and activities do not focus on its stated goals and mission, not only does the membership's interest flag, but the group loses influence.

A common sign that the advocacy group is in trouble is when the meetings turn into gripe sessions about personal grievances with the school or school system. This creates a negative feedback loop that not only repels outsiders (new members) but causes paralysis in the organization. The way to avoid this problem is to have yearly goals and an agenda for each meeting. Parents with personal issues should be referred to an advocate or to the appropriate school official who can facilitate a solution.

What the Law Says

State and local advocacy groups organized for educational purposes may qualify as charitable organizations with tax-exempt status. As charitable organizations, they may receive contributions from private parties that are tax-deductible for the contributor. To acquire nonprofit status, the organization must complete Form 1023 Section 501(c)(3) of the Internal Revenue Code.

There is a common misconception that nonprofit educational organizations cannot lobby elected officials. Nonprofit advocacy groups *may lobby elected officials*; the only limitations are related to the amount of money spent on lobbying. Lobbying is defined as any activity that attempts to influence the adoption or rejection of legislation. *Direct lobbying* is contacting members of a legislative body for the purpose of proposing, supporting, or opposing legislation. *Grassroots lobbying* is a public call to contact members of a legislative body for the purpose of proposing, supporting, or opposing legislation.

Political activity, however, is limited. All nonprofit organizations are pro-hibited from directly or indirectly participating in any political campaign in support of or in opposition to any candidate for elected public office. However, voter education activities, including presenting public forums and publishing voter education guides in a nonpartisan manner are allowed.

Advocacy groups interested in applying for tax-exempt status should visit the Internal Revenue System (IRS) Web site at http://www.irs.gov/charities/charitable. There is a fee required to complete the application and detailed information about the organization's goals and activities is required. Most advocacy groups will require professional legal assistance in completing the application.

Common Situations/Examples

The following examples illustrate two common problems that occur in local advocacy groups.

A school system is seeking to develop its programs and services for special education or gifted and talented students, so it convenes a parent advisory group to act as a "sounding board" for its plans. The advisory group, however, remains an "ad hoc" (improvised and often impromptu group formed for or concerned with one specific purpose) and does not develop a framework and objectives, or appoint a leader. After about a year, the group has served its initial purpose, begins to lose momentum, and eventually disbands. Without an organized parent advocacy group, the school system continues to move slowly to implement improvements for exceptional children, although periodically, a parent calls the school principal or central office to complain about the lack of appropriate services.

Another school system has a well-institutionalized parent advisory committee with a framework, mission, and goals. The committee has a yearly calendar of meetings, including an annual meeting with the school superintendent. However, a new advisory chair is appointed who strays from the meeting agendas, allowing the visitors to air personal grievances. The meetings begin to deteriorate into gripe sessions, making a poor impression on the superintendent. The advisory committee begins to lose influence, and as a result, system support for the existing programs begins to wane.

Implications/Tips to Avoid the Problem

Effective public advocacy will cause change and also must adapt to it. The following tips for public advocacy are drawn from change theory.

- *Portray the issues in language that outsiders can understand.* Education has a language of its own that can create a "secret society." We use terms like *differentiation* or *accommodation* that are not accessible to those outside our field.

- *Don't offend the people you are trying to convince.*

- *Identify the areas where change might happen the quickest—where the organization is the most flexible.*

- *Identify the next wave of change and "ride in on it."* Become informed about and involved in current reform initiatives that will affect programs and services for exceptional children. For example, the system may have convened a middle school task force that seeks input from diverse stakeholders.

- *See the issue from the other side.* You must understand the thinking of those you are trying to influence. What is important to them? Know the counterarguments and be prepared to counter them. Be ready to show how the policy change you are advocating ultimately is good for all kids.

- *Don't worry if your numbers are few.* Major changes can be enacted by small but well-organized groups. Power is not just about what you have, it's what your opposition thinks you have. A very small parent advocacy group can be successful in influencing one legislator who can introduce a bill that may later be enacted.

- *Be prepared to move quickly in times of change and reorganization.* When a new superintendent is appointed or new governing official is elected, waste no time in educating the new leadership about issues regarding exceptional children. One local parent advisory committee organized a half-day "retreat" for the new superintendent to present a history of the system's gifted and talented program, its strengths, as well as needs.

- *Connect problems to solutions and politics.* The launching of the Sputnik satellite by the Russians 50 years ago was a wake-up call to America's leaders. We were falling behind in mathematics and science achievement. Today, educational advocates have a similar opportunity to connect the dots for the legislators about what is needed to maintain our global competitiveness.

- *Insist that the school or system comply with the letter of the law.* Use the language in currently existing school system mission statements and policies in your arguments. For example, the system goal that achievement will improve for *each* student includes special education and gifted and talented students, and invites discussion about what is being done to support *their* achievement.

- *Bring in outsiders.* Sometimes the only way to think outside the box is to bring in new stakeholders from outside our box. Education is a unique business in that every person in society is a consumer of our product. Look for support outside the system.

- *Draw on the experience and interests of your members.* One local school system advocacy group chair became knowledgeable, through her personal experience with her own exceptional children, about their special needs in applying to colleges. The chair worked with the advocacy group to organize a systemwide college fair that became an annual event and continued long after her children had graduated from college.

- *Give members a reason to come to meetings.* Advocacy groups must have benefits of membership. These benefits will vary according to the personalities and motivations of the members. Members may ask, "What do I gain as a result of coming to this meeting?" One benefit is gaining new information, so meetings may feature an expert speaker. Task-oriented individuals will enjoy planning events such as conferences and meetings.

- *Emotional public campaigns can create policy change.* Consider the influence of advocacy organizations with an emotional message like Mothers Against Drunk Driving (MADD). In the field of gifted education, emotional arguments might present the plight of poor or minority gifted children, or the harsh economic realities of global competitiveness. *Emotions often trump experts.*

- *Change occurs through small inputs that cascade into major effects.* Each time a public advocate defends the needs of exceptional children, there is at least one more person who is better informed, armed with questions and language to frame new questions. These persons also are better prepared to understand counter arguments, and to propose constructive and sometimes low-cost solutions. *You never know who is in your audience.*

Framework for a State Advisory Council

Mission: The mission of the State Advisory Council for Gifted and Talented Education is to encourage and support the education of students who are identified as gifted and talented in accordance with the annotated code and national standards for gifted programming.

Guiding Principles:

- Gifted and talented students have outstanding talent and perform, or show the potential for performing, at remarkably high levels of accomplishment when compared with other students of a similar age, experience, or environment.
- Gifted and talented students need different services beyond those normally provided by the regular school program in order to develop their potential.
- Children with outstanding talent and advanced learning capabilities are present in all populations, across all economic strata, and in all areas of human endeavor.
- Equity of opportunity and access to high-quality programs and services, as defined by national standards, are necessary for all students requiring gifted and talented education.

Responsibilities:

The State Advisory Council for Gifted and Talented Education:

- Becomes informed about best practices for gifted and talented education and its role as an integral facet of education in the state.
- Advises the State Superintendent of Schools on issues and best practices relevant to the education of gifted and talented students.
- Supports the Department of Education and local leadership in developing, implementing, and monitoring plans and programs for gifted and talented education.
- Informs and educates parents and caregivers, educators, communities, and other stakeholders about the unique needs of gifted and talented students.
- Encourages the development and consistent implementation of comprehensive, high-quality services with regard to gifted and talented education in order to assure equity of access for all children throughout the state.

Actions

The State Advisory Council for Gifted and Talented Education:

- Analyzes data provided by the Department of Education with regard to gifted and talented education in the state.
- Prepares annual reports for the State Superintendent of Schools and the State Board of Education including a summary of the Advisory Council's findings regarding the status of gifted and talented education in the state.
- Receives periodic status reports as requested from the Department of Education with regard to implementation, completion, or projected timelines, and analyzes the progress in the implementation of recommendations previously accepted and/or adopted by the Board.
- At the request of the State Superintendent of Schools, presents publicly to the State Board of Education a progress report on the status of gifted and talented education and makes recommendations for Board consideration or action.

Membership

- The State Advisory Council for Gifted and Talented Education includes professional educators, parents, community members, and business stakeholders, representing all levels of education and the major geographic regions of the state.
- The Council Chair, in conjunction with Department staff, nominates individuals with regard to statewide representation. The State Superintendent of Schools, having received candidate nominations, makes the final appointments annually.
- The parent advocacy group, the Coalition for Gifted and Talented Education, maintains at least one seat on the Council.
- Members serve 3-year terms that are staggered so that one third of the membership is appointed each year. Members may be reappointed at the discretion of the Superintendent.
- The Advisory Council meets at least four times in an academic year. Additional meetings may be held to facilitate subcommittee work or research, and/or to address specific ad hoc issues or concerns.

Sample Organizational Framework for a Local Citizens' Advisory Committee

I. *Role of the Citizens' Advisory Committee*
  a. To educate committee members and the public concerning issues in special education both locally and nationally
  b. To serve as a channel and forum for concerns related to the special education program
  c. To collaborate in planning and implementing studies and presentations related to issues and concerns in special education
  d. To advise and make recommendations to the superintendent and staff concerning:
    i.   needs of students with disabilities
    ii. the degree to which these needs are being met by the school system

II. *Organization*
  a. No upper limits will be set on Citizens' Advisory Committee membership
  b. The number of professional members should not exceed the number of citizen members
  c. Professional members will be nonvoting members
  d. Five citizens-at-large positions may be designated in order to promote an advisory group that reflects the racial, ethnic, and socioeconomic compositions of the school system
  e. Citizen members will be appointed for renewable 2-year terms
  f. There will be an expectation of attendance at a minimum of 50% of yearly meetings
  g. Prospective committee members are recommended by
    i.   current members of the committee
    ii. self-nominations
    iii. the superintendent and staff

    h. Yearly self-evaluations will be conducted by the citizen members to assess group effectiveness

    i. A countywide committee of high school students in gifted and talented programs will provide the Citizens' Advisory Committee with student perspective and feedback on the program

    j. Nominations for the chairmanship will be submitted by the committee to the superintendent who will make the appointment

    k. The chairman will serve a renewable 2-year term

    l. The chairman, upon recommendation from the committee, will designate the vice-chairman

    m. The committee will develop its own operating procedures for monthly meetings

III. Members

    a. Representative from the PTA Council

    b. Members of the Office of Special Education serve as liaisons between the committee and the school system

    c. A minimum of three parents, one representing each educational level, from each geographic area

    d. Representatives of area colleges and universities

    e. Students with disabilities currently receiving special education services

    f. An elementary, middle, and high school teacher

    g. Representatives of Department of Curriculum and Instruction

    h. Representative from Guidance Office

Conclusion

Some of you may have read this book as a parent in order to get to know how best to advocate for your own child. Some of you may have read this as a teacher or other school system employee, in an effort to see how you can avoid conflicts and work in the best interest of your students. In either of those cases, we hope you have gained knowledge that will help you to work in the best interest of students.

Some of you have read this book as you prepare to advocate for the children of others. We caution you that reading this book, while an important first step toward being an educational advocate, should be just that, a first step toward working with families in a professional capacity. We encourage you to pursue further training through a variety of resources such as our own ABC Weinfeld-Davis Advocacy Training Institute, COPAA, Wrightslaw, or The Independent Educational Consultants Association. After completing a training program, we recommend that you spend some time working under the supervision of a professional advocate who can help you fine tune your skills. Then, you may be ready to go out on your own, if you choose, to have your own practice as an educational advocate.

Why is it important that we advocate for an appropriate education for every child?

We hope that reading this book has give you many answers to that question as well as many tools for making this happen. We'd like to leave you with James Gallagher's thoughts about the price of failure to help a child reach his potential. He called it

> . . . a societal tragedy, the extent of which is difficult to measure but what is surely great. How can we measure the sonata unwritten, the curative drug undiscovered, the absence of political insight? They are the difference between what we are and what we could be as a society. (National Education Association, 2006, p. ii)

Glossary

The following glossary has been compiled from our own experience and from wonderful glossaries and resources (Access Center, 2007; Barnes-Robinson & Jeweler, 2007; Bridges4Kids.com, 2007; Cooperative Service Agency No. 7, 2007; Council for Disability Rights, n.d.; Farlex, 2007; Renzulli, 1977; Wiggins & McTighe, 1998; Wilmshurst & Brue, 2005; Wright, Wright, & Heath, 2003; WrightsLaw.com, 2007a).

504 Plan: a written plan for individuals with disabilities qualifying under the U.S. Rehabilitation Act of 1973 that documents necessary accommodations or services.

accommodations: services or supports used to enable a student to fully access the subject matter and instruction. An accommodation does not alter the content or expectations; instead it is an adjustment to instructional methods. Accommodations should be specified in a student's IEP or 504 Plan. Examples include books on tape, content enhancements, and allowing additional time to take a test.

active listening: a process of hearing what is being said and understanding the message that is being sent. It is a helpful tool when interacting with others. It means making eye contact, acknowledging what is said, and being able to paraphrase back to the speaker the content of the message and his or her feelings.

adaptations: modifications of the delivery of instruction or materials used with a student.

adaptive behavior: a collection of skills learned in order to function in everyday life.

ADA (Americans with Disabilities Act): Federal legislation that gives Civil Rights protection to individuals with disabilities; enacted into law July 1990.

adequate yearly progress (AYP): as specified in No Child Left Behind, all children need to test as proficient on state tests of math, reading, and science by the year 2014. In the meantime, the gains the school must make between now and 2014 are broken up into equal increments for each group and measured accordingly. These groups are (1) school as a whole, (2) children with disabilities, (3) children learning English, (4) minority children, and (5) children from low-income families.

administrative review: a way of resolving special education issues by having supervisory personnel within the local school district or state review what has been done by the MDT.

adverse educational impact: in order to qualify for special education services, a student must have a disability that interferes with some aspect of learning.

advocate: a person who has a high degree of skill and knowledge about education and gives expert advice about this field for the purpose of supporting children.

alternative assessment: measures student performance on alternate achievement standards or for a functional life skills curriculum.

antecedent: something that comes before, precedes, or causes a behavior.

assessment: a collecting and bringing together of information about a child's learning needs; a process using formal and informal methods to determine an individual's strengths and weaknesses to plan, for example, his or her educational services.

assistive technology: an item, piece of equipment, or product system purchased commercially, modified or customized and used to increase maintain or improve functional capabilities of students with disabilities; also, services that assist students in selecting, acquiring, and using devices.

child find: the responsibility of the school district to locate, identify, and evaluate children with disabilities in their jurisdiction.

compensatory education: services determined to be necessary by the MDT as a result of failure of the school district to adequately implement the child's IEP.

consultant: person who gives expert or professional advice.

criterion referenced tests: assessment that compares a person's performance to some specific established level (the criterion) or a specific degree of mastery; his or her performance is not compared with that of other people.

curriculum-based measurement: an informal assessment approach emphasizing repeated direct measurement of student performance.

differentiation: a way of thinking about and planning in order to meet the diverse needs of students based on their characteristics; teachers differentiate content, process, and product according to students' readiness, interest, and learning profiles through a range of instructional and management strategies.

disability: a documented condition that results in restricted capability to perform a function of daily life; a disability is not a handicapping condition unless the individual with a disability must function in a particular activity that is impeded by his or her limitation.

dispute process: procedure to resolve disputes between parents and schools.

due process hearing: formal legal proceeding presided over by an impartial public official who listens to both sides of the dispute and renders a decision based upon the law.

eligibility: the process of qualifying for a service under one of the federally defined disability categories; a MDT meeting that considers that qualification.

enduring understandings: the big ideas, or the important understandings, that we want students to "get inside of" and retain after they've forgotten many of the details. Put differently, the enduring understandings provide a larger purpose for learning the targeted content. They implicitly answer the question, "Why is this topic worth studying?"

evaluation: to examine, judge, and analyze the data collected through the assessment process.

expert: person with a high degree of skill in or knowledge of a certain subject; having, involving, or demonstrating great skill, dexterity, or knowledge as the result of experience or training.

FAPE (free appropriate public education): the guaranteed right of children with disabilities to receive an education that meets their unique needs at no cost to parents.

FBA (functional behavior assessment): a systematic data-collection procedure conducted by the MDT, exploring the functions or reasons for students' interfering behaviors.

general education: a standard curriculum adopted by the state or local school district for all children from preschool to high school; the setting where this instruction routinely takes place.

highly qualified: relates to the teacher certifications requirements mandated by federal and state laws beginning in 2005.

identification: the process of locating and identifying children needing special services.

inclusion: The idea or philosophy related to students with disabilities participating and being educated in the general education classroom/program to the extent possible.

Independent Educational Evaluation (IEE): Federal law defines an IEE broadly as "an evaluation conducted by a qualified examiner who is not employed by the public agency responsible for the education of the child in question" (IDEA, 2006, section 300.503); it is provided either at parent expense or at public expense as a result of a parent's request or a due process hearing decision.

Individualized Educational Plan (IEP): a legal document designed by a team of educators, specialists, and the child's parent(s)/guardian(s) for students eligible as described in IDEA 2004; has many required sections, specifying many aspects of a disabled child's education.

Individualized Family Services Plan (IFSP): a legal document that specifies the plan for services for eligible children from birth to age 2 and often for children through age 5.

Individuals with Disabilities Education Improvement Act (IDEA): first enacted in 1975 as the Education for all Handicapped Children Act, and subsequently periodically reauthorized, it is a comprehensive federally funded law that governs the education of students with disabilities.

intelligence quotient (IQ): a standard score derived from psychological testing typically used to describe cognitive ability.

informed consent: signed parental agreement to an action proposed by the district after the parent is provided full information in a way he or she can understand.

interfering behavior: a child's behavior that gets in the way of his or her ability to access curriculum and/or participate in the classroom.

interim alternative educational setting (IAES): a setting, other than the student's current placement, that may be consider by the MDT as a result of disciplinary infractions, in which the child will continue to be educated and progress toward IEP goals.

intervention: action taken to correct, remediate, or prevent identified or potential educational, medical, or developmental problems.

Least Restrictive Environment (LRE): refers to the concept that children with disabilities should be educated to the maximum extent possible with children who are not disabled while meeting all their learning needs and physical requirements; the type of setting is stipulated in a child's IEP; LRE is an individual determination, where what is right for one student is not necessarily right for another.

local education agency (LEA): a school district, board of education, or other public authority under the supervision of a state educational agency having administrative control and direction of public elementary or secondary schools in a city, county, township, school district, or political subdivision in a state.

mainstream: the placement of a student with a disability into a general education classroom or any nonacademic setting (such as physical education, lunch, etc.) for any part of the school day.

manifestation determination: a process as a result of disciplinary actions that constitutes a change of placement whereby the MDT considers the relationship between the student's disability and the conduct in question and may adjust the disciplinary action, as well as the student's IEP, accordingly.

mastery criteria/mastery level: the cutoff score on a criterion-referenced test; the condition for mastery of an IEP goal.

meaningful progress: improvement in student performance individually determined to be sufficient to indicate that FAPE is being provided.

modification: changes to curriculum demand or assessment criteria such that the curriculum demand or assessment criteria are altered.

multidisciplinary team (MDT): a group including parents and professionals with different areas of expertise who come together for the purpose of looking at an individual child's educational program.

multiple intelligences: educational theory put forth by psychologist, Howard Gardner, which suggests that an array of different kinds of "intelligence" exists in human beings including: Verbal-Linguistic, Logical-Mathematical, Visual-Spatial, Musical, Bodily-Kinesthetic, Interpersonal, Intrapersonal, and Naturalistic.

No Child Left Behind: a United States federal law that aims to increase the standards of accountability for states, school districts, and schools, as well as provide parents more flexibility in choosing which schools their children will attend.

parent: a natural, adoptive, or foster parent; a guardian or individual acting in place of a natural or adoptive parent with whom the child lives or who is legally responsible for the child's welfare; a required member of the MDT team.

Present Levels of Academic Achievement and Functional Performance (PLOP): a statement in the IEP of the child's current baseline of strengths and needs as measured by formal and informal evaluations.

Prior Written Notice: required written notice to parents when the school proposes to initiate or change, or refuses to initiate or change, the identification, evaluation, or educational placement of the child.

procedural safeguards: rights regarding the special education of students who are either identified with a disability or suspected of having a disability; a booklet containing certain aspects of these rights required to be provided to parents once each year, as well as upon referral for special education, filing of a complaint, or upon parent request.

referral: a written request for evaluation or eligibility for special education and related services.

related services: services that are developmental, corrective, and other services required to assist a student with a disability to benefit from special education.

Response to Intervention (RTI): a process for increasing and/or changing supports, instruction, and interventions to address students' needs; under IDEA 2004, one of the preferred methods for identifying specific learning disabilities.

scientifically based: refers to the requirements in NCLB and IDEA 2004 that intervention to the greatest extent possible employs systematic methods of data analysis that are accepted by peer-reviewed journals or approved by a panel of independent experts.

screening: the process of administering global methods to determine if the child has a suspected disability and whether the child should have evaluations to determine if he qualifies for special education services and/or related services.

special education: specialized instruction specifically designed to meet the unique needs of a student with a disability, including classroom instruction, instruction in physical education, home instruction, and instruction in hospitals and institutions.

standardized tests: tests where the administration, scoring, and interpretation are set or prescribed and must be strictly followed; scores resulting from these tests are based on a normed population and compare students to their same-age peers.

stay put: commonly refers to the student remaining in his current educational setting while the due process complaint is being resolved, although there are important exceptions to this legal distinction.

supplementary aides and services: supports that are provided in the classroom, extracurricular, and nonacademic settings to allow a student with a disability to be educated with his nondisabled peers to the maximum extent appropriate; when possible these supports should be scientifically based.

transition services: a coordinated set of activities including special education and related services and community participation as listed in the IEP that facilitate the student's move to postsecondary options; may include vocational assessment, career exploration, and vocational education.

References

108th U.S. Congress. (2004). *Public Law 108-446, An act to reauthorize the Individuals with Disabilities Education Act.* Retrieved November 30, 2007, from http://www.nichcy.org/reauth/PL108-446.pdf

Access Center. (2007). *Enhancing access to the general curriculum for students with disabilities.* Retrieved December 4, 2007, from http://www.k8accesscenter.org/index.php

Americans with Disabilities Act, 42 U.S.C. §§ 12102 et seq. (1990).

Arlington Central School District Bd. of Ed. v. Murphy (No. 05-18), 402 F. 3d 332 (2006).

Barnes-Robinson, L., & Jeweler, S. (2007) *Conflict resolution: Teaching conflict resolution and mediation through the curriculum.* Hawthorne, NJ: Educational Impressions.

Board of Education of the City of New York v. Tom F. ex rel. Gilbert F., 107 LRP 58890 (U.S. 2007).

Board of Education of the Hendrick Hudson Central School District v. Rowley (80-1002), 458 U.S. 176 (1982).

Bridges4Kids.com. (2007). *Building partnerships between families, schools, and communities.* Retrieved December 4, 2007, from http://www.bridges4kids.org

Brown v. Board of Education of Topeka, 347 U.S. 483 (1954).

Burlington School Comm. v. Mass. Dept. of Ed., 471 U.S. 359 (1985).

Center for Effective Collaboration and Practice. (2001). *Functional behavioral assessment.* Retrieved December 6, 2007, from http://cecp.air.org/fba/default.asp

Cohen, L., & Spenciner, L. (2007). *Assessment of children and youth with special needs* (3rd ed.). Boston: Pearson.

Cooperative Education Service Agency No. 7. (2007). *Special education in plain language.*

Retrieved December 4, 2007, from http://www.specialed.us/Parents/plainlanguageindex.htm

Coping.org. (n.d.). *Nonverbal communication issues.* Retrieved December 3, 2007, from http://www.coping.org/dialogue/nonverbal.htm

Cornell University Law School. (n.d.). *Supreme Court collection: Florence County School District Four v. Carter, a minor.* Retrieved November 30, 2007, from http://www.law.cornell.edu/supct/html/91-1523.ZS.html

Council for Disability Rights. (n.d.). *A parent's guide to special ed/special needs.* Retrieved December 4, 2007, from http://www.disabilityrights.org/glossary.htm

Council for Exceptional Children. (1997). *Public policy & legislative information: Basic commitments and responsibilities to exceptional children.* Reston, VA: Author.

Council for Exceptional Children. (2007). *Policy and advocacy.* Retrieved December 5, 2007, from http://www.cec.sped.org

Csikszentmihalyi, M. (1998). *Finding flow: The psychology of engagement with everyday life.* New York: Basic Books.

Daniel R. R. v. State Board of Education, 874 F.2d 1036 (5th Cir. 1989).

Denckla, M. B. (1994). Measurement of executive functioning. In G. R. Lyon (Ed.), *Frames of reference for the assessment of learning disabilities: New views on measurement issues* (pp. 117–142). Baltimore: Paul H. Brookes.

Doe v. Smith, 486 U.S. 1308 (1988).

Education for All Handicapped Children Act of 1975, Pub. Law 94-142 (November 29, 1975).

Elementary and Secondary Education Act of 1965, §142, 20 U.S.C. 863.

Equip for Equality Legal Advocacy Program. (2007). *EFE fact sheet—Special education.* Retrieved December 1, 2007, from http://www.equipforequality.org/resourcecenter/spec_disciplineidea.doc

Farlex, Inc. (2007). *The free dictionary.* Retrieved June 1, 2007, from http://encyclopedia.thefreedictionary.com

Field, S., & Hoffman, A. (2002). Preparing youth to exercise self-determination. *Journal of Disability Policy Studies, 13*(2), 113–118.

Fitzsimmons, M. K. (1998). *Functional behavior assessment and behavior intervention plans.* Retrieved December 6, 2007, from http://www.cec.sped.org/AM/Template.cfm?Section=Home&TEMPLATE=/CM/ContentDisplay.cfm&CONTENTID=1742

Florence County Sch. Dist. Four v. Carter (91-1523), 510 U.S. 7 (1993).

Ford ex rel. Ford v. Long Beach Unified Sch. Dist., 291 F.3d 1086, 1089 (9th Cir. 2002).

Frank G. v. Board of Education of Hyde Park, 459 F.3d 356 (2d Cir. 2006).

Gardner, H. (1983) *Frames of mind: The theory of multiple intelligences.* New York: Basic Books.

Green, D. R., Trimble, C. S., & Lewis, D. M. (2003). Interpreting the results of three different standard-setting procedures. *Educational Measurement: Issues and Practice, 22*(1), 22–32.

Greer v. Rome City School District, 950 F.2d 688, 697 (1991).

Grenig, J. (2007). When does the Individuals with Disabilities Education Act permit tuition reimbursement? *Preview of United States Supreme Court Cases, 35*(1), 8–12.

Hager, R. M. (1999). *Funding of assistive technology.* Retrieved February 1, 2001, from http://www.nls.org/specedat.htm

Holloway, J. (2001). *Inclusion and students with learning disabilities.* Retrieved December 1, 2007, from http://www.ldonline.org/article/6297

Honig v. Doe, et al. (86-728), 484 U.S. 305 (1988).

Howard, P. (2004). Least restrictive environment: How to tell? *Journal of Law and Education, 33*, 167–180.

Hudson v. Bloomfield Hills Public Schools (96-1055), (6th Cir., 1997).

Hunter, M. (1982). *Mastery teaching.* Thousand Oaks, CA: Corwin Press.

Individuals with Disabilities Education Act, 20 U.S.C. §1401 et seq. (1990).

Individuals with Disabilities Education Improvement Act, PL 108-446, 118 Stat. 2647 (2004).

Individuals with Disabilities Education Improvement Act, 34 CFR C.F.R. § 300 and 301(2006).

J. L., M. L., and K. L. v. Mercer Island School District (C06-494P), W. D. Was. (2006).

Justin G. v. Board of Education of Montgomery County, 148 F. Supp. 2d 576, (D. Md. 2001).

Kitchelt v. Montgomery County Public Schools, 42 IDELR 58 (D. Md. 2004).

Lawrence-Lightfoot, S. (2003). *The essential conversation: What parents and teachers can learn from each other.* New York: Random House.

Larry P. v. Riles, 793 F.2d 969 (9th Cir., 1984).

LD OnLine. (2007). *IDEA 2004: Components.* Retrieved November 30, 2007, from http://www.ldonline.org/features/idea2004#components

Library of Congress. (2007). *Brown v. Board of Education: A chronological listing of related materials from the Library of Congress.* Retrieved December 7, 2007, from http://www.loc.gov/rr/program/bib/afam/afam-brown.html

Maryland State Department of Education. (2000). *Requirements for accommodating, excusing, and exempting students in Maryland assessment programs.* Baltimore: Author.

Mehrabian, A. (1972). *Nonverbal communication.* Chicago: Aldine-Atherton.

Mills v. Board of Education, DC, 348 F.Supp. 866 (D. DC 1972).

MM v. School District of Greenville County, 303 F.3d 523 (4th Cir., 2002).

Mr. and Mrs. I v. Maine School Administrative District 55, 04-165-P-H (U.S. District Court, Maine, 2006).

National Association for Gifted Children. (2005). *Mission statement*. Retrieved December 3, 2007, from http://www.nagc.org/index.aspx?id=661

National Center for Learning Disabilities. (2006). *IDEA parent guide*. New York: Author. Retrieved December 14, 2007 from http://www.ncld.org/images/stories/downloads/parent_center/idea2004parentguide.pdf

National Center for Learning Disabilities. (2007). *Student discipline addressing serious behavior issues and concerns*. Retrieved December 1, 2007, from http://www.ncld.org/content/view/911/456095

National Dissemination Center for Children With Disabilities. (2002). *Communicating with your child's school through letter writing*. Retrieved December 5, 2007, from http://www.nichcy.org/pubs/parent/pa9txt.htm

National Dissemination Center for Children With Disabilities. (2004). *Mental retardation fact sheet*. Retrieved December 5, 2007, from http://www.nichcy.org/pubs/factshe/fs8txt.htm

National Education Association. (n.d.). *Charter schools*. Retrieved December 4, 2007, from http://www.nea.org/charter

National Education Association. (2006). *The twice-exceptional dilemma*. Washington, DC: Author.

National Institute for Literacy. (2005). *What is scientifically based research?* Retrieved November 30, 2007, from http://www.nifl.gov/partnershipforreading/publications/html/science/stanovich.html

No Child Left Behind Act, 20 U.S.C. §6301 (2001).

Norlin, J. W. (2007). *What do I do when . . . The answer book on special education law* (5th ed.). Horsham, PA: LRP Publications.

Oberti v. Bd. of Educ. of Borough of Clementon Sch. Dist., 789 F. Supp. 1322, 1326 n. 7 (D.N.J. 1992).

Olson, D. H. (1999). Circumplex model of marital & family systems. *Journal of Family Therapy, 22*, 144–167.

ParentsUnitedTogether.com. (n.d.). *The legislative history of special education*. Retrieved December 7, 2007, from http://www.parentsunitedtogether.com/page15.html

Pennsylvania Association for Retarded Citizens v. Commonwealth of Pennsylvania, 334 F. Supp. 1257 (E.D. Pa. 1971).

Philpot, D. J. (2002). *Supreme Court cases in special education*. Retrieved November 30, 2007, from http://www.dphilpotlaw.com/html/supreme_court_cases.html

Polk v. Central Susquehanna Intermediate Unit 16, 853 F.2d 171 (3rd Cir., 1988).

Renzulli, J. S. (1977). *The enrichment triad model: A guide for developing defensible programs for the gifted and talented*. Mansfield Center, CT: Creative Learning Press.

Sacramento City School Dist. v. Rachel H., 14 F.3d 1398 (9th Cir. 1994).

Saphier, J., & Gower, R. (1997). *The skillful teacher: Building your teaching skills.* Carlisle, MA: Research for Better Teaching.

Schaffer v. Weast (04-698), 546 U.S. 49 (2005).

Section 504 of the Rehabilitation Act, 29 U.S.C. Section 706 et. Seq. (1973).

Silverman, S. M., & Weinfeld, R. (2007). *School success for kids with Asperger's syndrome.* Waco, TX: Prufrock Press.

Supreme Court of the United States. (2006). *Syllabus: Arlington Central School District Board of Education v. Murphy et vir.* Retrieved November 30, 2007, from http://www.supremecourtus.gov/opinions/05pdf/05-18.pdf

Supreme Court of the United States. (2007). *Transcription: Winkelman v. Parma City School District.* Retrieved November 30, 2007, from http://www.supremecourtus.gov/oral_arguments/argument_transcripts/05-983.pdf

TeacherVision.com. (n.d.). *Portfolio assessment guide.* Retrieved December 6, 2007, from http://www.teachervision.fen.com/assessment/resource/5942.html

Tomlinson, C. A. (1999). *The differentiated classroom: Responding to the needs of all learners.* Alexandria, VA: Association for Supervision and Curriculum Development.

Tomlinson, C. A., & McTighe, J. (2006). *Teaching for understanding.* Alexandria, VA: Association for Supervision and Curriculum Development.

Tuckman, B. W., & Jensen, M. A. W. (1977). Stages of small-group development revisited. *Group & Organization Management, 2,* 419–427.

U.S. Department of Education, Office of Special Education and Rehabilitative Services. (1998). *Letter dated April 29, 1998.* Retrieved December 7, 2007, from http://www.pattan.net/files/OSEP/CY1998/Garvin1.pdf

U.S. Department of Education. (2004a). *Four pillars of NCLB.* Retrieved November 30, 2007, from http://www.ed.gov/nclb/overview/intro/4pillars.html

U.S. Department of Education. (2004b). *Title I—Improving the academic achievement of the disadvantaged.* Retrieved December 7, 2007, from http://www.ed.gov/policy/elsec/leg/esea02/pg1.html

U.S. Department of Education, Office of Civil Rights. (2005). *Protecting students with disabilities.* Retrieved November 30, 2007, from http://www.ed.gov/about/offices/list/ocr/504faq.html

U.S. Department of Education, Office of Special Education and Rehabilitative Services. (2006). 34 CFR parts 300 and 301: Assistance to states for the education of children with disabilities and preschool grants for children with disabilities; Final rule. *Federal Register, 71,* pp. 46540–46845. Retrieved December 14, 2007, from http://www.nichcy.org/reauth/IDEA2004regulations.pdf

U.S. Department of Education, Office of Special Programs. (2007). *IDEA regulations: Disproportionality and overidentification*. Retrieved November 30, 2007, from http://www.ideapartnership.org/oseppage.cfm?pageid=41

U.S. Department of Health and Human Services. (2006). *Your rights under Section 504 of the Rehabilitation Act*. Retrieved November 30, 2007, from http://www.hhs.gov/ocr/504.pdf

U.S. Department of Justice. (2005). *A guide to disability rights laws*. Washington, DC: Author. Retrieved November 30, 2007, from http://www.usdoj.gov/crt/ada/cguide.htm#anchor62335

Weinfeld, R., Barnes-Robinson, L., Jeweler, S., & Roffman Shevitz, B. (2005). Enabling or empowering? Adaptations and accommodations for twice-exceptional students. *TEACHING Exceptional Children Plus, 2*(1), 1–19.

Weinfeld, R., Barnes-Robinson, L., Jeweler, S., & Roffman Shevitz, B. (2006). *Smart kids with learning difficulties: Overcoming obstacles and realizing potential*. Waco, TX: Prufrock Press.

Wiggins, G., & McTighe, J. (1998). *Understanding by design*. Alexandria, VA: Association for Supervision and Curriculum Development.

Wilmshurst, L., & Brue, A. W. (2005). *A parent's guide to special education*. New York: AMACOM.

Winkelman ex rel. Winkelman v. Parma City School District, 127 S.Ct. 1994 (2007).

Wright, P. W., & Wright, P. D. (2005). *Wrightslaw: IDEA 2004*. Hartfield, VA: Harbor House Law Press.

Wright, P. D., Wright, P. D., & Heath, S. W. (2003). *Wrightslaw: No child left behind*. Hartfield, VA: Harbor House Law Press.

WrightsLaw.com. (n.d.) *Passing grades, IQ scores & evaluations of students with learning disabilities*. Retrieved December 28, 2007, from http://www.wrightslaw.com/info/elig.sld.osep.felton.htm

WrightsLaw.com. (2007a). *United States Court, Western District of Washington at Seattle*. Retrieved December 3, 2007, from http://www.wrightslaw.com/law/caselaw/07/WA.jl.misd.htm

WrightsLaw.com. (2007b). *Glossary of special education and legal terms*. Retrieved December 4, 2007, from http://www.fetaweb.com/06/glossary.sped.legal.htm

Rich Weinfeld is the director of the Weinfeld Education Group, LLC, a group of educational consultants who provide advocacy to parents of student with special needs, as well as students who are gifted, training for school and parent groups, and consultative services to schools and school systems. Weinfeld is the coauthor of three previous books: *Smart Kids With Learning Difficulties*, *Helping Boys Succeed in School*, and *School Success for Kids With Asperger's Syndrome*. Rich was the first full-time coordinator of the Montgomery County, MD, gifted and learning-disabled program, and served in a variety of special education positions during his 30-year career in the public schools. He also has written numerous articles, presented at many national conferences, and taught a course entitled "The Gifted/Learning Disabled Child" at Johns Hopkins University. To learn more about his current endeavors, please visit http://www.richweinfeld.com.

Michelle Davis is an experienced leader and educator passionate about forwarding the civil rights of children. As a public school special educator, she advanced the learning of students in the classroom through training of other educators and working with families. In private practice, Michelle's consulting contributions include serving families and children across the nation, developing public and nonpublic school programs, and providing expertise to other educators through training and teaching higher education courses. Michelle is the proud recipient of awards and honors acknowledging her expertise in serving individuals with disabilities from universities, professional organizations, and school systems. Information about Michelle's consulting practice, ABC's for Life Success, LLC, can be found at http://www.abc4lifesuccess.com.

Rich and Michelle are the cofounders and directors of the ABC Weinfeld-Davis Advocacy Training Institute, providing extensive training for individuals (parents and professionals) who would like to effectively advocate for special needs children. Rich and Michelle's weekly radio show covers hot topics in education at http://www.voiceamerica.com. For information about their advocacy training institute, please visit http://www.specialneedsadvocacy.com.

About the Contributor

Jeanne L. Paynter, Ed.D., earned her bachelor's degree in English from Towson University, and her master's degree in gifted education and doctoral degree in teacher development and leadership from Johns Hopkins University. She served as the coordinator for K–12 gifted education and magnet programs in Baltimore County Public Schools, a large urban-suburban district of more than 107,000 students. In this position, she developed the local board polices and regulations for those programs. She has served on numerous advisory councils, task forces, and commissions that provided advocacy opportunities, including the Governor's Commission on Gifted and Talented Education and the Leadership Committee of the National Association for Gifted Children (NAGC). Currently she serves as the State Specialist for Gifted and Talented Education at the Maryland State Department of Education.